CLIMBING:
Training for Peak Performance

MOUNTAINEERS
OUTDOOR EXPERT
series

CLIMBING:
Training for Peak Performance

Clyde Soles

SECOND EDITION

THE MOUNTAINEERS BOOKS

Thanks to Cindy, my lovely wife and adventure partner,
who challenges and inspires.

THE MOUNTAINEERS BOOKS
*is the nonprofit publishing arm of The Mountaineers Club,
an organization founded in 1906 and dedicated to the exploration,
preservation, and enjoyment of outdoor and wilderness areas.*

1001 SW Klickitat Way, Suite 201, Seattle, WA 98134

© 2008 by Clyde Soles

Published simultaneously in Great Britain by Cordee, 3a DeMontfort Street, Leicester, England, LE1 7HD

Manufactured in Canada

Editor: Joeth Zucco
Cover and Book Design: The Mountaineers Books
Layout: Mayumi Thompson
Illustrator: Scott Bodell
Photographer: All photographs by the author unless otherwise noted.

Cover photograph: © Veer
Frontispiece: *The trail to the top of Gasherbrum II, Pakistan* © Clyde Soles
Back cover photograph: *Climbing in Indian Creek, Utah.* © Clyde Soles
Photographs on pages 93, 94, 97, and 98 by James Martin. Photograph on page 104 © Corbis

Library of Congress Cataloging-in-Publication Data
Soles, Clyde, 1959-
 Climbing : training for peak performance / by Clyde Soles. — 2nd ed.
   p. cm.
 Includes index.
 ISBN-13: 978-1-59485-098-1
 ISBN-10: 1-59485-098-4
 1. Rock climbing—Training. I. Title.
 GV200.2.S65 2008
 796.522'3—dc22
                    2008006009

Contents

Preface 8
Introduction 9

CHAPTER 1
Performance Fundamentals
Performance Fundamentals 12
The Aging Climber 16

CHAPTER 2
Nutrition Foundation
Nutrition Basics 18
Diet Basics 20
Sport Eating 27
Power Shopping 32
Fueling the Climb 44
Recovery Fuels 53
Supplements 55
Supplements with Potential 56
Dubious Supplements 63
Natural Supplements 66

CHAPTER 3

Mental Power

Mental Focus 72

Go With the Flow 74

Know Fear 75

Training Intuition 77

Accept Failure 78

CHAPTER 4

Aerobic Conditioning

Aerobic FUNdamentals 80

Follow Your Heart 83

Maximizing Performance 89

Cross-Play Exercises 92

CHAPTER 5

Climbing at Altitude

Change of Altitude 110

Very High Considerations 111

Going Low 112

Improving Altitude Performance 113

Expedition Nutrition 114

CHAPTER 6

Resistance Training

Strength Basics 120

Principles of Resistance Training 130

Gym Considerations 134

Weighty Concepts 147

Resistance Exercises 156

CHAPTER 7

Body Tuning: Joint Mobility, Flexibility, and Balance

Joint Mobility 190

Stretching 191

Stretching Routine 193

Stretches 195

Stretching Alternatives 203

Balance Training 205

CHAPTER 8
Recovery: Rest and Rehab
Rest Up 210
Massage 213
Rehabilitation 215
Common Climbing Injuries 222
After Major Injury 229

CHAPTER 9
Synergy: Coalescing and Planning
Putting It All Together 232
Training for Rock 233
Training for Alpine 236
Planning Your Program 237

Appendix A: Glossary 254
Appendix B: Product Sources 257
Appendix C: Suggested Reading 261
Index 265

Preface

This new edition of *Climbing: Training for Peak Performance* contains the latest advances in the sciences of nutrition and fitness. Since the publication of the previous edition, much has been learned about achieving optimal health and conditioning. Although a lot has changed, ultimately it requires work and dedication on your part—there are still no shortcuts!

This book is first and foremost for climbers. It applies to all ages, abilities, and interests—virtually anyone who wishes to improve their performance. It is for weekend warriors who enjoy 5.6 (UK 4b) yet desire to lead 5.10 (5b) and for mountaineers interested in moving faster at altitude. It is for ice climbers who want to move more efficiently over frozen terrain and big-wall climbers who want to increase their stamina. Even those only interested in clipping bolts on overhanging sport routes and cranking hard boulder problems can benefit.

The standard advice on training for climbing has long been, "Just climb!" While this may suffice for a few gifted individuals, that philosophy has also resulted in countless climbers reaching performance plateaus and suffering recurrent injuries. Even after the benefits of specific training were recognized, many of the regimens developed by climbers were physiologically unsound, or even downright dangerous, yet old concepts die hard.

Most climbing training books and articles focus on young advanced sport climbers with indestructible bodies and a lot of free time. That information is often ill-suited to middle-aged climbers with limited time, preexisting injuries, and other interests. This book is intended primarily for this latter group. Other outdoor recreationalists who play in the mountains, be they hikers, skiers, or cyclists, will also find the instructional material here useful because their sports share much in common with climbing.

Introduction

The guiding principle of *Climbing: Training for Peak Performance* is that training should be fun! While some people enjoy suffering, they are the exceptions. Many of us would rather eat junk food and lie on the couch than adhere to a strict diet and self-inflict torture. Although "to train" may seem the antithesis of "to play," they can be the same thing—with the right attitude and a good understanding of what you are doing.

In general, to achieve peak performance, your goal is to:

- enhance overall fitness and health.
- fine-tune aspects specific to your interests.
- peak for major excursions.
- prevent injury through a balanced program of exercise.

Think of climbing, outdoor recreation, and fitness as a year-round lifestyle—not just on-again, off-again activities. Even when the realities of life intrude, keeping this perspective will prevent major setbacks in your conditioning. When you think of climbing in a decade or three, and enjoying yourself even more, the efforts to improve your health and fitness seem all that much more worthwhile. Use this book to make educated decisions about your own life experiment. And have fun climbing better, stronger, and longer!

A NOTE ABOUT SAFETY

Safety is an important concern in all outdoor activities. No book can alert you to every hazard or anticipate the limitations of every reader. The descriptions of techniques and procedures in this book are intended to provide general information. This is not a complete text on climbing or training technique. Nothing substitutes for formal instruction, routine practice, and plenty of experience. When you follow any of the procedures described here, you assume responsibility for your own safety. Use this book as a general guide to further information. Under normal conditions, excursions into the backcountry require attention to traffic, road and trail conditions, weather, terrain, the capabilities of your party, and other factors. Keeping informed on current conditions and exercising common sense are the keys to a safe, enjoyable outing.

The Mountaineers Books

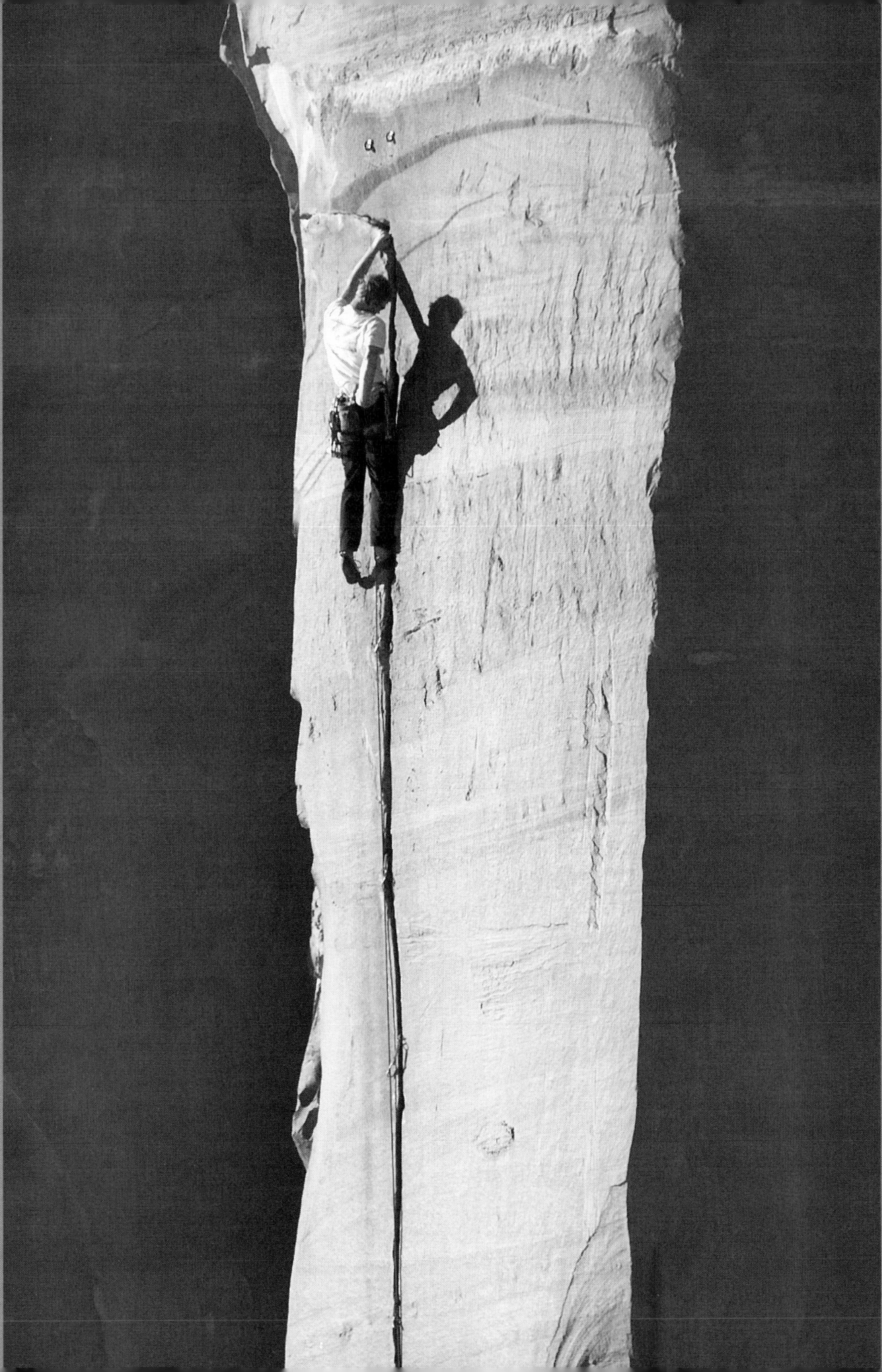

CHAPTER 1

Performance Fundamentals

There are no easy ways to improve your climbing performance. It will always require sweat and determination. To believe otherwise is folly. But by losing the ancient dogmas and applying sport science to your efforts, the rewards will come faster and with less effort.

Whether you prefer to focus on one aspect of the climbing spectrum, or tackle them all, you can only succeed with a solid foundation of fitness. Even the luck of the genetic draw can carry you only so far: a less gifted climber who trains smarter will blow you away.

The emphasis of this book is on sound nutrition and time-efficient training methods that will benefit "normal" people from late teens to octogenarians. This is based on the latest sport science—a rapidly evolving field that only began in 1927 and didn't get into full swing until the '60s. This new edition intermixes research and concepts that have emerged in the past five years. And, yes, there is a lot of new information!

Don't underestimate the value of training, either. A University of New Mexico study of twenty-four male and twenty female climbers evaluated a wide range of variables that can affect performance on sport routes. They determined that anthropometric factors (such as height, arm span, and weight) could account for only 0.3 percent of a climber's ability. Increased flexibility was a slight help at 1.8 percent. But training accounted for 58.9 percent of a climber's performance.

PERFORMANCE FUNDAMENTALS

Nobody consciously sets out to train "dumb." Ask most climbers and they will vehemently deny their training efforts have been a waste of time—and in the next breath admit they could be doing more. Most of us are guilty of training our strengths and not our weaknesses; this is only natural.

One of the hallmarks of world-class athletes is brutal honesty with themselves, which is not the same as relentless self-criticism. You need to evaluate yourself for both positives and negatives, solicit the opinions of friends, and perhaps even hire a coach or trainer, who can offer an unbiased evaluation. Find the areas where you can make the most gains, not just slight improvements, and the rest will fall into place on its own.

There is a world of difference between training harder and training smarter—the former is a path to mediocrity, the latter the route to the top. When you train and eat haphazardly, no matter how many hours you put in, you are climbing Mount Analogue and the summit will always remain untrodden.

When you establish specific goals, make a plan to achieve them, and fuel yourself accordingly, you'll get 80 percent of the reward with 20 percent of the effort. For many, if not most, this higher level of performance is sufficient since they are climbing better, feeling healthier, and still have time for a life. Others will want to apply themselves to their fullest to eke out that maximum performance edge.

There are many altruistic people in the fitness world who desire to make a decent living while helping others improve. These folks are genuinely pleased when their customers improve their health or performance.

However, the greedy side of the fitness industry has a secret that they'd prefer remains unspoken: almost anything works if you stick with it. When you see a product or coaching method that is hyped as "revolutionary" or "exclusive," there is a fair chance that the main goal is to reap financial rewards for the seller, not to help you with your goals. Sure, whatever they are selling (ab exerciser, miracle workout, magic potion, etc.) does something if you keep at it—and keep paying—but it often isn't the most time- or cost-effective means to achieve the desired results.

COACHING BASICS

It is important to distinguish between general and specific conditioning for a sport. During the former, you are working on getting stronger, improving flexibility, reducing weight, and so on. While working on the latter, you are actively refining movements and techniques that directly apply to your chosen activity.

At the elite level in many sports, athletes often have one coach for general conditioning and another coach to work on motor skills. The conditioning coach is usually educated at the college or graduate school level in sports science and works with many types of athletes. The sport coach is often a former competitive athlete with years of practical experience at the specific activity, who may or may not have a formal education or certification. It is rare that one individual can truly do both. Ideally, these two coaches collaborate and complement one another to help the athlete achieve his or her absolute best possible performance.

The training methods presented here, when thoughtfully performed, can make you stronger and healthier. But they will not necessarily make you a better climber. As part of the Mountaineers Outdoor Expert series, *Climbing: Training for Peak Performance* is intended to supplement the other titles, which focus on technique and safety in different aspects of the sport (trad climbing, ice climbing, alpine climbing, big-wall climbing, ski mountaineering, etc.). In essence, this book is the conditioning coach while the other books are the sport coaches. It is incumbent upon you to also learn how to move economically and safely in your chosen environment. Seek out these other books—they are excellent—and practice your skills.

PERFORMANCE BASICS

In case you haven't noticed, climbing is a sport that defies gravity. Since excess weight is a detriment, some climbers spend a small fortune on the lightest equipment. While high-tech gear can help performance, many of the climbers with the latest toys would do better to reduce their body fat.

Athletes can stay competitive and healthy down to about 5 to 6 percent body fat for men and 13 to 17 percent for women. However, that doesn't mean those are your optimal percentages. Many people require more fat for best performance—only *your* body knows what's best. With a thoughtful dietary plan, an ideal balance can be met while boosting performance.

Concurrent with losing extra fat, many climbers will benefit by building their muscles. Those who are past their mid-thirties have in all likelihood lost significant muscle mass since the days of youth. With intelligent resistance training, you can maximize your strength-to-mass ratio, boost your power output, and increase your metabolism.

Another important purpose of resistance training is to strengthen the ligaments and tendons that hold bones and muscles together. Climbers are frequently plagued by injuries of these connective tissues, either from overstraining or overusing them. To increase their size and strength requires high-intensity loading and sufficient rest.

Cardiovascular conditioning enhances all of the above basics of climbing fitness, even if your style of climbing is not very demanding on heart and lungs. Through aerobic training, you increase cardiac output, oxygen uptake, blood perfusion within muscles, breathing efficiency, and buffering capacity. All the while, you are burning calories and reducing stress.

Perhaps the most important aspect of climbing performance, and the hardest to master, is the mind. The mental games we must play with ourselves to accomplish a climb, or complete a workout, are substantial. Much of what we do as climbers defies any real logic: it borders on stupidity. To persevere in the face of adversity, and make suffering fun, takes willpower; this too requires training.

PLAY HOLISTICALLY

An absolute truth of climbing performance: everything works together. Even though few people would deny this, the concept is nonetheless downplayed to the point that it is often forgotten. It's common to see folks who practically live in the rock gym, yet they never seem to improve and often nurse injuries. Most books and magazine articles only focus on one aspect of performance, typically strength, perhaps in a paragraph or two mentioning that you also need to do other things like "eat right" or "go for a run." Yet failure and frustration come from concentrating on one aspect of fitness to the exclusion of others.

Much has been written in sports literature in general, and climbing literature in particular, about the need for specialization in training. This has been summed up by the acronym SAID—specific adaptation to increased demand. The vast majority of this specialization is due to neural changes, both within the brain and the musculature. Specificity is essential for competitive athletes who have already achieved a high level of performance.

However, specialization can be, and often is, taken too far. For recreational athletes, it can do more harm than good—insufficient all-around conditioning and a much greater risk of injury. Though they are very good within their specialties, neither 5.14 climbers nor sub-three-hour marathoners tend to be complete (or even healthy) athletes, and overuse injuries are rampant. Recall the old truism, "Everything in moderation, including moderation."

With the exception of high-end sport climbing and bouldering, which receive most of the hoopla in magazines, there is very little that is specific about climbing. All other forms of the games we play require greater depth of strength and power, muscular and aerobic endurance. For optimum climbing performance, you need to condition yourself to handle different levels and volumes of intensity. Along with this comes greater muscular efficiency—the economy of play.

Unlike many sports, which tend to have a single peak season, climbing is a year-round activity. The focus may change with the weather or a particular trip, but there is often less of a downtime for complete recuperation. During an extended break from activity, aerobic endurance declines much faster than strength. By cross-playing—using other sports for fun and relaxation—you can maintain a reasonable level of fitness with less risk of overtraining.

TRAINING CULTS

A recent fitness trend has been the emergence of training cults, with adherents who gush on and on about how their method is the "best" and anything else is garbage training. The most popular of these is CrossFit, which is essentially a business franchise masquerading as a new fitness program.

That is not to say CrossFit is all bad. Indeed, there are some very good aspects that the individual trainers, gyms, and websites offer. Perhaps the most valuable part of the CrossFit program is the motivation that comes from camaraderie. The underlying principle of high-intensity cross-training is also reasonably sound, though hardly new or innovative, and can lead to solid fitness gains if used wisely.

However, there is a high risk of acute injury from many of the exercises; some of which are frivolous. Due to the frequent high intensity of the workouts, without a good athletic base, there is also a potential for chronic fatigue. And optimal performance gains always come from addressing individual weaknesses and goals, not generic training programs.

The forums and newsletters contain good information scattered with unscientific nonsense about physiology and nutrition. Don't count on a well-educated instructor, either. It only takes attending a two-day class, with no written exam, to become a certified CrossFit trainer, which is weak compared to other standards. (See "Trainers" in chapter 6.)

If you inform yourself about the pros and cons of CrossFit or similar fads, and need the motivation of that style of training, the workouts and gyms can be helpful. For those adopting a periodized training program, high-intensity cross-training during the power endurance phase can lead to serious strength gains. However, joining a training cult on a year-round basis may not be in your best interests in the long run.

THE AGING CLIMBER

Sadly, we all grow older—at least in body. With advancing age comes wisdom and an inexorable physical deterioration. Large portions of these declines are the result of an increasingly sedentary lifestyle.

Many people have heard of osteoporosis, which is bone loss due to aging and poor nutrition. There is a lesser-known equivalent term for the loss of muscle mass with age, sarcopenia, from the Greek for "poverty of flesh." The two combined result in a frail elderly person, sometimes overweight, who can easily break a hip and has difficulty recovering from injury.

Between ages twenty-five and thirty-five, the average male gains 5 to 10 pounds of fat. Around our mid-twenties, strength and endurance begin to decline 1 to 2 percent per year; resting metabolic rate (RMR), the baseline energy requirement, decreases 1 to 2 percent per decade; aerobic capacity decreases about 10 percent per decade.

After around age fifty, the rate of decline speeds up as our production of testosterone, human growth hormone, and DHEA (a natural steroid precursor) slows down. Degenerating muscle fiber starts to be replaced by fibrous connective tissue (fibrosis), which reduces flexibility. Some studies have shown that after age fifty the fast-twitch muscle fibers (Type II) are more prone to decline noticeably than the slow-twitch (Type I) fibers.

As we ripen, our joints stiffen as ligaments become less elastic and synovial fluid thickens. The rate of sweating also decreases with age, so we become less tolerant to heat stress.

Among the most worrying facts: a six-year study of more than ten thousand middle-aged men and women demonstrated that low cardiorespiratory fitness is a strong predictor of metabolic syndrome. This term doesn't sound all that bad, but it translates to the nasty combination of medical problems associated with diabetes and heart disease.

The good news is that maintaining fitness slows the aging process. There is a growing body of evidence that memory and other intellectual functions are protected, and even improved, by staying fit and active. Indeed, some research indicates that increasing aerobic fitness leads to significant growth of several areas of the brain. Maintaining muscle mass with resistance training also helps retain bone mass, neither of which are aided by aerobic training alone.

The even better news is that you can reverse much of your losses if you've allowed yourself to slide—you *can* make yourself younger! Proper nutrition, including adequate protein intake, can ward off some of the unpleasant age-associated diseases. With endurance training, aerobic capacity can increase as much for people in their sixties as for kids in their twenties. Likewise, resistance training can increase muscle size and strength even when you're an octogenarian. Enjoy life—never stop playing!

CHAPTER 2

Nutrition Foundation

Hang around any major vertical destination and you'll discover that many climbers have a distaste for nutrition. What we eat and drink before, during, and after a climb is seldom given much thought regarding performance. Yet serious athletes in other sports, such as running and cycling, tend to pay greater attention to proper fueling.

This dichotomy exists partly because climbers often feel they are not mainstream athletes—and damned proud of it—and partly because of ignorance. Some would rather do ten thousand pull-ups than give up their breakfast of Kix cereal with chocolate milk. The magazines seldom run articles on improving performance through nutrition, and few training books consider it a worthy topic.

But the truth is you can climb better-faster-longer if you pay attention to what you eat. And it doesn't have to be bland, engineered crap either—quite the opposite.

NUTRITION BASICS

Accept that you are an athlete, no matter if you can redpoint 5.3 (UK 3b) or 5.13 (7a). The sooner you start eating like one, the sooner you can start making real performance gains. Whether you climb for fun, demons, or profit, all aspects of the sport are athletic endeavors that will benefit from healthy eating habits.

As an athlete, your nutritional needs are slightly different from those of the general population for whom recommendations are normally made. Obviously, you are working more, so you need to consume more calories and water. But compared to standard recommendations, climbers need approximately twice as much protein and possibly more antioxidants.

Shocking though it may sound, climbers do not need to buy specially designed "sport" foods or supplements. These products mostly offer convenient packaging but rarely provide anything that isn't obtainable from a normal, healthy diet. All too often, the marketing hype overwhelms reality. For example, minuscule quantities of supplements are often added simply as a sales gimmick; there isn't enough to have a real effect, or it takes many weeks of daily consumption to do anything, or an important facilitator is left out because it's too bulky or expensive.

DIET STYLES

With proper education and a modicum of restraint, an omnivorous diet is the easiest for meeting the nutritional needs of athletes. To be healthful, this features a lot of vegetables, fruits, and whole grains. The preferred source of protein is seafood, some skinless poultry, and occasional lean red meat. The things to avoid are the heavily refined sugars and fats that are so prevalent in commercial food. In general, a good sports diet tastes better, and is better for you, than the average Western diet that emphasizes convenience and value over nutrition.

Although vegetarians are sometimes annoyingly righteous about their food preference, no studies show that this diet style is healthier than a thoughtful omnivorous diet. However, there is considerable evidence that a vegetarian diet is healthier than that of the general public, which dines on the overprocessed "food products" shoveled out at fast-food restaurants and supermarkets.

From an athletic standpoint, vegetarians with the best chances of success are either semi-vegetarian (consume dairy products, eggs, and occasionally seafood and poultry, but no red meat) or lacto-ovo vegetarian (consume dairy and eggs but no meat or seafood). Both of these philosophies make it relatively easy to ensure adequate nutrition—if you pay attention!

Vegans, who consume no animal products of any sort, place themselves at a distinct performance disadvantage. Unfortunately, the most militant vegans are remarkably ill informed about biology and the scientific process (hint: correlation does not equal causation). While it is certainly possible for an athlete to perform well and stay healthy on a vegan diet, this requires a great deal of knowledge and effort. Don't undertake this lifestyle choice casually; consult a sports nutritionist. A particular danger is vitamin B-12 deficiency as well as possible deficiencies in vitamins A and D. On expeditions, the dietary constraints

of strict vegans can cause problems if they interfere with meal planning for the team.

If you don't like the taste of meat, or have moral qualms, that's fine. But make sure you offset the protein deficit with higher consumption of alternative protein sources (rice, beans, pasta, vegetables, fruits, nuts, and so forth). Though individually these lack adequate supplies of the essential amino acids, together they can supply all of your needs. Contrary to the old thinking, however, these do not have to be combined at the same meal.

While soy products (such as tofu and soy milk) have been championed as a complete protein, they also contain high levels of anti-nutrients (phytic acid in particular) that block the absorption of key minerals and enzymes. Fermenting soy, which removes the anti-nutrients, makes miso and tempeh. There are also lingering questions about high soy consumption and hormonal balance and doubts about its efficacy in preventing cancer.

Vegetarian female athletes must be even smarter about their diet because low protein, which often accompanies low calories, can result in disrupted menstrual cycles. If this is your preferred diet style and you wish to climb hard, it is imperative that you do a lot of research on eating smart.

According to Suzanne Girard Eberle, author of *Endurance Sports Nutrition*, "I meet vegetarians with unhealthy, unbalanced diets all the time—especially athletes who lack cooking or meal preparation skills or the desire to apply them. Dairy and eggs are poor sources of iron and zinc.

Also, most people don't eat eggs daily (as we do with meat) or drink enough milk (3 glasses = 24 grams of protein = chicken breast the size of a deck of cards) to meet their increased protein needs. Especially for women, the easiest and most practical way to consume readily absorbable iron (and zinc) is lean red meat. Bottom line: If you want to be vegetarian and an athlete, you'll have to be extra vigilant about your diet."

DIET BASICS

The amount of misinformation about diets and dieting floating around is downright scary. Much of this is fueled by the mega-billion-dollar diet and supplement industry, an industry which would disappear if its products really worked. No wonder many of us are confused to the point of giving up.

DIET CHICANERY
The goal of nearly all diet plans is to lighten your wallet, little more. If you escape by only purchasing a book, then you're just out some time and money. The real scams are the ones that try to hook you on their products; multilevel marketing schemes are the worst offenders.

If a company's literature includes the words "secret," "miracle," "magic," "rejuvenates," "detoxification," or "adaptogen," you are virtually guaranteed there is no solid science behind the products. Testimonials and endorsements aren't worth the paper they're printed on, no matter how famous the celebrity or team.

A patent only proves the company has mixed ingredients in a different ratio than anyone else. The patent offices in the United States and most other countries do not require any evidence that a product is safe or even effective. In the supplement world, a patent makes for great marketing but means nothing.

Beware the pseudoscience found on many websites and infomercials; these can be filled with technical-sounding jargon to hide the truth. Before committing your body and cash to the latest diet fad or supplement, check the science. Skip the hogwash on their website and go straight to their references. Examining the research, or lack thereof, behind the product can save you a lot of time and money.

First look at the names of the journals (are they widely read and recognized in their field?), then the years published (anything over a decade old in the nutrition world should be suspect), and finally the title of the paper (is it relevant?). Pay attention to who wrote the study; often you will find that one of the owners of the company is listed among the contributors (sometimes not as the primary author so it is less obvious). References to articles in consumer magazines or popular books are just window dressing and should be ignored.

If the purveyors happen to post the entire study, go to the section after the conclusion to see who paid for the research. If the company is involved, the study could still be legit but requires an extra careful read to be sure. Frequently, company-funded studies are poorly designed and have a small number of subjects to reach astounding conclusions.

Look up significant citations to read the abstracts on PubMed, a free internet resource with more than 17 million medical references (www.ncbi.nlm.nih.gov/sites /entrez); if there is anything to the claims, the research should be there. Sometimes the references on a website don't include follow-up studies that proved the theory wrong but these will show up in a search.

There is no legitimate reason for serious research to be hidden from peer review or the public. Assertions that the research is unpublished because it's proprietary, or that the study is in progress, are essentially the same as saying, "Give us your money and trust us, fool." Often studies used to tout the success of a diet are based on self-reporting, which is notoriously unreliable. Seldom do they pass muster when subjected to metabolic ward studies with strictly controlled intake.

Another common ploy is to take the results of a legitimate study out of context. Sometimes they will draw conclusions from a test-tube study (*in vitro* instead of *in vivo*, meaning the whole animal). Often claims are based on the assumption that mice and rat (murine) studies will give the same results in humans; many times this is false. A common tactic is extrapolating data from geriatrics or the seriously ill to a younger, healthier population; these studies often don't mean much.

What many promoters fail to mention is that you can lose weight via countless schemes—but keeping it off is a different story. And most diets and weight loss supplements are intended for couch potatoes who buy books. Few fad diets even consider the energy needs of an athlete and some supplements have killed people who were exercising.

The Zone Diet (aka, the 40-30-30 plan based on the ratio of carbohydrates, protein, and fat) is a classic example of bad science that has been thoroughly debunked for sport performance yet still lingers among desperate athletes. This diet essentially restricts calories by cutting back on carbohydrate consumption to a point that your body doesn't get enough fuel. Despite a lot of hype, the Zone Diet can help with weight loss, temporarily, but has not been shown to improve athletic performance in controlled studies.

The Paleo Diet (20–35 percent carbs, 20–35 percent protein, and 30–60 percent fat with most calories coming from animal sources) is based on the supposed eating plan of early humans. The basic rules require eliminating all grains, beans, dairy foods, salt, fatty meats, and alcohol. While long on hype, the actual research showing improved performance is remarkably paltry, and genetic studies show that humans have evolved considerably since Paleolithic times. It is now recommended that some of the rules be broken for athletes. Overall, the Paleo Diet is probably healthier than many of the other fads, but the evidence that it is superior to a healthful omnivorous or vegetarian diet is totally lacking.

Another popular fad is the Atkins Diet, which has been advocated in various forms for over a half century and periodically makes a comeback (the South Beach Diet is the latest permutation). But they offer no metabolic advantage and all fall flat for athletic performance. Indeed, eating according to these high-protein/high-fat schemes can reduce endurance, decrease maximal output, and even be harmful to your health. For endurance athletes, there is a greater risk of dehydration and stress on the kidneys due to the high nitrogen levels in the blood that must be excreted.

Raw food diets (uncooked fruits and vegetables) are sometimes touted as the ultimate in nutrition. But the reality is that this eating style has no scientific justification and several flaws, such as inadequate protein intake, greater bacterial intake due to lack of sterilization, and reduced phytochemical activity. Eat raw foods, yes, but cooking is good for you too.

It's also helpful to remember that the media and conventional wisdom are often wrong. The media loves to jump on a bandwagon long before it's ready to roll. The devil-may-care attitude toward headlines has led to general confusion among the public: let's see, are eggs good or bad this week? Answer: good, in moderation (four per week). And conventional wisdom's selective memory is both amazingly long- and shortsighted. (See Appendix C, "Suggested Reading," before committing yourself to the latest fad.)

DEFINING PROGRESS

First things first: throw away that old scale! Losing weight is not the goal; reducing body fat while building muscle is your objective.

A normal scale only provides trivial information that is often discouraging. One of the paradoxes of weight loss is that you can build muscle faster than you lose fat, especially when starting a training program. Thus you could trim a pound of fat while adding 2 pounds of muscle and a normal scale would deliver bad news when it's actually great; you're stronger and leaner. (Muscle is about 18 percent denser than fat, so an equal weight takes up less volume.)

If you are serious about becoming lean and mean, consider purchasing a body fat scale to monitor your progress in reducing body fat and use it every day. One research study showed that using a scale daily greatly helped people from backsliding on weight loss compared to those who used it sporadically.

The best-known brand of body fat scales is Tanita, though others include Digiweigh, Omron, Taylor, and Terraillon. These range in price from around $50 up to $150. The higher-priced models have useful features but are not necessarily more accurate.

Body fat scales use bioelectrical impedance analysis (BIA), which compares the resistance to flow of a small electric current through different body tissues. Muscle, which is 74 percent water, conducts electrical flow more effectively than fat, which is about 10 percent water (bone is 32 percent and blood is 93 percent). The technique can be quite accurate if you are consistent in using the scale.

For BIA to be effective, you need to keep the variables to a minimum: same time of day (it's most accurate in the evening), same part of the menstrual cycle, same hydration level (go to the bathroom first and avoid excessive hydration). The body fat scale is very easy to use by yourself—just stand on it for a few seconds. Better models offer different calculations for athletes and non-athletes; many climbers will be in the middle.

If you have a normal scale that you just can't give up, a reasonable alternative to a body fat scale is a skinfold caliper. Accu-Measure and Slim Guide are two good consumer brands (around $20 to $30); professional models cost several hundred dollars. These are used to take measurements from three to nine places on your body (more is better). However, skinfold measurement can be difficult to do on yourself since some of the locations are hard to reach. Plus it's important to use the correct amount of pressure and the proper equation (there are several). Digital models are more convenient (they do the math) but not necessarily any more accurate.

With proper technique, both skinfold measurements and body fat scales provide about a 3 percent range of error. So a reading of 13 percent means you are between 10 percent and 16 percent body fat. Here's the thing: The actual day-to-day number is less important than the trend over weeks and months.

If you really need to know your body composition, other methods—such as underwater weighing, air displacement (Bod Pod), and DEXA scans—can be more accurate (around 1 percent error range). But these cost significantly more and are not available in many places.

A commonly mentioned, yet useless, measure is the body mass index (BMI). This is derived from a formula dating back to the nineteenth century that relates your height and weight to determine how close you are to your ideal weight (BMI = lbs ÷ in^2 x 703 or = kg ÷ m^2). A score above 25 is considered overweight and over 30 is obese. Unfortunately, because it is so simplistic, the mass media and countless, clueless websites have made a huge deal about the BMI.

There are so many factors that the BMI formula does not account for that athletes shouldn't take it seriously. A six-foot-tall muscular man who weighs 200 pounds has a BMI of 27, but you probably wouldn't call him fat to his face. This index tells you much less than standing naked in front of a full-length mirror—the true body fat test.

LASTING LEAN

Reducing excess body fat is central to better performance for many climbers. But it's well documented that radical diet plans don't work in the long run. The quicker the fix, the faster the weight will return—with a vengeance since fat can replace lost muscle. If you lose more than 1 or 2 pounds per week, the majority of it comes from water, muscle glycogen, and lean muscle mass—not fat.

Strict low-calorie diets (such as Jenny Craig and Weight Watchers) both reduce your resting metabolic rate (RMR) and do not provide sufficient energy for effective workouts. Studies on healthy women in metabolic chambers show that a bare minimum of 1,200 calories (1,500 for men) is required to sustain body weight without any exercise. Yet many diet plans are at or below this level and the victims are somehow supposed to lead a normal life—short-term results and long-term failure is almost guaranteed.

Shocking though it may sound, exercise alone frequently does not lead to significant fat loss. Nor will exercise always keep fat off once it has been lost. The problem is that the exertion also makes us hungrier so we consume more calories. Of course there are many reasons to exercise but losing excess pounds isn't foremost among them.

Pssst . . . wanna know the real secret to permanent weight loss? The surefire formula, proven by numerous controlled, independent studies? Burn more than you eat. The critical corollaries: gradually make small changes, cut back on refined sugars, and get plenty of sleep. No gimmicks, no quackery, no extra money involved. Just honest-to-goodness sound medical advice.

You won't see overnight results, and that's the point. You didn't gain the fat overnight either. Don't eat less than about 8 calories for every pound of body weight to ensure adequate fuel for maintaining muscle (e.g., a 180-pound man needs at least 1,440 calories per day).

By reducing your current average daily consumption by only 10 percent—easy once you start thinking about it—you will maintain muscle mass and have energy to play hard. Cutting by 20 percent requires a bit more careful shopping but still isn't that hard and doesn't compromise flavor. Since you are not making drastic diet changes, or even forsaking favorite foods, the minor alterations become acceptable and sustainable.

Here's a bonus tip: Research has shown that eating in a brightly lit room can reduce the temptation to binge heavily during meals. Dim light is disinhibiting, so you tend to eat more at that candle-lit restaurant.

The great part about basing your diet on energy balance is all the things that you don't have to worry about. How much you eat on a particular day doesn't matter: savor a gourmet meal if you want, just don't do it often. What counts is that the number of calories consumed in a week is less than calories burned.

Myths abound about when to work out, but here's the truth: It doesn't matter if you exercise in the morning or evening, before or after a meal. The minor differences in calorie burning are insignificant in the grand scheme of things. What's important is that you make regular exercise part of your lifestyle.

Likewise, there are many rumors floating around about the best and worst times to consume foods. A commonly encountered falsehood is that you shouldn't consume snacks before going to bed. The reality is too many calories make you fat, not when you eat them.

Don't fear the fats! This fairly recent obsession has led to bigger guts everywhere. Eating fats won't necessarily make you fat—the body just doesn't work that way—but eating too many calories will. To make them somewhat palatable, those low-fat and fat-free "diet" foods can be packed with nearly as many calories (often simple sugars) as real food. Since many people are fooled into thinking the stuff is better for them, and it's less filling, they chow down more—and gain weight.

FINDING BALANCE

Although permanent weight loss (for those without medical conditions) is truly just a matter of consuming less energy than you expend, counting calories—the old standby of perpetual dieters—doesn't need to be a daily exercise in mathematics.

Unless you are fanatical about it, there is little chance you'll include all that you consume; hidden calories are everywhere so we typically underestimate intake. On the other side of the formula, research has shown that most people tend to overestimate their energy expenditure.

None of the charts that estimate calories burned by different exercises are even close to accurate (look carefully at the comparisons to see what a joke they are). The guesses by most heart rate monitors and exercise machines are also pretty worthless; they ignore too many factors such as weight, body fat, and fitness level. Don't let the minutia overwhelm you.

That said, it is helpful to have a general idea of the amount of calories you need based on overall activity level. The table in figure 1.1 below can give you a ballpark figure. Multiply your weight by the calories per pound to get a rough estimate of your daily requirement (reduce the total if you're carrying more body fat than you should). If the intensity of exercise is low or high, you might move a level accordingly. For example, 90 minutes of low intensity drops you from High to Moderate activity level; the same time at high intensity puts you in the Extreme level.

It's also wise to have an idea of where the calories come from, and the ubiquitous Nutrition Facts label on the packages of food you buy is a great resource. Get in the habit of reading it. To calculate calories in each "serving" (as defined on the label), multiply the grams of carbohydrates and protein by 4 and the grams of fat by 9 (this last calculation is done for you). Be sure to multiply this result by the number of so-called servings you actually consume!

Figure 1.1 Estimated Caloric Requirements		
Activity Level	**Exercise**	**Calories Needed Per Pound**
Low	Minimal to none	14 to 15
Moderate	45–60 min. moderate intensity	16 to 20
High	1–2 hrs. moderate intensity	21 to 25
Extreme	2+ hrs. moderate intensity	25 to 30

HIT IT HARD

We'll talk about this more in chapter 4 but it's important to dispel the "fat-burning zone" myth now because it is so prevalent in diet discussions. The concept of low-intensity exercise promoting a higher proportion of fat utilization is yet another case of the abuse of science misleading the public.

Any diet program that promotes working out in a long and slow fat-burning zone is fundamentally flawed. What is proven to work for reducing excess fat, by numerous studies, is high-intensity training (HIT). Eating properly and either moderate intensity with no breaks or fast and hard exercise, with brief breaks is the surest way to fat loss.

FASTING LEAN

While energy balance is the key to keeping the excess fat off permanently, there is increasing evidence that short-term fasting can give your weight loss goals a boost. Importantly, this is achieved by burning fat while sparing muscle and you can still exercise and live your life normally.

Whereas long-term fasting is all about deprivation for days or weeks on end, going without food for 16 to 24 hours once or twice a week does not require eliminating anything. Since a good portion of this intermittent fast occurs while you sleep, and you can consume non-caloric fluids (such as coffee and tea without milk or sweetener) the rest of the time, it isn't as harsh as some might think. These short, occasional fasts, essentially just skipping breakfast, appear to promote production

of adipose triglyceride lipase (ATGL), a protein that helps breakdown fat, and human growth hormone (HGH), which helps preserve muscle.

This is a controversial topic and the science is still emerging. As usual, there is a lot of hype for schemes, such as alternate-day or everyday fasting (bad ideas), and programs that require your monetary input for results. There is no performance or health benefit to long-term fasting.

DISORDERLY EATING

It's a dirty secret in the climbing world that quite a few elite sport climbers suffer from eating disorders. Some of the men and women you might recognize from magazines and posters are seriously anorexic or bulimic. Nobody likes to talk about it—even his or her friends and parents are in denial. Sponsors too often care only about results and publicity.

This problem doesn't stop with the elites; eating disorders are widespread throughout the sport climbing community, which places a high premium on low body fat (much like gymnasts, dancers, and runners). Eating disorders, which affect men too, are a serious psychological issue, fostered by our society and the demands of sport. Since the victim is often unaware or unable to escape, this condition almost always requires intervention and counseling.

Young female climbers in particular face a very real danger from the female athlete triad: disordered eating, amenorrhea (loss of menstrual period), and osteoporosis (brittle bones). Individually, each of these is a serious problem; together the health risks are severe.

Climbers must be realistic in their expectations about body weight. There is only so little you can weigh without sacrificing performance and health. If you come from a long line of large ancestors, no amount of wishful thinking or starvation will make you diminutive.

For an approximation of your ideal minimum weight, use the following formulas and allow a range of error of 10 percent for bone structure. Men: start at 106 and add 6 pounds for each additional inch past 5 feet (therefore, a 6-foot male should weigh around 180 and be between 160 and 195 pounds). Women: start at 100 and add 5 pounds for each additional inch over 5 feet (thus a 5-foot, 6-inch female should weigh about 130 and be between 117 and 143 pounds). If you think you can climb your best at 20 percent below that figure (144 and 104 respectively), faggetaboutit! On the other hand, you may feel just fine at 20 percent heavier (216 and 156 pounds).

SPORT EATING

Since most of your meals are consumed at home, that is where you build the foundation for improving your climbing performance. No matter your diet philosophy—omnivore or vegetarian—the basics of healthful eating are the same.

In general, you should aim to get 50 per-cent of your calories from carbohydrates, 25 percent from fats, and 25 percent from protein. This differs from the old 60-25-15 guideline but is less radical than most fad diets. It doesn't really matter much if you consume three meals per day or more, as long as the total calories are the same. Some people will do better with more frequent, smaller meals while others are just fine with a few larger meals.

An active person on a low-carb diet needs a minimum of 1 gram of carbohydrates per pound of body weight every day to avoid ketosis (a metabolic state in which performance suffers). Most climbers eating a healthy sports diet should take in two to three times that amount daily while serious endurance fiends need to increase the rate to 3 or 4 grams per pound or they'll bonk.

While the macronutrients receive most of the attention, an aspect of nutrition that scientists are increasingly focusing upon concerns feeding our guests. There are roughly ten times more microbes in the body than there are human cells. The total mass of all those microbes is around 2.5 pounds (1.1 kilograms); nearly as much as the brain.

Increasing evidence is showing that all those bacteria (more than one thousand species) are vital to good health. Thus greater attention is now being paid to prebiotics (foods that feed the good flora) and probiotics (foods or supplements that contain healthy bacteria). This is one more reason to consume less refined products from a wide range of sources.

BREAKFAST RULES

You may be tired of hearing that "breakfast is the most important meal of the day." Moms around the world use this refrain—then fill their children up with candy (aka, kids' cereal loaded with sugar) before packing them off to school. Despite this hypocrisy, the basic advice holds true and is especially important for athletes—that would be you. Don't even think about complaining that a climb is too strenuous if you didn't eat a real breakfast!

It isn't just a matter of starting the day off well fueled, though that's certainly a big performance help. Eating a good-size (500+ calorie), breakfast rich in carbohydrates and protein can reduce your daily calorie consumption by about 5 percent without the usual diet suffering. You won't feel as much need to snack on junk food and sodas in the afternoon and are less likely to overindulge at dinner.

Cereals with milk or yogurt are still the kings of breakfasts since they're convenient and contain mostly carbs with a bit of protein; adding fruits is a bonus. Although the cardboard box may be more nutritious than many of the cereals at the supermarket, you can find some healthy ones that actually taste good; it just takes a bit of looking and testing.

The main cereal ingredients should be whole grain oats, whole grain wheat, or bran flakes. When comparing the Nutrition Facts labels, first multiply the grams of sugars by 4 to get the number of sugar calories, then compare that to the total number of calories. It should be less than a quarter—though it's about half in many kids' cereals. Ideally each serving should contain at least 5 grams of fiber. And there should be less than 8 grams of sugar, 3 grams of total fat, and 250 mg of sodium.

It's ironic that granola-crunchers have earned a reputation as healthy, back-to-nature types since most granolas are fairly high in fats and sugars; the few granolas that are actually better for you tend to taste like cow fodder. Instead, try muesli, a cereal made from toasted whole oats, nuts, fruit, and wheat flakes.

If you need to reduce calories, consider trying lower fat milk: start with 2 percent, then move to 1 percent. In cereal, you'll hardly notice the difference and eventually won't even miss whole (3.3 percent) milk.

Soy "milk" is another alternative that can be tasty but, contrary to the advertising, is not any healthier than cow's milk unless you are lactose intolerant. Indeed there is increasing evidence that the negatives of high soy intake (blocking uptake of nutrients, high estrogen content, blood-clotting component, genetic modification, and pesticide content) may outweigh the positives (high content of polyunsaturated fats, fiber, vitamins, and minerals, and low content of saturated fat). And 87 percent of the soy grown in the United States is genetically modified.

An excellent choice to accompany muesli or other cereals is whole or low-fat yogurt with fresh fruit. The milk is cultured with probiotic bacteria, but many of the mass-produced brands kill these off with pasteurization. For the most health benefit, look for "Live and Active Cultures" on the label; some companies add additional strains of bacteria to enhance their beneficial effect on the digestive system. Yogurt is high in calcium and also contains protein, B-12, riboflavin, potassium, magnesium, and zinc. Beware that most of the non-fat yogurts with processed fruit on the bottom have so much sweetener in them that they should be considered dessert instead of health food.

If cereal just isn't your thing or you need variety, there are a lot of other options besides greasy egg dishes, bacon, sausages, hash browns, croissants, and all the other traditional gut-bombs that slow you down. These are still better than nothing, if consumed in moderation, but the tendency is toward excess. When heading out to play in brutally cold weather, a high-fat breakfast can even be the best choice.

More athletic options for warm weather include a bagel with lox and low-fat cream cheese; poached eggs and whole grain toast or muffin with fruit preserves; Canadian bacon and whole grain waffles or pancakes with maple syrup; or even a breakfast drink. A grapefruit sprinkled with brown sugar is a popular choice: opt for a ruby-red instead of a plain to get nearly 50 times more beta-carotene and 1,700 times more lycopene.

MIDDAY REFUELING

In terms of calorie content, lunch should be the same size as breakfast and dinner.

But this doesn't have to be in one sitting. If you're going to work out in the afternoon, it's often better to eat a light lunch or simply graze on healthy snacks throughout the day, since a full stomach isn't conducive to exercise. Snacking on protein can prevent hunger binges and maintain your energy level—no post-lunch coma—better than carbohydrates or fats.

There are a lot of good midday snacks that are fast and easy: soups; fruits (fresh and dried) and fruit smoothies; raisins and prunes; mixed nuts; yogurt or frozen yogurt; low-fat cottage cheese and carrot sticks; celery and hummus; stone-ground crackers and sugar-free peanut butter; whole-grain bread with tuna fish and mayonnaise; whole-grain bagel and cream cheese; baked potato with plain yogurt or mustard; zucchini bread.

Some snacks, like low-salt pretzels, rice cakes, and air-popped popcorn, don't provide much calorie content (if you don't overdo it) or protein but do help fill you up. Drink several glasses of water throughout the day; use a carbon filter on your faucet if taste or chemical contaminants are a problem in your area (bottled water has no salubrious effects but does cost more). Try to avoid junk such as soft drinks (diet or not), potato chips, French fries, and many of the popular entrees served at fast-food restaurants.

If you've eaten well earlier in the day, you won't feel the need for that huge dinner that may have been your mainstay. By eating a smaller supper, you'll sleep better and wake up hungry for a good breakfast.

DINING OUT

When you dine out, especially if you're traveling, it's more difficult to control your diet. If you normally enjoy a healthful diet, there are no forbidden foods for the climber in training—just fewer high calorie indulgences. And keep exercising while you travel.

American

Better: grilled, baked, or broiled fish; barbecued or grilled chicken sans skin; turkey; lean steak (filet mignon or sirloin); roast beef or tri-tip; lean hamburger; veggie burger; soups sans cream; whole grain bread sans butter; salad bars (careful with the dressing and toppings); baked or mashed potato; baked sweet potato; roasted garlic; rice; steamed veggies; sherbet; angel food cake with fruit.

Worse: fried anything; most toppings on baked potatoes; pot pies; fatty steaks (New York strip, porterhouse, T-bone); grilled cheese or Philly cheesesteak sandwich; Caesar salad; creamy salad dressings; buffalo wings; potato skins; ice cream; crème brûlée; cheesecake, mousse.

Chinese

Better: stir fries; chow mein; chop suey; moo goo gai pan; Mongolian beef; black bean and garlic sauce; hot and sour or wonton soup; spring rolls; steamed brown rice (order extra); steamed dumplings; fortune cookie (just one for good luck).

Worse: fried rice; crispy or batter-coated dishes; egg rolls; fried wonton; lo mein; pork ribs; duck; sweet and sour dishes; kung pao dishes; cashew, lemon, or sesame chicken (okay if not fried); orange beef; General Tso's chicken; lobster sauce; MSG.

Fast Food

Better: submarine with lean meat; veggie pizza (request half the cheese); soft taco; broiled or grilled chicken (remove skin); chicken burrito; roast beef sandwich; chili and crackers; single broiled or grilled burger; baked potato sans topping; pancakes, bagel, breakfast burrito; low-fat milk shake.

Worse: super-size meals; French fries or onion rings; extra hamburger patties; bacon cheeseburger; fried chicken; fish sandwiches; special sauce and mayo; sodas; milk shake; granola; kids' cereals; breakfast biscuit; hash browns; muffins; Danish pastries; donuts.

Indian

Better: tandoori chicken; shish kebabs; curries sans coconut milk; biriyani; tikka and vindaloo dishes; chapatti, naan, and roti breads; steamed rice; mulligatawny and dhal soups; low-fat lassi (yogurt drink).

Worse: pakori, samosas; paratha; poori; palak and saag paneer; dishes with makkhani (butter) or malai (cream).

Italian
Better: pasta with red, primavera, or clam sauce; veggie pizza; chicken cacciatore; minestrone; bread sans butter.
Worse: calamari; antipasto; garlic bread; bread dips; alfredo or pesto sauce; cannelloni, lasagna, ravioli, and tortellini; parmagiana dishes; pepperoni or sausage pizza; parmesan topping.

Japanese
Better: sushi and sashimi (from a reliable source); edamame; sunomono (cucumber salad); tofu dishes; soba noodles; ramen; sukiyaki; yakitori; green tea.
Worse: tonkatsu (fried pork); tempura; agemono; smoked fish.

Mediterranean
Better: gyros; cucumber salad; baba ghanoush; tabouli; hummus; olive bread.
Worse: feta cheese; spanikopita; falafel; baklava.

Mexican
Better: grilled fish and chicken; rice and bean burritos; tostadas; soft tacos; fajitas; tamales and enchiladas sans cheese; salsa and baked chips; guacamole (in moderation); gazpacho and bean soups; ceviche; black or red beans; refried beans sans lard; Spanish rice.
Worse: fried chips; nachos; sour cream; normal refried beans (with lard); mole; chimichangas; chili relleno; hard tacos; quesadilla; flautas; fried ice cream.

Snacks
Better: fresh fruit (apple, banana, berries, grapes, orange, pear); fresh vegetables (broccoli, carrots, celery, grape tomatoes) with hummus dip; raw nuts (almonds, cashews, pecans); roasted peanuts; pre-popped popcorn (low salt, trans-fat-free oil); dried peas with wasabi; can of tuna (packed with water); whole-grain crispbread with cottage cheese; low-fat yogurt; quick breads (pumpkin, zucchini, banana, bran); dark chocolate (at least 50 percent cocoa); low-salt pretzels; natural peanut butter; natural beef jerky.
Worse: potato chips; corn chips; donuts; cookies; cake; milk chocolate; microwave popcorn; peanut butter (most have a lot of sugar added); ice cream.

Thai
Better: tom yum soups; pad Thai; Thai salads (many have meat or seafood); steamed brown rice; curries sans coconut milk; gratium (garlic pepper) sauce.
Worse: tom kha gai (coconut chicken soup); satay with peanut sauce; mee krob; gang, massamon, and panang curry; Thai iced tea.

DINING TIME

For most of us, the largest meal of the day is in the evening.

Whether by choice or necessity, we don't always eat at home. This doesn't mean you have to give up all hope of healthy nutrition, even if you don't know what the menu means. Following a few simple guidelines can make your meals healthier.

- Try to cover half of your plate with complex carbs (vegetables, beans, grain-enriched pasta, brown rice, potato with skin, whole-grain bread, fruit), then make sure you have adequate protein represented; the fats will usually take care of themselves.

- Make fish and seafood your main dietary priority, followed by poultry, then red meats. Select organic free-range meats to reduce consumption of antibiotics.

- When possible, opt for baked, broiled, or grilled entrees versus fried or sautéed to eliminate hidden fat calories.

- Remove the skin from chicken and trim the fat from steaks.

- For maximum nutritional value, select vegetable courses that are raw or lightly steamed versus cooked to death. If it's limp and pallid, it's been ruined.

- Don't smother baked potatoes with cheese, butter, and sour cream, but do eat the skin. Better yet, order a sweet potato; it's packed with vitamins.

- When grazing at the salad bar, go for the dark green and colorful vegetables (spinach, broccoli, carrots, peppers, tomatoes), plus cauliflower, beans, chickpeas, mushrooms, and sunflower seeds. Go light on the pale lettuce, celery, cucumbers, radishes, zucchini, and alfalfa sprouts; pallid vegetables tend to add weight but little nutrition.

- Watch out for the heavy dressings (which can add more than 800 calories) and fatty toppings (cheese, greasy croutons, marinated artichokes) that can nullify many of the health benefits of a salad. Request dressings on the side and then add sparingly.

- Avoid excess alcoholic drinks. Some wine with dinner is arguably a good thing, particularly red wines since they are high in antioxidants. Beer can be okay if you choose wisely (see "Fermented Malt Beverages" later in this chapter) and do not drink too many. Mixed drinks, however, tend to be high in calories with little nutritional benefit.

Although alcohol itself does not create the dreaded beer belly (little is converted directly to fat), the by-product of conversion in the liver is acetate, which greatly reduces fat burning. Consumption of excess alcohol (read: getting drunk) also reduces levels of testosterone and increases cortisol, leading to decreases in muscle mass. Worse yet, studies have shown that an aperitif enhances appetite so you consume more calories at a meal—part of the reason restaurants encourage that pre-dinner cocktail.

POWER SHOPPING

The bulk of your food probably comes from the grocery store, so that's where good nutrition begins. It takes a little longer to be a smart shopper—you have to read the labels— but the rewards are worth it. Of course, if you have a local farmers market, by all means take advantage of it; everything is fresher, healthier, tastier, and often cheaper.

The main rule of thumb: the less processed, the better. When selecting breads, crackers, and cereals, always opt for whole grain instead of enriched white or just "wheat"; these have more vitamins, minerals, and fiber. Brown rice is more flavorful and nutritious than white rice, which has the bran removed.

Foods with a lower energy density (number of calories per gram) are generally more filling and nutritious than high-density foods. Simply divide calories by weight to do a quick comparison.

Pasta is not usually considered a health food. Although whole-wheat pasta is somewhat healthier than traditional durum wheat (semolina), the latter cooks better because of higher gluten content. Soy and rice pastas turn to mush and taste bland, so they are only recommended for those with wheat allergies.

However, a relatively new pasta, Barilla Plus, is a multigrain product that actually tastes as good as the normal variety. This blend of semolina includes lentils, chickpeas, oats, spelt, barley, egg whites, ground flaxseed, and wheat fiber and has 30 percent more protein, 75 percent more fiber, and 100 percent more omega-3 fatty acid.

ORGANIC VS. LOCAL

This may sound like heresy, but organic foods are not necessarily more nutritious or flavorful than those offered by the agrochemical industry. Some of the claims by starry-eyed advocates are inaccurate or wildly blown out of proportion.

Although some studies tout the nutritional superiority of organic fruits and vegetables, most did not take into account variables such as time of harvest, freshness, storage, and weather. The best study to date showed that when these variables are controlled, organic wheat, tomatoes, potatoes, cabbage, onions, and lettuce have 20 to 40 percent more nutrients than non-organic produce, while organic milk contained 50 to 80 percent more antioxidants.

While encouraging, more depends on where it comes from and freshness than how the food was grown. In some regions, it isn't possible to grow certain produce without the use of pesticides. It is better for you and the planet to consume fresher, local fruits and vegetables than organic ones trucked in from a thousand miles away.

Though nutrition may not be a sure thing, there are still good reasons to purchase organic products. Eating fewer toxic chemicals is probably good for your health since low doses can accumulate in tissues. There is also no question that organic farming is better for the planet; in some cases, it can even be more productive per acre of land. Unfortunately, the major food corporations care more about profits than nutrition, so they emphasize taste (add sugar and salt), eye appeal (add coloring), and long shelf life (strip the good stuff and add the periodic table).

Every visit to the store is an opportunity to vote against spraying pesticides, depleting topsoil, contaminating water, and shortsighted greed. Now that the Pandora's box of genetically modified organisms (GMO) has been opened, there are even greater health and safety concerns, with very few assurances, about our food supply. Yet there currently are no regulations on labeling of GMOs, so there is little choice about eating them.

Since organic products tend to cost 50 to 100 percent more than conventional products, going totally organic can be cost prohibitive for many people. If you simply choose one additional organic item per shopping trip, the impact to your wallet will be minimal but the cumulative effect can be major.

The best overall value is in organic meats (free-range animals grown without steroids or antibiotics), omega-3 enhanced eggs (from chickens that eat feed high in canola oil), and milk. Other good organic values because the conventional products are often contaminated include apples, cherries, peaches, potatoes, spinach, and strawberries.

According to the Environmental Working Group (a relatively unbiased source), there is little point in purchasing organic asparagus, bananas, broccoli, cauliflower, corn, or peas because the conventionally grown produce is essentially pesticide free. Organic seafood is so mired with misleading labels that it is not worth spending extra to purchase.

SMART READING

Pay attention to the Nutrition Facts label on the back or side of the packaging, not the advertising hype on the front. First, look at the serving size and see how much you will actually eat. Then find out how many calories are in a serving and do the math. Next find out how many calories come from fat, the total grams of fat, and the total grams of protein. The amount of sodium and saturated fats should be close to zero. With practice, it doesn't take long to scan a label to find the good, the bad, and the ugly.

Protein

It is often said that proteins are the building blocks of the body. While a bit of an exaggeration, the amino acids they provide are vital for growth, maintenance, and repair of muscles and tissues such as tendons, ligaments, and skin. Protein is also important for the production of enzymes, hormones, neurotransmitters, and hemoglobin.

Considerable evidence indicates that, to maintain muscle mass (neutral nitrogen balance) or build muscles (positive nitrogen balance), most climbers need about twice as much protein as the recommended daily allowance for sedentary adults (0.36 gram per pound of body weight, or 0.8 gram per kilogram of body weight). Thus you should strive to consume 0.72 to 1.0 gram of protein per pound of body weight—a 176-pound (80 kilogram) person needs about 127 to 176 grams per day.

For most athletes, this amount of protein is easily achieved with a standard, healthy diet. However, those who are on severe diets that are not carefully planned place themselves at risk of deficiency. Also, during phases of very intense strength training, the body may require even higher levels of protein. Insufficient protein will hamper your recovery, prevent strength gains, and reduce resistance to colds and flu.

Although some debate remains, most of the evidence indicates there is no benefit to endurance when protein is consumed during exercise as long as adequate carbohydrates are available. It is also doubtful that ingesting protein immediately after exercise speeds recovery or aids muscle adaptations as long as plenty of carbs are consumed.

Contrary to claims of the protein-pushers, there is no evidence that consuming more than 1 gram per pound will make you huge or do anything else except drain your wallet. With a proper diet, there is almost never a need for any outdoor athlete to purchase protein powders or amino acid supplements. Omnivores may even need to cut back on some protein sources since many are also high in fat calories.

Vegetarians, especially vegans, have to be more careful about protein intake since they need to consume large portions of alternative sources because plants just aren't as protein-dense as animals. Those who don't eat meat must learn about complementary proteins and include a variety of beans and grains in their diet.

Fat

Possibly the most confusing nutrition topic of all is "good fats" versus "bad fats." This subject has received a lot of attention in recent years, and as is common in this field, what we were told a few years ago (and which is still widely held) is at odds with what is being said now by the experts.

Even cholesterol may not be the heart-killer that drug companies would like everyone to think—it is far from being an open and closed case. Indeed, low levels of cholesterol can impair brain function, muscle and bone growth, and immune protection. Eating foods high in cholesterol has no effect on blood levels for most people. And for the one-third who do respond the bad low-density lipoprotein (LDL) particles get bigger so they are less likely to cause problems.

There are four main categories of fats: saturated, monounsaturated, polyunsaturated, and trans fatty acids (more commonly known as trans fats). Then there are two types of polyunsaturated fatty acids (PUFA), called omega-3 and omega-6, which are frequently termed "essential fatty acids."

In general, the ones to avoid are the processed trans fats, which tend to be solids at room temperature. The most common source of trans fats in the modern era is partially hydrogenated oil, which is darn near everywhere in processed foods (Crisco has been around since 1911).

In January 2006, the U.S. Food and Drug Administration (FDA) began requiring food labels to list the amount of trans fats on the nutrition label. The American Heart Association has recommended that trans fats should be limited to 2 grams per day. Here's the catch: the FDA allows a package to claim zero trans fats if a single serving has less than half a gram. But we all know you can't eat just one, so by the time you've polished off a bag of potato chips with "zero trans fats," you've actually exceeded your daily allotment!

Saturated fats have been vilified for over fifty years but more recent research is showing they may not be as evil as many believe. What was once dogma is now being questioned again as the blame shifts to trans fats.

When shopping it helps to know the marketing lingo: "Reduced Fat" (25 percent less than the original product); "Lite" (one-third the calories or half the fat, not both); and "Fat-Free" (half gram or less per serving). These products tend be less filling and guilt-free, so people eat more. Many people consume more calories and sodium than if they'd gone with the "evil" original.

When it comes to oils, they all contain about 120 calories per tablespoon, but some are better than others. The ones to shun are commercial lard, partially hydrogenated oils, and refined oils, all of which are unhealthy.

The debate over whether butter or margarine is healthier has gone back and forth for decades. The new trans-fat-free margarines in a tub (not a stick), taste issues aside, are a pretty good choice. But butter, in moderation, is still a decent choice because it helps you absorb vitamins and is a good source of conjugated-linolenic acid (CLA), which helps fight cancer.

The best choices for cooking are olive oil, coconut oil, peanut oil, leaf lard and ghee (clarified butter). Avoid corn, refined canola, palm, sunflower, and safflower oils; the latter two are associated with allergies and inflammations. Extra-virgin, cold-pressed, first-pressing oils (such as olive, avocado, and walnut) retain more flavor and nutrients than those extracted with heat or chemical solvents but need to be refrigerated and protected from light.

In the typical Western diet, the ratio of omega-6 to omega-3 PUFA is often greater than 10 to 1 because we don't consume enough of the latter. Numerous studies have shown that a ratio of 4 to 1 or less is strongly associated with healthier hearts, reduced risk of cancer, and fewer problems with asthma, arthritis, and depression. Some scientists are even arguing that the ratio is less important than the total amount of omega-3 in the diet.

The best source of omega-3 is cold water fish such as salmon and tuna, which are high in DHA (docosahexaenoic acid) and EPA (eicosapentaenoic acid). Ideally, fish should be consumed once or twice per week; unless you are pregnant you would have to eat far more than that to be concerned about contamination.

Fish oil isn't used for cooking but may be added to foods to boost omega-3 fatty acids. Thankfully, you don't have to take your Grandma's advice (though it was excellent) of a daily dose of cod liver oil. Now there are plenty of fish oil capsules available that are inexpensive and don't taste horrific. But don't forget that all fats are still 9 calories per gram, so this is not a case of "more is better."

If you can't or won't consume fish, then you should try to boost omega-3 consumption by including alpha-linolenic acid (ALA) in your diet. Good sources of this include flaxseed, flax oil, expeller-pressed canola oil, and walnuts; these are common ingredients in fortified foods.

Sugar

When it comes to sugars, it's best to think of what you consume on a daily basis and also what you select for athletic performance. For your daily diet, try to eliminate as much added fructose as possible. In this day and age, that's easier said than done. Beware that the Nutrition Facts label only lists "total sugars," which includes both added and naturally occurring sugars, so you must read the ingredients list to find out what is hidden inside.

Among the most pervasive additives is high fructose corn syrup (HFCS); it is merely a cheaper alternative for table sugar. In 1974, the average American consumed 1.5 pounds per year. By 2000, they were eating 62.7 pounds of the sweetener.

GLYCEMIC INDEX

While carbohydrates are classified as simple (1 to 5 molecules) or complex (hundreds of molecules), this does not describe how quickly they are absorbed. The glycemic index is a rating system developed for diabetics to approximate how fast sugars enter the bloodstream; 0–60 is low and slow, 60–85 is moderate, 85–100 is high and fast.

Unfortunately, recent research has shown that the variance of reactions to foods is highly individual. For example, white bread is typically given a GI of 70 but the bodies of some people treat it as 44 and others as high as 132. Another problem is different charts often provide different values for the same item, sometimes varying widely, due to the particular test procedure and brand or freshness of food.

Some foods also change properties depending on how they are prepared. For example, a baked potato is usually considered to have a high glycemic index but cooling it for a salad doubles the amount of natural resistant starch, which reduces the insulin spike.

Furthermore, adding fats and proteins will lower the GI of carbohydrates so the index value is invalid for nearly all meals. Adding vinegar or lemon juice to a meal also lowers the glycemic load (GI x grams of carbohydrate/100).

This means that any diet based purely on glycemic index or glycemic load is flawed from the get-go. Most healthy people don't have real problems with an insulin spike and the ensuing sugar crash, so there is little need to stress over glycemic charts. In general, however, opting for lower glycemic foods is a good idea because they tend to be more nutritious. Only those with a great deal of excess body fat (30 pounds or more) will really need to pay attention to the glycemic load of their diet.

While of limited value for planning meals, the GI values can be helpful for athletes during and immediately after exercise. For a quick pick-me-up during the day, moderate- to high-GI fuels will enter your bloodstream faster. Following a hard effort, consuming high-GI foods can restore muscle glycogen faster so you'll be ready to go again the next day.

As you can imagine, high fructose corn syrup is everywhere, and it's difficult to avoid. Worse, HFCS may be unhealthier than sugar, also known as sucrose. Though chemically similar (the most common HFCS breaks down to 55 percent fructose while sucrose contains 50 percent fructose—the rest is glucose), the stronger bonds of sugar make it more stable.

Other commonly added sweeteners include honey, brown and raw sugar, brown rice syrup, evaporated cane syrup, apple juice, and white grape juice. Products containing these are often labeled as "natural," implying they are somehow better, but they have insignificant nutritional value over table sugar. Essentially, all of these sugars are "junk calories" that merely improve taste.

Probably the most common artificial sweetener, aspartame (aka, Equal and NutraSweet), is actually a molecule of two amino acids that is 180 times sweeter than table sugar but follows a different metabolic pathway. Diet sodas, usually made with aspartame, cut about 150 calories per can from your diet, and are okay in moderation. But plain old water or flavored seltzer is still the best way to slake your thirst. Some people have negative reactions to aspartame and may experience migraines, hives, swelling, or hyperactivity. However, most of the myths floating around on the internet about the dangers of aspartame are just that.

For a training diet, you should pay attention to the specific sugars in the products, particularly energy bars and sports drinks. The types of sugars included can directly affect your performance due to how quickly they reach your bloodstream and depending on how your stomach handles them.

All carbohydrates are ultimately broken down in the small intestine into glucose (blood sugar), which is then converted to glycogen; however, the body handles the sugars differently. While glucose is actively absorbed into the bloodstream, fructose (fruit sugar) diffuses so it doesn't provide a fast energy spike. This is good for some people, but too much fructose may cause cramps or diarrhea in others. Combined with other sugars, small amounts of fructose give a bigger energy boost than either alone.

As a sports fuel, honey can be a good natural source of energy for working hard due to its mix of sugars; typically around 38 percent fructose, 31 percent glucose, and 10 percent other sugars. Indeed honey has a carbohydrate profile almost identical to some of the most popular sport gels that come in expensive packages.

Maltodextrin is another form of sugar, a glucose polymer, that is not as sweet as many others, which allows it to be used in higher concentrations for high-energy foods and drinks. Maltodextrin is easily digestible so it is less likely to cause stomach problems when you are exercising hard.

Another popular source of sugar in workout drinks is brown rice syrup, which is roughly 50 percent soluble complex carbohydrates, 45 percent maltose, and 3 percent glucose. This combination gives a quick energy boost from the glucose while the maltose takes about an hour to digest and the biggest molecules take two or three hours to break down. Thus brown rice syrup offers a steady energy supply instead of the fast spike followed by a crash associated with simple sugars.

Other sources of easily consumed carbohydrates include agave syrup (derived from the same plant used to make tequila; about 85 percent fructose and 8 percent glucose) and barley malt syrup (also used to make high quality beer; 65 percent maltose and 30 percent complex carbohydrate). Both of these contain larger sugar molecules so they take longer to break down for a slower energy release. They also have unique flavors that can help spice up bland recipes.

A carb that has received a lot of hype is waxy maize starch, which is made from a special variety of corn. The only controlled study so far showed that it does not empty from the stomach or replenish glycogen faster than maltodextrin. None of the other fanciful claims have been backed up by science either, yet it sure costs a lot more.

Salt

As with sugars, it is best to think of your salt intake on a daily basis as separate from that needed during hard exercise. While sodium is essential in small amounts (around 2 grams per day), many people consume between 8 and 12 grams per day. Bear in mind that table salt is just 40 percent sodium by weight, the rest is chloride.

Meanwhile, we are not getting enough potassium in our diets; the recommended amount is 4.7 grams per day (up from the former 3.5 gram recommendation) and most of us fall far below that. The best solution is consuming more spinach, beans, cantaloupes, almonds, Brussels sprouts, mushrooms, bananas, oranges, grapefruits, and potatoes, which are all high in potassium.

The problem with too much sodium is that your kidneys can only process so much before it starts to accumulate in your blood. This excess mineral is hydrophilic, so it attracts and holds water, which increases your blood volume. This in turn raises pressure in your arteries and makes the heart work harder because it is moving more blood. Everyone has their own sodium limit, so what is fine for some will cause bloating, higher blood pressure, and heart and kidney problems in others.

Many of us have been admonished to cut back on salt at the dinner table, yet that only accounts for about 6 percent of our daily sodium intake. In the typical U.S. diet, the vast majority (about 77 percent) of the excess sodium comes in prepared or processed foods. Selecting low-sodium foods whenever possible will give you the biggest health benefit.

Table salt is pretty much pure sodium chloride, stripped of all minerals, with some anti-caking additives. However, the powers that be in North America ensure that iodine is added, while in Europe and Latin America fluoride is added to offset supposed health concerns—the science is dubious at best but it's good propaganda.

A slightly healthier, and certainly tastier, alternative for both cooking and at meals is sea salt, which contains trace amounts of iron, magnesium, calcium, potassium, manganese, zinc, and iodine. Beware the latest health fad for "Himalayan salt," which is purely a way to extract exorbitant sums of cash from your pocket with zero benefit.

The best way to combat sodium loss from exercise is by consuming a variety of foods. Old-fashioned salt tablets are obsolete and should be avoided. Even modern electrolyte replacement drinks and tablets are unnecessary, despite the marketing.

Fiber

Dietary fiber, also known as roughage, is an important part of a healthy diet. This is the plant stuff that isn't broken down in the stomach and absorbed by the small intestines. What remains is passed into the large intestines where it mingles with bacteria to ferment and release gases and short-chain fatty acids, such as butyric acid. These fatty acids play important roles in controlling blood glucose and lipid levels, regulating immune response, and maintaining colon health.

A diet with sufficient fiber is associated with reduced risk of heart disease, high blood pressure, stroke, diabetes, constipation, diverticulitis (inflamed pouches on the colon), and cancer. The recommended daily intake for men aged fourteen to fifty years old is 38 grams while women in that age range should consume 25 grams. Over age fifty, the recommendation drops to 30 and 21 grams, respectively. Unfortunately, most Americans only consume about 15 grams per day, so there is a lot of room for improvement.

Dietary fiber is commonly divided into three types: soluble, insoluble, and resistant starch. These are present in all plant foods, though the exact amount varies. Rather than thinking about consuming one type or the other, it is best to seek out foods high in fiber in general.

A category of fiber receiving more medical attention these days is known as prebiotic because it stimulates the growth of healthful bacteria and impedes harmful bacteria in the colon. Many of the typical fiber sources are prebiotics, but one compound that appears particularly beneficial is inulin (no relation to insulin), which is found in onions, garlic, chicory, and Jerusalem artichoke (a type of sunflower).

Many health products contain added fiber that is extracted or modified from plants (e.g., green bananas and potatoes) or animal sources (e.g., chitin and chitosan that come from crab and lobster shells). The FDA allows foods with 5 or more grams of fiber per serving to be labeled "high fiber." If the food contains 2.5 to 4.9 grams per serving, it may be termed a "good source of fiber."

For your daily diet, you should strive to include more whole-grain breads and pasta, brown rice and quinoa, cereals with bran or fiber (or sprinkle wheat bran and berries on your normal cereal), beans of all types, plenty of fruits (both fresh and dried), and vegetables (carrots, broccoli, potatoes with the skin, etc.). For snacks, look to whole-grain crackers, nuts and seeds, wasabi peas, low-fat popcorn, and oat bran muffins.

However, prior to a strenuous workout, high fiber foods may not be your best choice. During exercise, these have a tendency to cause intestinal discomfort.

WALKING THE AISLES

The tricks of the supermarket trade make healthy shopping more difficult. Notice how the lighting is just right (so you don't blink or squint), the music is soothing (so you'll relax and linger), and the in-store bakery and chicken rotisserie are always on (so the smell will make you hungry and buy more food). At most stores, products at eye level and at the ends of aisles have paid a premium for that location. If a product is discontinued, it may have sold well but the manufacturer didn't pay the slotting fee charged by the store.

To defeat these tactics, the smart shopper prepares a list, sticks to it, and doesn't go to the store on an empty stomach. Get in, get out. Ignore the store's layout—though fresh products are often on the perimeter—and shop according to the food pyramid: start with grains, move to produce, and finish with dairy and meats. Resist the temptation of coupons and specials, since you often end up buying more and getting a less-healthy product. Compare the unit price on the shelves; bulk isn't always a good value.

Cereal Aisle

▨ Pick cereals that contain at least 5 grams of fiber and no more than 8 grams of sugar, 3 grams of total fat, and 250 mg of sodium per serving.

Bread Aisle

▨ Look for whole grain as the main ingredient but keep fat to less than 2 grams per slice. Pass on any white or "wheat" breads.

▨ Consider purchasing an automatic bread machine and making your own fresh whole grain breads; simple and delicious.

▨ Avoid the high-fat treats such as croissants, muffins, and pastries.

Produce Aisle

▨ Fill your basket with fruits and vegetables. Consider organic to reduce your pesticide intake. Prewashed and packaged salad mixes cost more but make your hectic life easier.

▨ Select darker green vegetables whenever possible because they tend to be much higher in important nutrients. For example, romaine lettuce is far healthier than pale-green iceberg.

▨ Choose red or yellow peppers over green. It's the same plant, but the former are more mature and contain twice as much vitamin C, four times more vitamin E, and eight times more beta-carotene.

▨ Avocados are not only tasty but contain beneficial phytochemicals and monounsaturated fat.

▨ White potatoes can be as nutritious as sweet potatoes if you eat the skin and hold back on the fatty condiments. The nutrition profiles are different so choose both.

▨ Fresh fruit and vegetable juices are a tasty and convenient way to get your daily quota, though you miss out on the fiber in the real thing.

Canned-Foods Aisle

- Stock up on soups, but avoid those with a cream base, MSG, or high sodium content.
- Select canned tuna packed in water for an excellent, low-cost source of protein.
- Canned vegetables contain nearly as many nutrients as fresh, but watch out for sugar, salt, and other additives.
- Canned fruits are often packed in syrup that is basically liquid sugar; look for fruits packed in their own juices.

Ethnic Aisle

- Choose the vegetarian refried beans without the hydrogenated lard.
- Opt for multigrain or whole-grain pasta over plain semolina varieties.
- Many pasta sauces and salsas contain a surprising amount of sodium and hidden sugars; compare nutrition labels when deciding.
- Pesto sauce typically contains 50 percent more calories than tomato sauce.
- Coconut milk is healthy but high in calories; choose the light version if available.

Dairy Aisle

- Work your way down to 1 percent milk. Some milk is now fortified with DHA, an omega-3 fatty acid that is important for optimal brain function.
- Although soy milk is heavily marketed as healthful, there is increasing doubt about these claims. Consider unsweetened soy milk an occasional taste change rather than a substitute for real milk.
- Select cheese made with low-fat milk when the recipe allows. If the cheese is labeled, look for those with less than 5 grams of fat per ounce. Nonfat cottage cheese is a good source of protein.
- Yogurt is an excellent source of protein and calcium, as well as probiotic bacteria. Look for less than 200 calories, 2 grams of saturated fat, 40 grams of sugar, and no artificial sweetener. The best option is plain yogurt (containing live cultures) mixed with fresh fruit.
- Butter or trans-fat-free margarine is the best choice for daily consumption; avoid hydrogenated or partially hydrogenated oils.

Frozen-Foods Aisle

- Select calcium-fortified orange juice and any other that is 100 percent fruit juice.
- Frozen entrees from the natural foods case or the "health" section will usually have reduced saturated fats and can be quite tasty. However, they may also be loaded with calories, so check the labels.
- Frozen vegetables are nearly as nutritious as farm fresh—and more nutritious than store fresh during the off-season—but beware the sauces. Vegetables with a "U.S. Fancy" shield on the box tend to have higher nutrient value than those labeled "U.S. No. 1" or "U.S. No.2."
- Frozen yogurt often contains as much sugar as ice cream. Whichever you choose, try to keep total fat to less than 5 grams per serving. However, it's better to indulge in a super-premium ice cream once a month than in a low-fat one a couple of times a week.

BETTER LIVING THROUGH PLANTS

Numerous compounds in plants, generically called phytochemicals, are emerging as potential insurance against a host of diseases. It's best to get the original sources rather than purchasing expensive (and sometimes ineffective) supplements. Here are some of the goodies that have been identified and their possible benefits:

Plant	Compound	Action
broccoli, cauliflower, kale, cabbage	isothyocynates, indoles	block synthesis of estrogen associated with breast and ovarian cancer; prevent carcinogens from harming cells
carrots, cantaloupe, apricots, parsley, vegetables	carotenoids	formation of vitamin A; immuno-protection
chile peppers	capsaicin	anticoagulant
citrus fruit	terpenes, limonoids	prevent growth of tumors
flaxseed, walnuts	omega-3 fatty acids	block estrogen activity; immuno-protection
garlic, onion	allylic sulfides	reduces blood pressure and cholesterol; formation of glutathione, a powerful antioxidant
rosemary	quinines	inhibits carcinogens
spinach, collard greens	lutein	antioxidant; eye health
strawberries, pineapple	chlorogenic acid	prevents formation of carcinogenic nitrosamines
tea, red wine, fruits, berries, vegetables, chocolate	flavonoids	antioxidants; inhibit carcinogenic hormones; protects memory
tomatoes	lycopenes	antioxidants
vegetable oils, almonds, peanuts, sesame and sunflower seeds	vitamin E	antioxidant

Meat and Seafood Counter

■ Try to make the fish counter your main source of protein but check the Seafood Watch on the Monterey Bay Aquarium website (www.mbayaq.org/cr/seafood -watch.asp) for an updated list of fishes to avoid (it's grim). Nutritious seafood with healthy populations that are caught with minimal by-catch (other sea life) or are farmed with minimal environmental impact include albacore tuna (North America only), catfish, crab, Pacific halibut, mahi mahi, rainbow trout, striped bass, farmed shrimp (U.S. only), swordfish (U.S. only), tilapia, wild salmon, and yellowfin tuna.

■ Seafood to avoid: bluefin tuna, Atlantic cod and halibut, Chilean seabass, orange roughy, red snapper, farmed salmon, shark, imported farmed shrimp, and imported swordfish.

■ Commercially raised chickens are not kept in cages nor are they fed hormones (by law), but they do consume antibiotics. Organic and free-range chicken isn't necessarily better but can't hurt. Purchase skinless or remove the skin.

■ Turkey is another good protein source. However, processed turkey (bologna, sausage, hot dogs) is often high in fat.

■ Pork tenderloin and Canadian bacon are both fairly low in fat. Minimize your consumption of bacon and hot dogs.

■ Choose lean steaks (sirloin, top round, roast beef) or extra-lean hamburger, preferably from "natural" farms. Grass-fed beef is higher in omega-3s and CLA than beef from feed lots (even organic) but it

can be harder to find. Avoid the fatty grilling steaks (New York strip, porterhouse, T-bone) and regular hamburger.

Cookie and Snack Aisle

■ Journey not into the valley of temptation. But if you must stray, read the nutrition labels and try to minimize the damage.

■ Most peanut butter is loaded with sugar and hydrogenated oil. Select a natural brand without any additives. Pour off the oil and replace it with flax oil to get some good fat in your diet. Almond butter is also tasty and does not contain aflatoxins, known carcinogens produced by molds that grow on some crops.

■ All of the sodas and most of the fruit juices (unless labeled 100 percent) are merely liquid candy that deter people from healthier alternatives.

FUELING THE CLIMB

For normal training and climbs, you don't need to alter your standard diet—as long as it's healthy. However, if the next day will include a very demanding route or long alpine ascent, you can give yourself an edge by eating smart in advance.

The day before the climb, have a good breakfast and a hearty lunch, with some snacks along the way so you don't feel a need for a massive dinner. Start filling your tank early by hydrating all day long and avoid alcoholic beverages that will cause dehydration; you should urinate more often than usual.

Make your evening meal high in carbs but avoid gaseous foods (beans, broccoli, cabbage), especially prior to alpine climbs. It's best to stick with familiar foods that aren't too spicy so you don't have an unexpected surprise on the approach. Don't pig out since a massive meal can disrupt your sleep, which is often hard enough to come by prior to an alpine start.

Endurance athletes often "carbo load" prior to a big event to increase energy stored in the form of glycogen. After the carbohydrates you ingest are broken down into glucose, unused blood sugar can be converted to "animal starch," which is a fast but finite supply of power. Muscle glycogen supercompensation, as carbing up is properly called, can increase endurance for long events up to 20 percent, although there is no benefit for short-duration events.

However, carbo-loading is seldom practical for climbers since our main event doesn't always start at a set time on a specific day. To be effective, it takes at least three days with minimal activity and very high carb consumption (over 70 percent); much more complicated schemes involving depletion days provide slightly greater gains. Loading can also add five or more pounds of extra weight (mostly water) and may cause gastrointestinal problems, both of which can hinder your climbing. If you wish to try it, experiment with carbo-loading well before a major climb.

If you plan to start exercising within an hour or two of waking, it's best to just have a small (200-calorie), carbo-rich breakfast (bowl of bran cereal or bagel with jam, yogurt, and orange juice) that will replenish liver glycogen lost during the night. If you don't eat anything, you may not think straight since the liver maintains blood sugar required by the brain.

On the other hand, too many calories (big ol' stack of pancakes or an omelet with hash browns) will slow emptying from the stomach so the food may slosh around on the approach and not provide the energy when you need it. If you're a bit queasy, try a breakfast shake or meal replacement drink, since liquids empty faster from the stomach. Keep hydrating: drink water, fruit juice, coffee, or tea.

POWER UP: MID-CLIMB FUELING

No matter what you do, even with the most brutal training and carbo-loading regimens, your body can only hold enough glycogen for 90 to 120 minutes of vigorous exercise. The amount you stow away is roughly the same as your daily carbohydrate intake (depending on such factors as lean muscle mass and fitness). For example, a climber who consumes a 3,000-calorie diet that is 60 percent carb might store 1,800 calories: 1,400 as muscle glycogen, 320 as liver glycogen, and 80 in blood.

The meter starts running when you begin working hard and muscle glycogen is consumed. Once this supply is exhausted, you hit the infamous "wall" where suddenly everything seems much harder—your muscles are literally out of fuel. You can keep going a little longer because of the glycogen reserve in your liver. But it won't last long and then you "bonk"—there's no fuel for the brain, and coordination and thinking suffer (irritability, indecisiveness, confusion, and lethargy are common). This is particularly dangerous in an alpine environment because low blood sugar impairs shivering so there is a greater risk of hypothermia.

To skirt the wall and prevent the bonk, you must consume about 40 to 65 grams of carbohydrates per hour while working at moderate intensity. If it will be a very intense day, such as carrying massive loads to a high camp in subzero temps, you may need to triple this intake to stay fueled. However, it truly takes practice to consume 200+ calories per hour while working hard; you must force yourself.

Climbers tend to be haphazard about their rest/fuel breaks and this leads to decreased performance. You can decidedly increase your energy level by getting a head start on fueling and sticking to an eating game plan.

The best way to prevent fatigue is to start ingesting at least a half hour before you feel tired. Rather than one big munchie break every hour or so at the belay, it's better to have small snacks three to four times an hour. This will prevent your muscles from having to compete with the digestive track for blood. Attach a pouch to your climbing harness or the hip belt of your pack so there is a ready supply of carbs (plus sunscreen, lip balm, etc.).

Bars and Gels

Despite the copious advertising hype, you really don't need any of the energy bars or gels. The only thing they offer is convenience—but that's a huge plus for many of us. There is minimal evidence that any of the sport products actually increase performance over thoughtfully selected normal food.

As you've probably discovered, some bars taste like sawdust-flavored shoe leather, others are sickeningly sweet, and several can solidify into jawbreakers in the cold. Many also contain questionable ingredients—such as vitamins, minerals, and herbs—added by the marketing department. Even if an ingredient has been shown to enhance performance, there is rarely enough to make a difference (for example, a product may have 25 to 50 mg of caffeine when it takes about 400 mg for a significant effect).

The best of the energy bars are about 70 percent carbohydrates (about 45 grams; the source doesn't matter that much) and low in fat (less than 5 grams) and protein (less than 10 grams). Recent research has shown that adding protein does not offer any benefit during exercise.

For optimal performance, avoid the low-carb bars that follow the 40-30-30 Zone Diet marketing scheme (such as Balance Bars and PR*Bars). These are slow to digest (fat takes 2 to 4 hours), low on the quick fuel you need, and do not promote fat burning.

If you find energy bars that you like and can get them cheap, great—but don't waste money on any that don't suit your tastes. Real food can be just as effective at keeping your blood sugar up and far less expensive than the fancy bars. If practical, try eating a variety of fruit (fresh or dried), fig bars, bagels, graham crackers, gorp (dried fruit, chocolate, and nuts), or hard candies. If you don't care about maximum energy efficiency, you can even enjoy a Snickers bar, which is 49 percent carbohydrate, 43 percent fat, and a heck of a lot cheaper and tastier.

Sport gels do have the advantage that they are absorbed faster, are easier to consume when you are puffing hard, and usually don't freeze. Gels also can be less irritating to the stomachs of runners because solids can jostle around a lot. Each packet contains about 25 grams of carbohydrate, so it's easy to monitor intake. But be sure to drink two cups of plain water with each gel for the fastest absorption and hydration.

DRINK UP

Water is our second most essential nutrient, after oxygen; even a small deficit has a significant effect on performance. Depending on size, gender, and leanness, your body holds about 30 to 60 liters of water. Men are composed of around 60 to 65 percent water while women are 50 to 55 percent due to less muscle mass.

Unfortunately, there are a lot of myths about dehydration, some of which are perpetrated by companies selling sport drinks (who fund faulty research). For example, dehydration does not cause a significant rise in core temperature; this is a function of metabolic rate (how hard you are working) and environmental factors. Also, a loss of body weight during an event is a poor indicator of hydration status because fuel is also consumed and can account for 30 percent of that drop.

Perhaps the most prevalent myth about hydration is that we should drink eight glasses of water every day. In fact, there is no science to support this exhortation, and there is no health benefit to overconsumption of fluids in healthy adults. The "8 x 8 rule" (eight, 8-ounce glasses) merely results in more trips to the restroom and a lot more overpriced bottled water sold to the gullible.

It is also claimed that our thirst mechanism is poorly tuned, typically stated as, "if you wait until you are thirsty, it is too late." Actually our body is very sensitive to plasma osmolality (the concentration of substances in the blood) and, with only a 1 percent increase, will release antidiuretic hormone (ADH) to prevent urination. As osmolality increases (due to exercise) to around 3 percent, our thirst mechanism kicks in. All of this is independent of weight loss and occurs well before dehydration becomes an issue. *Optimal fluid intake is achieved simply by drinking when you are thirsty.*

Contrary to common wisdom, urine color is a rather poor indicator of hydration. The yellow in urine mostly comes from the breakdown of hemoglobin resulting in a pigment called urochrome; the longer you go without urinating, the more it accumulates. Certain foods (such as asparagus, beets, and carrots) and food colorings can also darken urine. And as anyone who takes a mega-dose vitamin knows, excess riboflavin (vitamin B2) turns urine bright yellow, and excess vitamin C turns it orange, no matter how much fluid you have consumed.

DO-IT-YOURSELF SPORT FUEL

By making your own sport fuel, you can save considerable money while getting better taste and equal performance compared to commercial products. Because these recipes lack preservatives, it is best to store them in airtight containers (wrap the bars individually) in a refrigerator or freezer until ready for use. Experiment!

Energy Drink

4 cups hot water
2 tablespoons lemon juice or ¼ cup orange juice (7 grams carbohydrate)
4 tablespoons sugar (48 grams carbohydrate)
³⁄₁₆ teaspoon sea salt (440 mg sodium)

Dissolve the sugar and the salt (⅛ teaspoon plus half that makes ³⁄₁₆ in the hot water before adding the fruit juice, then refrigerate. This makes a solution with a carbohydrate concentration of 6 percent with an energy source consisting of about 45 percent glucose and 55 percent fructose. One cup provides 55 calories (14 grams carbohydrate), 110 mg sodium, and 30 mg potassium.

Energy Gel

1½ cups brown rice syrup
1 cup honey
1 teaspoon sea salt
4 NoDoz tablets, crushed (optional)
1 Rolaids tablet, crushed (optional)
¼ teaspoon vanilla extract or natural flavoring (optional)

Heat the rice syrup and honey in a saucepan on medium heat until liquid (about 5 minutes). Dissolve the salt, NoDoz (caffeine), and Rolaids (calcium and magnesium) into the mix. Add vanilla extract or other natural flavoring to taste, if you wish. While the mix is still warm, pour it into two Coghlan's squeeze tubes and install the clip. Each tube holds about 300 grams, which is the same as ten gel packets.

This recipe gives you energy in the form of complex carbohydrates, maltose, fructose, and glucose, so there will be a quick pick-me-up followed by a steady boost. You can substitute agave syrup for the honey but only use ¾ cup to reduce the amount of fructose. Maltodextrin powder can be dissolved in water to replace the rice syrup if you prefer less sweetness. Barley malt syrup can replace the rice syrup for a different taste.

Raisin Energy Bars

1 cup dark raisins	¼ cup toasted wheat germ
½ cup golden raisins	½ teaspoon ground ginger
⅓ cup butter	½ teaspoon salt
½ cup sugar	½ teaspoon baking soda
½ cup molasses	½ teaspoon baking powder
1 egg	½ cup milk (liquid, not powdered)
1¼ cups whole wheat flour	1 cup quick-cooking oats
½ cup nonfat powdered milk	1 cup sliced almonds

Chop the raisins into small pieces. Mix the butter, sugar, molasses, and egg until smooth. In a separate bowl, combine all the dry ingredients. Blend the two mixtures and the skim milk, then stir in the oats, raisins, and half the almonds. Pour the batter into a greased 13x9-inch baking pan and spread evenly. Sprinkle with remaining almonds. Bake at 350°F (175°C) for approximately 30 minutes. Cool in pan and cut into 1x4-inch bars. Each bar offers about 135 calories with 66 percent coming from carbohydrates and 32 percent from fat.

Crispy Cereal Bars

6 cups Kashi Puffs cereal	¾ cup, slivered almonds
3 tablespoons walnut oil	⅓ cup, dried cranberries
1 tablespoon honey	⅓ cup, dried cherries
4 cups mini marshmallows	⅓ cup dried blueberries

Toast the almonds on a baking sheet in a 350°F (175°C) oven for approximately 10 minutes. Chop the dried fruit. Heat the oil and honey in a large glass bowl for 30 seconds in a microwave oven. Add the marshmallows, toss to cover, and heat for 90 seconds until melted. Mix in the cereal, almonds, and fruit. Pour the mixture into a greased 13x9-inch baking pan and spread evenly. Bake at 425°F (220°C) for about 9 minutes. Cool in pan until firm, then cut into 2-inch squares. Each square is roughly 100 calories with 69 percent as carbohydrates and 25 percent as fat.

Rice Cereal Bars

½ cup sesame seeds	1 cup old-fashioned oatmeal
½ cup raw, hulled sunflower seeds	7 cups Nature's Path Rice Puffs cereal
1 pinch salt	1 cup honey
½ cup dates	¼ cup brown sugar
½ cup raisins	1½ cups unsweetened crunchy peanut butter
½ cup dried apricots	1 cup nonfat powdered milk
½ cup dried cherries	1 teaspoon vanilla extract
½ cup semisweet chocolate chips	½ teaspoon almond extract

Toast the sesame seeds and sunflower seeds in a skillet over medium heat for a couple of minutes until brown. Salt lightly and set aside to cool. Combine the dates, raisins, apricots, cherries, chocolate chips, and toasted seeds. Chop finely, preferably in a food processor. In a large bowl, combine chopped mixture with the oats and rice puffs. In a saucepan on medium heat, melt the honey, brown sugar, and peanut butter. Stir in the powdered milk and vanilla and almond extracts. Now mix all the ingredients together, pour into a greased 13x9-inch baking pan, using wet hands to press firmly into pan. Allow to cool for several hours and then cut into 2-inch squares. Each square is roughly 250 calories with 55 percent as carbohydrates and 37 percent as fat.

Granola Bars

1¾ cups old-fashioned oatmeal	2 tablespoons butter
1 cup sliced almonds	2 teaspoons vanilla extract
½ cup raw, hulled sunflower seeds	½ teaspoon salt
½ cup wheat germ	½ cup dried blueberries
½ cup honey	½ cup raisins, chopped
¼ cup brown sugar	½ cup dried cranberries, chopped

Preheat the oven to 350°F (175°C). Spread the oats, almonds, sunflower seeds, and wheat germ on a baking sheet and toast for about 10 minutes, stirring two or three times. After cooling, chop the toasted mixture into smaller pieces (a food processor helps). In a large saucepan on medium heat, mix the honey, brown sugar, butter, vanilla, and salt until melted. Combine the two mixtures and add dried fruit, pour into a 13x9-inch greased baking pan and with wet hands press firmly into pan. Bake at 300°F (150°C) for 25 minutes. Cool the pan for at least 3 hours, and then cut into 2-inch squares. Each square is roughly 200 calories with 62 percent as carbohydrates and 31 percent as fat.

Sweat loss is highly variable among individuals and depends upon intensity of work, level of fitness (sweating increases with better conditioning), temperature, and humidity. Even though women have more sweat glands, men tend to sweat more. It's typical to lose about 1 liter per hour when playing hard, but this can easily increase to 2 to 3 liters an hour in extreme conditions, such as running on muggy days, baking on a Yosemite wall in July, or humping up a glacier in the sun.

Cold weather and altitude compound the water loss due to heavy ventilation in the dry air; up to 1.5 liters a day may be lost just from breathing. Climbing on windy days, and speed sports like cycling or track skiing, can fool you because evaporation occurs faster.

Sodium Status

Even though your sweat may taste salty (due to evaporation of water, which makes it more concentrated), it still has a much lower concentration than your blood; 20 to 60 milliequivalents per liter (mEq/L) of sodium in sweat versus 140 mEq/L in plasma. Because of this difference, the more you sweat, the more concentrated the sodium becomes in your blood.

Most of the time, you do not need extra electrolytes (sodium and potassium) since there are plenty in your diet. It takes about 3 grams of table salt to replace that sodium lost in a liter of sweat. The dash of salt in sport drinks merely improves taste, which helps you drink more, and speed absorption of fluid from the gut. (See "Salt" in the "Power Shopping" section.) None of the sport drinks contain sufficient electrolytes to off-set the volume of water they contain when you drink more than you need.

Despite what you may have heard, muscle cramps are not caused by a shortage of electrolytes or water. Eating a banana to ward off cramps falls under the old-wives'-tale category.

However, if you are exercising hard for more than four hours and ingesting a lot of water or sport drink, there is a risk of hyponatremia, a potentially fatal condition involving a low sodium concentration in the blood. Although rare, this sometimes happens to marathon runners, triathletes, and Grand Canyon hikers who consume too much water. The lesson here is for climbers to eat a variety of snacks containing salt and drink when thirsty when working hard for hours on end—too much fluid can be dangerous.

Drinking Strategy

The wise climber drinks early and drinks often. The day before a big climb, increase your normal fluid intake and consume a half liter of water before going to bed. When you wake, drink another half liter of fluid (yes, coffee or tea counts). Then top off the tank an hour before your workout.

When you are climbing, drink whenever you are thirsty. Drinking a liter quickly makes you pee more, so you don't hydrate as well as spreading the dosage out. Instead of guzzling a full bottle, it is better to take smaller sips throughout the day. In general, if you aren't thirsty, there is no reason to force fluids down—drink to thirst.

The major exception is when climbing at high altitude. (See "Improving Altitude Performance" in chapter 5 for more details.) In that situation, you may need to force yourself to drink more than you feel like. Plan ahead to ensure that you have adequate water; this may require stopping to melt snow, hauling extra, or detouring to a stream.

Among the best inventions of the last decade is the hydration bladder, which encourages you to sip continuously from a hose running into your pack. While many companies now offer them, most of the systems are poorly designed and result in frustration particularly in cold weather. Be sure that it has a large-diameter hose with a high-flow nipple (that won't dribble) or you'll feel like you're sucking through a tiny straw.

Avoid putting anything but water in a bladder; sport drinks leave a permanent taste and breed nasty creepy crawlies. If you must add carbohydrates, be sure to rinse and dry the system thoroughly afterward.

To prevent freezing, keep the bladder near your back and blow air back into the tube (the insulated tubes work poorly). But you should also have a wide-mouth plastic bottle on hand in case the bladder becomes inoperable.

For any exercise bout lasting an hour or less, there is no advantage to sport drinks: imbibe water. Right from the faucet is fine in many locations, but some areas have "hard" water with a high mineral content that tastes lousy. A sink filter with activated carbon can improve taste.

Bottled water is convenient and that's about all—it doesn't improve health unless your tap water is really bad, in which case, a reverse osmosis filter for the sink is a good investment. The new "fitness waters" are just about taste and marketing, not performance; there is zero benefit to adding vitamins during a workout.

When your climbs or workouts extend into the time where glycogen depletion becomes a factor, then you should consider your alternatives. Sport drinks can be a good choice if you are not consuming any other food. The ad hype never mentions that combining products, as most people do in the real world, can decrease performance.

The American College of Sports Medicine (ACSM) recommends a carbohydrate concentration of 4 to 8 percent for fastest hydration and energy replenishment (10 to 19 grams per 8 ounces water). More than this will slow gastric emptying, which means the fluid stays in your stomach where it sloshes around and is not absorbed. If you eat energy bars or gels and then wash them down with a sport drink, the high carbohydrate concentration can *increase* dehydration because water is drawn into the small intestines. It's best to consume a sport drink on its own (without dilution) or to eat bars and gels with just plain water.

Proper hydration means frequent urination: be sure that your clothing and climbing harness are designed to work together for this basic bodily function! Many of the outdoor companies choose fashion over function and make taking a piss difficult for men and women; zippers are often too short or difficult to operate. Women might consider using a pee funnel; they can make life easier but true woman-specific outdoors clothing is the best option.

BIG-WALL FOOD

Life on a big wall is essentially vertical backpacking: the major difference is that you usually must haul all of your water. Frequently, climbers balk at the weight of the gear they have to schlep to the base of the route and, in an effort to cut back, they jettison fluids. There are countless stories of teams in Yosemite that ran out of water part way up; sometimes they tough it out, often they bail.

Most climbers who have run dry swear they will never make the mistake again. Even though the approach will suck, it's definitely better to take more water than you think you'll need; once you start hauling, the extra weight won't make that much difference and the load gets lighter as you get higher. If it looks like you'll have a surplus before you top out, you can be an unsung hero and leave a cache for unfortunates who have calculated poorly. Carry water in 2-liter plastic soda bottles wrapped with duct tape to attach a clip-in loop (or equivalent bombproof containers) in the bottom of several haul bags (read: don't put all your chickens in one basket).

In cool weather, as a bare minimum, you should carry 3 liters of water per person per day (6.6 pounds). If the route gets a lot of sun, add at least another liter (1 gallon total, 8.4 pounds) per person per day. For an El Cap wall in July, don't even think about going up with less than 6 liters of water (13.2 pounds) per person for each day. On alpine wall climbs, you may be able to melt snow but you'll also be toting a hanging stove and fuel, so the weight savings isn't as much as you'd wish.

These water rations assume you are also consuming hydrated foods such as cans of soups, stews, tuna, fruit cocktail, and possibly a daily tallboy, too. A day's ration of canned food weighs about 3 pounds per person; a team of two climbers should expect to haul about 17 pounds of food and water per day. Other popular wall entrées include pre-made burritos (tortilla, refried beans, rice, cheese, and salsa wrapped in foil, then stored in a resealable plastic bag); Tasty Bites (prepackaged gourmet meals found at some groceries) with a pre-baked potato; and bagels with sausage and cheese. You're limited only by your imagination, but it's best to select foods that are relatively crushproof and require no cooking.

Beware that some energy bars are virtually inedible without water to wash them down, so gels may be a better alternative for fast, convenient energy. Take some hard candies to combat dry mouth and, if possible, fresh oranges and apples—they will be unbelievably delicious after a few days on the big stone. For hygiene, bring premoistened towelettes or baby wipes to clean your hands after making a "wall burrito."

RECOVERY FUELS

Following a good session of hard exercise, it normally takes at least 20 hours for glycogen to restore completely. If you intend to play again the next day, it's important to get a head start. Once your workout is over, there is a 30-minute window of opportunity to significantly hasten recovery. During this time, when your muscles are still warm and circulation is enhanced, the muscle cells readily suck up any carbohydrates that you ingest.

For the most part, it doesn't matter what kind of carbohydrate you eat or drink as long as you consume at least 50 grams in that first half hour. An exception is fructose, which does not replenish muscle glycogen as quickly, so avoid sodas, fruit juice, and drinks with high fructose corn syrup.

Some research has indicated that it may help to include about 10 to 20 grams of protein to enhance muscle recovery. However there does not appear to be any scientific support for a 4:1 carb to protein ratio that some companies tout. Indeed, a recent study showed that low-fat chocolate milk was equal for recovery to Endurox (and both were better than Gatorade). As long as you consume plenty of calories right away following a tough workout, your recovery will be aided.

High-carb recovery drinks (20 to 25 percent carbohydrate; 48 to 60 grams per 8 ounces) offer convenience but there is nothing magical about them. You can recover just as effectively by eating real food such as a bagel sandwich with hummus or lean meat; fruit, cheese, and crackers; or a tray of sushi—all washed down with water or iced tea.

Don't stop grazing after your initial round of post-climb snacking. Over the next two hours, you should try to ingest another 50 to 100 grams of carbs, as well as 10 to 20 grams of protein, whether from engineered drinks or real food. If you don't maintain this carbohydrate influx, that climb the next morning is going to be a lot tougher!

FERMENTED MALT BEVERAGES

The puritans assert that there is no value in the consumption of beer after a day of climbing. This defies a century of tradition and isn't entirely true. Mass-produced "beer" that nutritionists and aficionados revile is made with rice, corn, coloring, flavorings, and enzymes. This insipid drink is the equivalent of white bread—bland and lacking most of the good nutrition. A 12-ounce can contains about 1 gram protein, 25 mg sodium, and only a trace of potassium or B vitamins.

But a finely crafted beer is only made with barley, wheat, hops, and water. This is akin to good whole-grain bread, better tasting and better for you. A good microbrew contains about 2.2 grams protein, 75 mg sodium, 195 mg potassium, and 5 to 15 percent of the DRI for riboflavin, niacin, folic acid, and vitamin B-6. Plus the high hops content contains nine flavonoids that you won't find in sport drinks. Even better, if you can find them, are cask-conditioned ales, which are unfiltered and naturally carbonated; rather like fine artisan bread pulled fresh from the oven.

Beer contains zero fat and zero cholesterol; moderate consumption may even raise your level of HDL (the good cholesterol). The typical 12-ounce serving of light beer has about 100 calories; a normal beer is around 150 calories; stouts run around

225 calories; and a triple bock or barley wine is upwards of 330 calories. Although two-thirds of the carbohydrates in a beer come from alcohol, which does not convert to glycogen, you still get about 12 grams of restorative carbs per bottle.

No, beer isn't the ultimate recovery drink—but you could do worse. It's the French fries and nachos that really get you into trouble. To offset the slight dehydrating effects of alcohol, it's a good idea to consume one glass of water for each beer consumed.

SUPPLEMENTS

Athletes are notorious for looking for the quick fix that will deliver better performance: the first case of Olympic organizers banning competitors for using supplements (mushrooms and animal protein) occurred in 300 BC. Climbers are certainly no exception in their desire for magic elixirs. Yet the utter disregard for health and common sense shown by athletes is truly amazing. On little more than rumor and bad science, North Americans and Europeans waste billions of dollars each year and get little more than expensive piss.

The truth is that most athletes have minimal need for extra vitamins or minerals simply because these are not burned by exercise and we eat more than the average person. Assuming you consume a balanced diet (no bizarre eating habits) and consume more than 1,500 calories per day, which is likely even if you're trying to lose fat, then you are probably well above the dietary reference intakes (DRI) on just about everything.

Quite simply, if you gobble non-prescribed pills by the handful, you've likely been suckered. That wouldn't necessarily be bad, assuming you have the disposable income, but there are considerable risks besides pissing away your money.

The evidence for ergogenic effects (enhanced performance) or health benefits by supplementation of most vitamins, minerals, and micronutrients beyond dietary amounts is scanty at best. The body has large stores of fat-soluble vitamins (A, D, E, and K), and even the water-soluble vitamins (B-complex and C) won't show a deficit over a month of no intake. If you binge on junk food for a few days, get stressed at work, or wake up with a hangover, popping a supplement pill won't do any good. Supplementation is only beneficial for correcting long-term deficiencies from an inadequate diet.

Even the media hysteria over antioxidants has been blown out of proportion. Although free radicals (molecules with unpaired electrons) sound scary and can do nasty things in a test tube, the body is better able to cope with them than once thought.

There is no solid evidence that taking additional antioxidants will increase performance or speed recovery. While antioxidants may prevent some chronic diseases, the research does not support overdoing them, or overspending on them, the way the vitamin industry would like. Indeed, there is increasing evidence that excess antioxidants may do more harm than good.

The dangers of overdosing on vitamins can be greater than the consequences of not taking extra. Too much vitamin A and beta-carotene may increase the risk of heart disease and lung cancer; chronic megadoses of vitamin B-6 can result in neurotoxicity; high levels of niacin has a host of side effects including decreased fat burning and possible liver damage; megadoses of vitamin C combined with excess iron can become a pro-oxidant (increasing free radicals and oxidative damage) and cause kidney stones and heart failure; too much vitamin D can be toxic and reduce bone mass; and overdoing vitamin E can exacerbate bleeding and possibly suppress your immune system.

Likewise, megadosing on minerals can lead to unpleasant complications. As mentioned, iron can be highly toxic. Men should have a blood test for serum ferritin (more sensitive than a serum iron test) before taking extra iron—and should not exceed 45 mg per day. While calcium is important, overdoing it reduces zinc absorption. High intakes of zinc can result in a copper deficiency; don't use the cold lozenges for more than a week. Magnesium can also be overdone, resulting in kidney problems. Too much chromium may interfere with iron in the blood. There is some evidence that excessive phosphorous can lead to bone loss. Selenium is the easiest mineral to overdose, with toxic results such as vomiting and hair loss.

SUPPLEMENTS WITH POTENTIAL

Those vast aisles of bottles at health food stores and supermarkets are less intimidating once you know what to avoid. Most of the stuff is expensive snake oil. Before spending a lot of money on supplements, consider joining Consumerlab.com; their independent tests may give you some assurance that you get what you pay for. Once you have optimized your diet, you *might* be able to boost performance with these supplements. But ya gotta plug the big leaks before fixin' the little drips! None of these can make up for an inadequate diet or overcome inefficient training—sorry, no miracles in a bottle.

Multivitamins. Even if you're doing everything "right," it's still a good idea to take a daily multivitamin/mineral supplement with a meal. This ensures that most of the essentials are covered without pushing you over the limit (remember, those DRIs are *total* daily intake). Unless you are on a fad diet, lactose-intolerant, or have food allergies, there is no legitimate reason for the megavitamin horse pills or many-per-day supplements that the scammers swear are necessary.

When selecting a multivitamin/mineral supplement, examine the label to make sure the pill will dissolve completely— guaranteed by USP (United States Pharmacopeia) approval. A simple test is to place a pill in a half-cup of vinegar and gently stir occasionally; it should disintegrate within thirty minutes.

Most of the ingredients should be about 100 to 150 percent of the recommended daily value, though none will contain enough calcium or magnesium since you wouldn't be able to swallow the pill. Avoid any multivitamin with ultra high doses—they don't help and could hurt. Men should avoid iron unless they have been cleared by a blood test. Active women, especially those who may become pregnant or are pregnant, need extra folate.

There are differences in the quality of mineral supplements based upon their rate of absorption (bioavailability). As you might guess, the cheaper supplements contain ingredients that your body has a harder time using. The higher quality supplements will include the following words on the label: ascorbate, citrate (e.g., magnesium citrate), fumarate, malate, picolinate, succinate, and tartrate. The cheaper supplements use carbonate (e.g., calcium carbonate), aminoate, oxide (e.g., magnesium oxide), chelate, sulfate, gluconate, and phosphate. Beware that copper, iodine, and iron are oxidants that can degrade the other vitamins in the pill

Similarly, the quality of the vitamins included can vary. Better quality products will offer vitamin B-2 in the form of riboflavin 5-phosphate and vitamin B-6 as pyridoxol 5-phosphate. The natural forms of vitamin E (d-alpha or RR-alpha tocopherol) are about a third more potent than the synthetic versions (dl-alpha or all-rac alpha tocopherol) and come with related chemicals that may be beneficial.

Beyond these basic requirements, you can ignore the hype: there is no practical advantage of "natural" vitamins (except vitamin E); chelated supplements don't absorb better; time-release isn't superior; sugar or starch are fillers that don't affect anything; liquids aren't better than pills; brand names are no better than generics as long as the quantities are right.

Antioxidants. Although the evidence for additional antioxidants is far from conclusive (much of it is based on cellular studies), it's sufficient for the U.S. Olympic Sports Medicine Committee to recommend somewhat higher dosages for athletes.

Since your multivitamin already contains the RDI of vitamin A (5,000 IU) and too much is toxic, there is no need for more. Beta-carotene is a related, even stronger antioxidant that has no DRI because supporting data is lacking. Besides, it's just one of over 600 carotenoids—eat your veggies.

Climbers might consider 250 to 500 mg per day of vitamin C to boost immune protection, especially during cold season or if you are doing a brutal, multiday route. But citrus fruits, strawberries, kiwi fruits, raw broccoli, and red peppers are all better sources than a pill. There is no proven benefit to high doses of vitamin C (1,000 mg and upward), which are associated with diarrhea and kidney stones.

Even with a healthy diet it can be difficult to meet the DRI for vitamin E, and there may be benefits from ensuring an extra 100 to 400 IU. However, a study of triathletes showed that supplementing with 800 IU of vitamin E actually increased oxidative stress.

Herbal antioxidants receive a lot of media attention and enormous marketing hype despite very sketchy science. There are many natural sources of antioxidants, though little research has compared them against each other or simple vitamin supplements that are less expensive. When tea leaves are dried instead of fermented,

SUPPLEMENT DOSAGE

The Food and Nutrition Board (FNB) of the Institute of Medicine (IM), made up of scientists in Canada and the United States, has developed replacement guidelines based on the most recent research, termed Dietary Reference Intakes (DRI), that started coming out in 1997. In addition, the committees have provided a Tolerable Upper Intake Level (UL) that is considered the maximum safe level in your diet. It is termed "tolerable" because the science does not support higher dosages than the DRI.

These DRIs are for healthy adults ages nineteen to fifty. Your needs will be different if you are younger, older, pregnant (or thinking about it), lactating, or have a medical condition. If in doubt, consult your doctor.

	DIETARY REFERENCE INTAKE	TOLERABLE UPPER LIMIT INTAKE
VITAMINS		
Vitamin A	900 mcg (3000 IU) men, 700 mcg women	3,000 mcg (10,000 IU)
Vitamin C	90 mg men, 75 mg women	2 g
Vitamin D	5 mcg (200 IU)	50 mcg (2,000 IU)
Vitamin E	15 mg	1 g
Vitamin K	120 mcg men, 90 mcg women	Not determined
Thiamin	1.2 mg men, 1.1 mg women	Not determined
Riboflavin	1.3 mg men, 1.1 mg women	Not determined
Niacin	16 mg men, 14 mg women	35 mg
Vitamin B-6	1.3 mg	100 mg
Folate	400 mcg	1,000 mcg
Vitamin B-12	2.4 mcg	Not determined
Biotin	30 mcg	Not determined
Pantothenic acid	5 mg	Not determined
Choline	550 mg	3,500 mg

	DIETARY REFERENCE INTAKE	TOLERABLE UPPER LIMIT INTAKE
MINERALS		
Calcium	1,000 mg	2.5 g
Chromium	35 mcg men, 25 mcg women	Not determined
Copper	0.9 mg	10 mg
Fluoride	4 mg men, 3 mg women	10 mg
Iodine	150 mcg	1,100 mcg
Iron	8 mg men, 18 mg women	45 mg
Manganese	2.3 mg men, 1.8 mg women	11 mg
Magnesium	420 mg men, 320 mg women	350 mg as a supplement
Molybdenum	45 mcg	2,000 mcg
Phosphorus	700 mg	4 g
Selenium	55 mcg	400 mcg
Zinc	11 mg men, 8 mg women	40 mg

which turns them black, they retain their antioxidant properties. You'd have to drink five to ten cups of green tea every day to get an effect, so extracts (125 to 500 mg per day) are more practical. Grape seed extract (50 to 100 mg per day) is an alternative to drinking red wine every day, though human studies are lacking at present.

Caffeine. Long popular with athletes for boosting performance, caffeine has proven to increase power output and endurance but has no effect on maximal strength. There is also evidence that caffeine enhances our ability to absorb carbohydrates during exercise. In 2004, the World Anti-Doping Agency (WADA) removed caffeine from the list of banned substances.

Even if you are a habitual coffee or tea drinker, you can get a slight performance boost by supplementing with 2.5 mg of caffeine per pound of body weight (about four NoDoz or two Vivarin tablets) about an hour before a long endurance climb. Because of other compounds that moderate the effect, drinking coffee or tea does not offer the performance effect provided by caffeine supplements. One note of caution applies to people with coronary disease: avoid caffeine prior to exercise because it impairs blood flow to the heart, especially at altitude.

Contrary to popular belief, caffeinated drinks do not cause dehydration. The diuretic effect is actually very weak in healthy adults, and drinking coffee and sodas does help you hydrate, just not quite as much as fluids without caffeine.

The evidence supporting caffeine as a "fat burner" is equivocal at best, though the combination with ephedrine appears more effective. These stimulants can make you wired and sweaty and should not be taken in excessive dosages or at all if you have high blood pressure. There is a risk of unwittingly overdoing it since they are hidden in many products under innocuous names (see cautions on ephedrine in "Natural Supplements," later in this chapter). The results also appear to vary widely, so many people suffer the jitters yet realize no fat loss.

As far as coffee and tea go, for those who consume them in moderation (two to three cups per day), they are a major source of antioxidants. An overwhelming body of evidence indicates that the health benefits of coffee consumption are considerable while the negatives are minor. Among the advantages are reduced risk of diabetes, heart problems, Alzheimer's and Parkinson's diseases, and several types of cancer.

Calcium. Calcium has many functions besides bone growth, such as helping muscles contract, so it's important for optimal performance. Even if you are not lactose-intolerant or vegan, it can be difficult to get adequate calcium from a normal diet if you don't pay attention.

To make the quota, you need to consume three cups (24 ounces) of milk, or fortified orange juice each day. Other good options include yogurt (one 6-ounce container is a third of the DRI) and tofu made with calcium sulfate (five times more calcium than regular tofu; 6 ounces meets your need). Some vegetables contain calcium but you have to eat a lot. Cheese and ice cream contain calcium but come with a price (lotsa fat calories).

If your diet is still insufficient for calcium, you can fill in the deficit with a supplement (500 mg maximum per dose). However, those made from bonemeal, dolomite, or oyster shells may contain lead. And taking too much calcium (over 2,500 mg per day) can result in kidney stones.

Creatine. Among the most talked about, and advertised, sport supplements is creatine, a naturally occurring substance found in meat and fish. Due to the water weight gain associated with creatine loading, it is generally a bad thing for climbers on a routine basis since we must fight gravity. Some boulderers and sport climbers have experimented with it and have come to the general conclusion that it isn't worth messing with.

While creatine is considered useful for athletes requiring short, explosive strength (six- to thirty-second duration) such as sprinters and power lifters, it may help to raise the performance threshold (see "Aerobic FUNdamentals" in chapter 4) and enhance the quality of workouts for endurance athletes too. When resistance training for maximal strength, you can get a few extra repetitions per set. Thus creatine can benefit climbers if used judiciously once or twice a year during specific training phases.

Vegetarians are most likely to see the biggest boost in performance, since their diet is lacking in creatine. About a quarter of the people who try it see no results. To prevent excess water gain, take six 1-gram doses per day for five to six days, then 2 grams per day for maintenance. Despite the hype, there is no significant difference between the various brands of powdered or liquid creatine, except how much you pay.

Iron. Roughly a quarter of female athletes may be iron deficient, partly due to menstruation but also because many are vegetarians on calorie-restricted diets. Male climbers, especially vegetarians and endurance fiends, may also be iron deficient. If you are often tired and feel weak and fatigued, it may be an indication of deficiency instead of overtraining, but a blood test is the only way to be sure.

If you eat red meat a few times a week, there should be no problem. Many plants contain a form of iron (non-heme) that is less bioavailable (only 2 to 10 percent is absorbed), so try to purchase iron-fortified breads and cereals and consume them with a source of vitamin C. Using a cast-iron skillet will also boost iron intake.

There is no benefit to supplementing iron if your supplies are adequate (above 50 nanograms per milliliter of blood for athletes). Worse, too much iron can be dangerous since it can impede absorption of calcium and zinc.

Women can safely include 15 mg of iron in their multivitamins because their monthly menstrual cycle removes excess. However, men (and postmenopausal women) should only do so after a serum ferritin blood test. Hemochromatosis (iron overload) is among the most common of all genetic disorders, affecting about one in two hundred people, particularly those with northern European ancestry. It can lead to cirrhosis of the liver, liver cancer, heart attack, diabetes, and erectile dysfunction. Because of the risk and there being no other way to remove excess iron, it is wise to donate blood several times a year.

If you will be training at high altitude or going on a months-long mountaineering expedition, it is may be worthwhile to supplement iron because it is needed for production of red blood cells.

Probiotics. Capsules containing "good" bacteria can help you fight off illness and diseases. Particularly after a course of antibiotics that tend to wipe out your gut flora, you should try to ingest probiotic supplements. Other good sources are yogurt and kefir with live and active cultures and Emmenthaler cheese.

When selecting supplements, look on the label for the specific species of bacteria (the more, the merrier) not just the genus (such as *Lactobacillus* or *Bifidobacterium*). The label should also state the number of colony-forming units (CFU) as well as the total milligrams. Most probiotics require refrigeration and are age-sensitive, so be careful of the source and how you store them.

Phosphorus. This mineral is used for energy production, lactate buffering, and release of oxygen to the muscles, plus strong bones and teeth. Most people get more than enough from their diet, so there is little need to supplement. But a fair amount of research shows that up to 4 grams per day of sodium phosphate for three to four days can slightly improve endurance. Too much on a routine basis can lead to calcium deficiency.

Protein Powder. Active climbers have a higher protein requirement than the DRI (see "Protein" earlier in this chapter). Most athletes on a normal diet consume adequate protein (about 1.5 grams per kilogram of body weight) and shouldn't waste money on powders. However, during periods of strength building and high-intensity climbing, supplementing with protein powders to achieve a 2-grams-per-kilogram total daily intake might help with recovery.

Whey protein, a by-product of the cheese industry, is the most common protein supplement, but the processing can vary widely (30 to 90 percent concentrations). The most expensive form, ion-exchange whey protein isolate, may also enhance immune protection. Casein (milk curd) is another protein supplement that absorbs more slowly, which helps increase amino acid levels. Soy protein isolates contain isoflavones that may protect the heart, but also contains estrogen that may cause other problems. The bioavailability of all these protein sources (that is, the body's ability to use them), based on the most recent rating system, is comparable. All of these contain BCAAs (branched chain amino acids), so there is no need to take both at the same time.

The patented or proprietary protein supplements are merely different blends of various sources with scanty evidence to prove they are better than others. None of the formulations have actually been tested against each other in well-documented independent studies. Blending is a marketing trick that lets them list protein first on a label; the ingredients would be lower down (below all the sugar) if listed separately.

Glucosamine and Chondroitin. Among the most common buzzwords in the over-forty crowd are glucosamine and chondroitin, which appear to be as effective at relieving joint pain as ibuprofen; they may even assist in rebuilding damaged cartilage. Although many people swear by it, fueling a market approaching $1 billion, the research is still inconclusive. A large twenty-four-week study funded by the National Institute of Health found that glucosamine or chondroitin or a combination of the two was no better than a placebo for mild pain. However, they may be beneficial to those with moderate to severe pain and longer-term effects remain unproven. While not a cure for arthritis, glucosamine/chondroitin could be worth a try if you are experiencing joint pain. However, if symptoms persist, you definitely need to see a doctor!

Non-Steroidal Anti-Inflammatory Drugs (NSAIDs). Many climbers take "vitamin I" (ibuprofen) to ease their aches and pains. While effective at reducing swelling, this exceedingly popular NSAID does not promote healing and can be more dangerous than you realize. It's debatable whether ibuprofen masks pain sufficiently for a climber to aggravate a preexisting injury, but the possibility exists. However, combining ibuprofen and alcohol (three or more drinks per day) is known to cause stomach bleeding. Since ibuprofen is cleared through the kidneys, avoid taking it when they are stressed during ultra-endurance events. (See "Rehabilitation" in chapter 8 for more details on NSAIDs.)

DUBIOUS SUPPLEMENTS

In 1994 a federal law (Dietary Supplement Health and Education Act) reclassified dietary supplements so they were no longer "food additives" that were controlled by the Food and Drug Administration. This left the industry virtually unregulated regarding product claims and helped make it extremely lucrative—annual sales were around $22.5 billion in 2006.

The supplement companies are frantically looking for the next creatine—that product's annual sales jumped from $50 million to $400 million in just five years—and are promoting products long before they're ready for prime time. Since there is no reporting of adverse effects, the safety of many herbs and supplements is unclear.

It's a rare race package, climbing competition, or outdoor event that doesn't provide samples of "sports enhancers" and "nutraceuticals" with ingredients you probably haven't heard about. Most of these exotic ingredients are backed by little more than glowing testimonials with unbelievable before and after photos. Invariably when somebody claims a product gave them great results, they were manipulating several variables at once, such as diet and exercise, in addition to taking the supplement.

Even if the word hasn't reached the pill-pushers at "nutrition centers," many of these popular supplements have proven to be ineffective in well-controlled studies. Don't be swayed by claims of faster or superior absorption for liquids or unique blending processes and formulations: three times zero is still zero.

BCAA. Branched chain amino acids (BCAAs; leucine, isoleucine, and valine) may help with mental fatigue and prevent muscle breakdown during two or more hours of endurance fun. The theory holds that high levels of BCAAs will reduce free tryptophan, which is a precursor of serotonin (the brain hormone associated with fatigue).

At present, most studies have shown that BCAA supplementation is no more effective than ensuring adequate carbohydrates. In low doses, as is found in some sport drinks, it has no effect on serotonin, and high doses can cause stomach problems. If you experiment, purchase prepackaged BCAAs, not the individual amino acids, to get the proper ratio.

Bicarbonate. Supplementing with baking soda (sodium bicarbonate) has the potential to increase performance for events that stress the lactate system (e.g., those that last one to seven minutes). It acts as a buffer against acid building up in the muscles. While this may sound attractive to climbers, the associated gut problems probably don't make bicarbonate worth your while. The recommended dose is about 5 teaspoons along with 1 to 2 liters of water within an hour or two of exercising.

Carnitine. Carnitine is used in the oxidation of fatty acids, so it is vital for energy production. However, our bodies produce all that we need. Although carnitine supplementation in several forms (L-, alpha L-, or the synthetic D-) is marketed as improving endurance and fat loss, substantial independent research shows that it has no effect.

Chromium. This mineral has a function in insulin regulation. One company holds the patent on chromium picolinate and has promoted it heavily. Most independent studies show it doesn't aid fat loss, build muscles, or do anything except spot-reduce your bank account.

Coenzyme Q10 (ubiquinone). A ubiquitous antioxidant (hence its name), CoQ10 is used by mitochondria to create energy. Produced by your body and found in fish and meat, there is no evidence CoQ10 is lacking in healthy adults. Claims for improved endurance and increased weight loss remain weak. However, CoQ10 does appear to aid recovery after exercise, reduce migraine headaches, and help sufferers with chronic fatigue syndrome or fibromyalgia. It is also helpful for people with high blood pressure and those who are taking cholesterol-lowering medications. If you decide to try it, there appears to be no harm other than spending $50 to $200 per month. The crystal-free variety is best for maximum absorption.

Conjugated Linoleic Acid (CLA). CLA is a category of essential fatty acid (it's actually a healthy trans fat) found in dairy products and meat. There are twenty-eight types of CLA that don't all act the same in the body; which ones are in a particular supplement is anybody's guess. Builds muscles, reduces fat, and protects against cancer—if you're a rat. Human research is not very encouraging; some studies show no effect while others support fat loss claims with a dosage of 3 to 4 grams per day.

HMB. HMB is a metabolite of leucine (a BCAA). Nearly all the research showing that HMB aids muscle growth or endurance performance comes from the university lab that holds the patent. Independent human studies haven't shown any benefit, though more research is needed.

Glutamine. Another amino acid that might help performance is glutamine, which is normally abundant. However, levels of glutamine are severely depressed following intense endurance exercise, overtraining, and severe stress. It has been suggested, but not conclusively proven, that supplementing with 5 to 20 grams of glutamine might increase glycogen stores, improve recovery, and boost the immune system. Be warned that most "sports foods" contain nowhere near this amount, which makes its inclusion mostly for show. Glutamine absorbs best when combined with other amino acids.

Glycerol. A non-intoxicating alcohol, glycerol may help you stay hydrated during endurance events in the heat. The research is far from conclusive, but there may be some benefit to 2 liters of a glycerol solution a couple of hours prior to a long climb in the sun. However, possible side effects include headaches and blurred vision due to a drying effect on your brain and eyes as well as nausea and vomiting.

Lactate. Lactate is one of the most easily absorbed and utilized sources of energy. In fact, when working at high intensity, glucose must be converted to lactate. Unfortunately, ingested lactate causes intestinal discomfort at fairly low doses so it is not a good sport fuel. Calcium lactate and magnesium lactate are good sources of calcium and magnesium so they are often taken by those needing more of these minerals. One company is marketing a lactate supplement (SportLegs) for preventing muscle burn. However, it is merely an expensive mineral supplement without any credibility for helping athletes other than serving as a placebo. Various Cytomax products also contain lactate, but the benefit of that particular ingredient is dubious.

Magnesium. Magnesium is an essential mineral used in many processes throughout the body, such as helping muscles relax. Some companies have suggested supplementation can enhance endurance, but little evidence supports this. Magnesium is widely available in a healthy diet; whole grains and brown rice are excellent sources. If you are under a lot of stress or eat poorly, make sure your multivitamin contains magnesium (most do). Taking too much (over 350 mg per day) causes diarrhea and can create an imbalance with calcium.

MCT Oil. Medium-chain triglycerides are fats, with 6 to 12 carbon atoms, that act more like carbohydrates (fast absorption and quick burning). Although it's claimed to reduce body fat and increase endurance by sparing muscle glycogen, several well-controlled studies show that MCT does nothing and can even harm performance.

Prohormones. A prohormone is a precursor in the body to a hormone. Androstenediol, commonly called "Andro," is one step away from testosterone and comes in several forms (norandro, 1-AD, etc.). Another prohormone, DHEA (Dehydroepiandrosterone) is the precursor of androstenediol and is hyped as a "natural" steroid because it can be made from wild (Mexican) yams.

All of these prohormones are banned by the World Anti-Doping Agency (WADA), and most have nasty steroid side effects with no real evidence supporting the claims of muscle growth or fat loss.

Pyruvate. The end product of glycolysis, pyruvate is claimed to aid fat loss and improve endurance (the so-called exercise in a bottle), but this is based on a few flawed studies. No good evidence exists that pyruvate supplementation is effective.

Ribose. A simple 5-carbon sugar that is a precursor of adenosine, ribose is used to make ATP (adenosine triphosphate). Theories abound that d-ribose supplementation will increase energy stores and speed recovery. Most of the research that showed promise was on cardiac patients, but one well-controlled study on healthy subjects found no effect on performance.

Vanadyl Sulfate. Vanadium (named for a Scandinavian goddess of beauty and youth) is an essential trace mineral found in a wide variety of foods that has an insulin-like effect on regulating glucose. Widely hyped for muscle building, but for non-diabetic humans, the main result is a smaller bank balance. Besides the lack of efficacy, there is a risk of toxicity.

Other Supplements. There are too many unproven supplements to detail them all. Among those that stretch the limits of scientific credulity or fiscal practicality are Anator P70, arginine, boron, choline, chrysin, enterostatin, growth hormone releasers, glutathione, gugglesterone, HCA, inosine, KIC, MSM, OKG, orchic substance, ornithine, SAM-e, taurine, and ZMA. Don't waste your money until they show a *lot* more serious proof.

NATURAL SUPPLEMENTS

These days, most sports food contains at least a few herbal ingredients. Usually, there is little evidence to back up the marketing, just a lot of mumbo-jumbo and pseudoscience. Often there isn't even a biologically credible explanation of how the ingredient is supposed to work.

With many herbal supplements, there are risky drug interactions since they contain so many compounds—and many people don't just take one supplement but a smorgasbord. Some, such as St. John's wort, can counter the effects of prescription drugs, including oral contraceptives.

Among the most hyped category of products are "adaptogens," a term coined by Russian scientists in the 1950s, though the Chinese have used the herbs for millennia. These products are said to offer systemwide healing, stress reduction, and "balancing" without any specific site of action or detrimental effects. Unfortunately, the science behind these claims has never been verified in controlled, peer-reviewed studies published in major international journals. The promoters all hide behind vague references to Soviet or undocumented research.

Beware the testimonials for herbal products. Usually the people who offer these testimonials, even if they aren't paid, also made other fitness improvements at the same time. Many herbal products are said to take up to six weeks before effects can be seen—plenty of time for training and proper nutrition benefits to show.

Sometimes there is a grain of truth to

the statements—but the products often do not contain enough of the herbal ingredient to be effective, or it's of the wrong species, or the quality is poor. Standardized extracts may be the most reliable form for ensuring you're receiving a proper dosage, but there is no guarantee you're getting what you pay for. Tests of herbal products routinely find that they contain a fraction of (or many times) what is stated on the label.

It is quite likely that some of the compounds in the following natural supplements will eventually prove to have merit. But at present, virtually none of them have demonstrated their efficacy at anything except making a few people wealthy.

Alfalfa (*Medicago sativa*). A fiber-rich plant in the legume family that is commonly used as animal fodder (the name in Arabic means "father of all foods," since it appeared to make horses run faster). Claims include increased energy, reduced fatigue, lower cholesterol, and liver detoxification, yet virtually no clinical evidence backs this up. One study showed lowered cholesterol from ingesting 120 grams per day, but most dosage recommendations are only 2 to 3 grams per day.

Astragalus; Huang qi (*Astragalus membranaceus*). The dried root of this Chinese herb is used, often with other adaptogens, to make energy tonics. There are no studies that demonstrate it increases performance, and evidence for immune protection is sketchy.

Bee Pollen. It's actually flower pollen collected from bees returning to the hive. It's

called the "perfect food" by hucksters because it's supposed to have a magical blend of nutrients. Groovy. No proof it does anything, but there is a risk of allergic reaction.

Blue-green Algae (Spirulina; *Aphanizomenon flos-aquae*). Several species of expensive pond scum are a source of nutrients already abundant in a healthy diet that includes vegetables. Despite copious hype and fanciful claims, there are no controlled studies published in reputable journals that show blue-green algae does anything special.

Chitosan. Crab and shrimp shell extract that is purported to bind with fat to prevent absorption (the "fat trapper"). Sketchy evidence, with the minus of reduced calcium and vitamin E, plus constant diarrhea.

Chlorophyll (wheatgrass, chlorella, etc.). Because this plant molecule is similar to human hemoglobin (it contains magnesium instead of iron), some have theorized that it speeds the production of red blood cells, cleanses the liver, and fixes nearly everything. Long on talk, pathetically short on solid science. Wheatgrass and chlorella (green algae) are favorite sources for this scam, but it takes weeks of daily consumption of vile-tasting products before it's supposed to do anything.

Colloidal Silver. A favorite of the charlatans, this is merely silver suspended in water that is supposed to cure everything. Silver is not an essential element, and it's only effective as an antibiotic in amounts that are toxic to humans. No benefits have yet been proven.

Colostrum. This is the pre-milk produced by the mammary glands of mammals during the first few days following birth. It is a very nutritious liquid for newborns that is very high in protein, antibodies, and growth factors. The stuff sold by the purveyors comes from cows (bovine) and is sold in capsule or powdered form.

Of course, the claims for this mother's gift are many (immune protection, ergogenic enhancement, etc.) but the support is totally lacking. To achieve the dosage that showed any effect in the few studies that exist would require taking thirty to sixty capsules or six to twelve scoops per day.

Cordyceps. Originally collected from dead Tibetan caterpillars, this fungus is supposed to increase energy, sexual and otherwise. So far, minimal evidence substantiates claims that it can enhance oxygen utilization and athletic performance.

Echinacea. A fair amount of evidence supports the claims of immune-boosting properties for this plant. However, other studies have shown no effect, so the jury is still out. In theory, it can both decrease symptoms and shorten the severity of colds and flu. Research on echinacea's preventive capabilities is inconclusive and little has been done on goldenseal, which often is mixed in the pills and potions.

Once you feel something coming on, take either the liquid or pill form of the standardized extract according to the instructions (pills don't require counting drops). However, avoid echinacea if you have pollen allergies or are asthmatic because it could make matters worse.

Ephedrine. This stimulant is derived from herbs such as Ma Huang (*Ephedra sinica*) and bala (*Sida cordifolia*). Ephedrine used to lurk in diet products that claimed to boost your metabolism. Frequently combined with caffeine (or guarana) and aspirin (or white willow bark), the "ECA stack" can be effective for weight loss by giving you the constant jitters.

Although generally safe when taken in proper dosages by healthy individuals, there are many contraindications including high blood pressure. Due to the great danger of excessive dosages, the FDA banned ephedrine in 2004. Synephrine from a fruit called zhi shi or bitter orange (*Citrus aurantium*) has a similar effect. Even if you ignore the warnings, your body builds a tolerance to these stimulants and the fat will return once you stop.

Germanium. A trace element that is supposed to facilitate oxygen uptake, correct your electrical fields, and prevent cancer, there is no good evidence it is lacking in diets or that supplementation helps anything.

Ginkgo Biloba. This tree has been around for 200 million years, and the Chinese have used the nuts as medicine for nearly 5,000 years. Now, extract from the leaves is proving effective against problems associated with blood flow (microcirculation in small capillaries); taking it with aspirin may cause problems with excessive bleeding. Ginkgo is also a powerful antioxidant though not necessarily one superior to countless others. Research is still ongoing in many fields, but 200 mg per day (half in the morning, the rest before dinner) seems to be effective for most people. The inclusion of ginkgo in sports drinks is purely for marketing purposes.

Ginseng, Asian; Ren Shen (*Panax ginseng*). This is the classic ginseng that is claimed to improve performance and have adaptogenic properties. Though there is a lot of research on *panax*, much of it is poorly designed and conflicting. American ginseng (*Panax quinquefolium*) is closely related but has slightly different properties.

Ginseng, Peruvian; Maca (*Lepedium meyenii*). This root related to turnips was eaten by Inca warriors before battle to boost strength and stamina. The main claim to fame is as an aphrodisiac and adaptogen though all of this is purely anecdotal; no human studies yet offer corroboration.

Ginseng, Siberian; Ciwujia (*Eleutherococcus senticosus*). A distant relative of *panax*, it is also an adaptogen that is claimed to improve endurance by reducing lactate production and raising the anaerobic threshold. As the main ingredient of Endurox and PrimeQuest products, *eleuthero* is also supposed to burn more fat, increase muscle oxygenation, and hasten acclimatization. Sounds great but the oft-cited research is mostly from Soviet and East German sports labs from three decades ago. Recent studies in mainstream, peer-reviewed journals do not support the claims of increased performance.

Golden Root (*Rhodiola rosea*). A "second-generation" adaptogen from Russia, it has even less research supporting it than the "first-generation" ginsengs. Increased oxygen uptake, fat burning, and mental power are some of the unconfirmed claims.

Guarana (*Paullinia cupana*). An Amazon berry that produces an overpriced form of caffeine (guaranine), guarana is used to make a product sound exotic or natural.

Hornet Juice (*Vesper mandarin japonica*). The grubs of three-inch-long wasps digest insect meat and then regurgitate a clear liquid that serves as food for the adults. Gross, and no evidence it does anything for humans.

Maral (*Rhaponticum carthamoides*). Another adaptogen from Siberia that is supposed to build muscles, prevent muscle breakdown, and increase energy. While the claims are abundant and fanciful, the hard evidence is nonexistent.

Maté; Yerba Maté (*Ilex paraguariensis*). The leaves of this South American tree are sold as an energizer and fat burner. There are cheaper ways to get caffeine, antioxidants, and an "herbal high."

Milk Thistle (*Silybum marianum*). Reputed to protect the liver, a meta-analysis in 2000 of all the research concluded that the clinical evidence is inconclusive. Milk thistle appears to be safe and has no major side effects, so it falls into the "can't hurt and may do some good" category, particularly if you drink alcohol. For preventive purposes, typical recommendations are about 280 mg of 80 percent extract per day.

Reishi Mushroom; Ling-zhi (*Ganoderma lucidum*). Considered the king of herbal medicines by ancient Chinese, it is now marketed as a cure-all that, among other things, can prevent altitude sickness and increase endurance. Unfortunately, trustworthy studies on humans are entirely lacking.

Royal Jelly. The spit that worker bees feed to bee larvae is claimed to have all manner of health benefits, which is true—if you're a bee. No major journal has ever published a human study that supports the hype. There is nothing mysterious in the product, and there is a chance of allergic reaction.

Wheat Germ Oil; Octacosanol. A single study more than two decades ago showed an increase in grip strength, but little else, after eight weeks of supplementation. No other studies have demonstrated any effect that enhances athletic performance.

Yohimbe. An extract from African tree bark marketed for weight loss and as a "natural Viagra." The active ingredient is a stimulant with many unpleasant side effects. Clinical studies show the rewards are minimal to nonexistent.

Other Herbs. Look at the label on many herbal supplements marketed for athletes and you'll find a wide variety of unproven ingredients, including anterior pituitary, beet root powder, eurycoma (aka, tongkat ali, longjack, Malaysian ginseng), fo ti, garcinia, forskohlin root, gotu kola, hawthorn berry, hoodia, Indian berry, kava, kelp, kola nut, murira puama, nettle, oat straw extract, pumpkin seed, sarsaparilla, saw palmetto, tribulus terrestris. Caveat emptor.

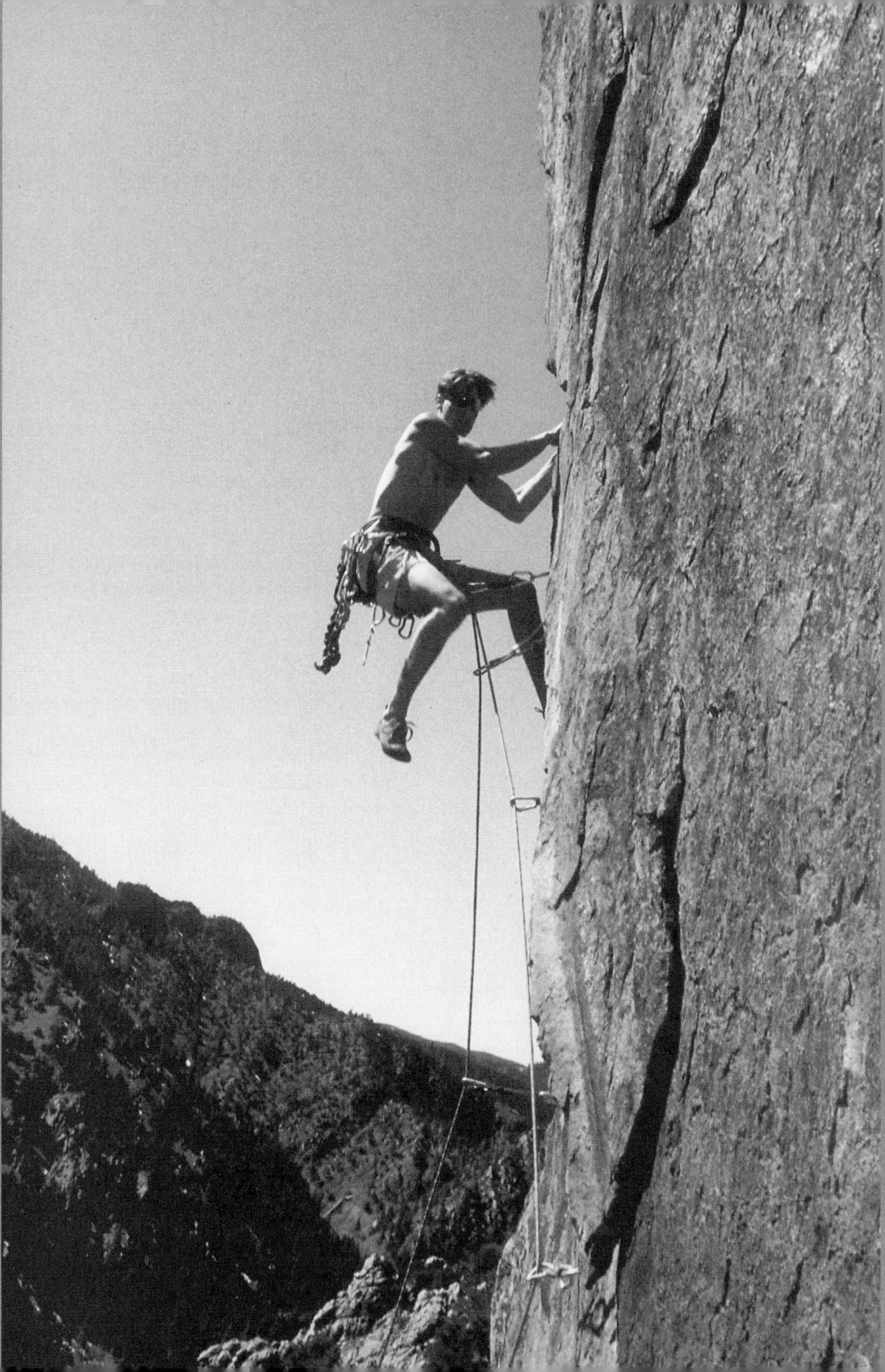

CHAPTER 3

Mental Power

It takes much more than good physical conditioning to be a successful climber. In truth, it's the power of the mind that separates the elite of the climbing world from the rest of us. When the crux is upon them, they can recruit a mental strength with immense energy.

Fortunately you can train your mind as well as your body. Many of the teachings of martial arts and yoga forms are centered on this point—indeed, many climbers practice these disciplines. While it is not necessary to become an Eastern adept, you can improve your climbing performance by stretching both your mind and body. Conveniently, you can do both at the same time.

While it may sound pithy, there is scientific evidence to support claims of increased power from mental preparation. For example, one study showed that "psyching-up" for a bench press allowed subjects to achieve about 8 percent more peak force than when using an attention placebo and 12 percent more force than when the subjects were mentally distracted ahead of time.

Another study has shown that our body actually anticipates upcoming exercise and begins ramping up ahead of time. Blood tests of athletes revealed that about 10 minutes prior to a hard resistance workout, the nervous system begins producing large amounts of adrenaline and related compounds (called catecholamines). These are the chemicals the body uses for stressful physical activity, commonly associated with the flight-or-fight response.

It has even been demonstrated that the mind can trick the body into getting into shape without changing the level of activity. In a unique study, hotel maids were given health exams and then divided into two groups. One group was the control and the other was told that their normal work is good exercise. After four weeks, the informed group had lost body fat and lowered their blood pressure simply because they believed they were exercising more. This was a clear demonstration that placebos can be used to our advantage.

MENTAL FOCUS

Few activities draw upon your mental powers like climbing on the sharp end. The complete concentration and focus required is what attract many people to the sport. Jobs, relationships, and everything else in life are quickly shoved aside for the business at hand. Yet if you examine the accidents you've suffered, the odds are high that few occurred when you were completely focused. It's the momentary lapse that fills the history of climbing with disasters; outside factors are but minor players in most of the dramas.

Veteran climbers who have developed their technique often find that the most difficult part about returning to the rock after an extended absence isn't a lack of strength. Recovering their "lead head," the ability to think when leading a pitch, can be more problematic. Without exercise, your mental muscle can also atrophy.

Walking a slack line—a length of webbing loosely strung between two trees, a foot or so off the ground—has long been a popular form of training for climbers. While many think of this as a balance exercise, for which it is indeed useful, you will also find it requires a great deal of concentration. When your mind wanders, you're on the ground in the blink of an eye.

Although focus is critical to all aspects of climbing, you must learn to use it like a zoom lens. This comes only with practice. When performing at your highest standards on the relative safety of a sport climb, zoom in and isolate only that which gets you to the top: your movements and breathing, the features of the rock, and clipping the draws. Everything else—wind, heat, sounds, smells—is mentally blotted out.

However, this level of attention can get you killed in the more dangerous arenas of traditional and aid climbing, so you mentally zoom back to a "normal" perspective that includes the quality of gear placements, how the rope is running, the security of the belay.

When you enter the alpine environment, you must pull back even further to get the "wide angle" big picture. All of the above factors are still important, but to survive, your mind also is aware of the weather, the safety of the snowpack, the feel of the ice, the per-formance level of you and your partners.

Your ultimate goal, Grasshopper, is to master this mental zooming to the point that you can be focused and aware simultaneously. You must also learn to deal with distractions, both external (such as weather, noise, other climbers) and internal (self-doubts, emotions, past falls). Focusing on things that are beyond your control will merely drain your energy.

One way to cope with distractions is to anticipate them and how you will respond. Make a list of things that might distract you during a climb and how you would typically react. Then, using the same situations, think about how you would like to react for a better outcome. Perhaps think about how one of your heroes would react; what would Messner do? Or Sharma? Or (insert name of choice)?

Often, there are critical moments in a climb when your utmost focus is required for optimal performance or even survival. Examples include when you tie into your harness, place protection in a pumpy location, miss a clip, are making the crux move, or transitioning at the belay. It can help to identify these moments ahead of time and plan on where your focus needs to be and the best course of action. Then employ a focus cue to get you back on task.

A focus cue might be a positive verbal command to yourself such as "Focus!" "I'm in control," or "I've trained hard." The cue can also be a physical action such as taking a few deep breaths, shaking out the hands, or chalking up. The focus cue can even be a mental image that helps you relax or a quick look at your tie-in knot. Any of these verbal, physical, and visual cues can be combined too, such as taking a deep breath and thinking "Power!" right before making a crux move.

To be effective, focus cues must be practiced and used every time a situation arises. With frequent use, they can become a powerful technique to refocus your attention and clear detritus from your mind at the critical moment.

GO WITH THE FLOW

Few drugs are as powerful and intoxicating—or as elusive—as "flow," the mental state where everything comes together. When you're in it, you know it. Once you've felt it, you'll want it again. It's that ecstatic feeling after you just floated up a pitch, ran with wings on your shoes, skied the perfect line. Psychologists define flow as the ideal performance state: movement is seemingly effortless and graceful, actions are automatic, attention is focused, fears are suppressed, you have a feeling of control, and time seems to slow.

Although there is no single path to the flow state, you can facilitate its arrival by training for relaxation, pre-visualizing, and establishing goals.

RELAXATION

Learning to relax at will, even when your senses are screaming to do otherwise, is one of the most essential talents for a climber. This saves you valuable mental and physical energy, which are always in short supply. Athletes choke when they overanalyze themselves during performance.

Practicing relaxation in a non-stressful environment makes it easier to summon when under pressure. This is essentially a form of meditation, though you need not chant mantras, ring bells, or burn incense (unless desired). Normally we breathe shallow about fourteen times per minute—but taking deep inhalations only six times per minute synchronizes cardiovascular rhythms, calms the mind, and increases concentration.

It's no coincidence that reciting prayers in many religions tends to create a relaxed mental state. Research has shown that reciting the Catholic prayer Ave Maria in Latin or the Buddhist mantra om-mani-padme-om result in the speaker breathing six breaths per minute. Additionally, both are often recited for roughly 15 minutes.

Find a comfortable place to sit or lie down where you will not be distracted. Begin by inhaling smooth, deep breaths through the nose and exhaling slowly through the mouth. Concentrate on the rhythm and fullness of each breath; actively think about pulling your diaphragm downward with each inspiration. When thoughts intrude, acknowledge them and return to focused breathing.

After a few minutes of meditative breathing, begin to notice any tension in your body—a clenched jaw, tight shoulder muscle, tense back—and release it. Practice relaxation by tensing a muscle very tightly for a few seconds, then quickly releasing it, and notice the smooth feeling that ensues.

Learning to pay attention to your body for unnecessary tension and teaching yourself to relax at a moment's notice with a few deep breaths is essential for optimal performance in all sports.

VISUAL IMAGERY

Visualization is a well-proven method for improving performance; it is well documented that intensely thinking about an activity stimulates nerves in the associated muscles. There are multiple theories on how the use of visual imagery results in better performance but almost universal agreement that the effects are real.

When you visualize a climb, don't just study a topo or photo; imagine yourself there overcoming the obstacles. It can even help to create a meta-picture where you view yourself in action like in a movie. If you see something you don't like, go back into your body and make the changes, then play the scene again to see that you have improved.

During this mental exercise, include full details: how you feel, rock texture, temperature, sound of the wind, light reflecting off a carabiner, reaching the top, the descent. This process helps eliminate self-doubt and calm fears because you have already rehearsed the route.

Using visualization can also help instill mental toughness and motivate you through a workout. If you are rehearsing a route that requires many attempts, for example, it can help to create a mental image of yourself floating through the crux and making the final moves to the top. Or if you are doing laps on a climbing wall for endurance, imagine yourself five or ten laps ahead of your current point and still feeling strong.

GOAL SETTING

All aspects of your training become easier when you establish a major goal and a time frame. This goal needs to be specific, such as "do The Nose in a day next summer," "climb the Cassin Ridge in June," or "redpoint Just Do It this September." And your goal should be realistic, a good fit with your level of experience (the climbs just mentioned are only for veteran climbers), and meaningful.

Once you've picked your objective, write it down. Then divide it into necessary subgoals, along with definite measurements for your progress. The more accurate you are in defining the required steps to achieve the goal, the more likely you are to succeed.

To add extra motivation, post your goal in a place where you will see it every day—on the bathroom mirror or refrigerator door. Tell your friends and family your intentions and reap the benefits of their support: a little needling is sometimes good.

KNOW FEAR

Never climb with anyone who is fearless: it's just a matter of time until they become a statistic. The best climbers are intimately familiar with fear—it keeps them alive—but they do not let it control them. Fear becomes panic when it prevents action or causes critical thinking to falter. Learning to keep that knot in the stomach as a tight little ball comes from experience, but there are some guidelines that can help.

While it should be obvious, it's easy to overlook the fact that building a base of confidence makes fear more manageable. This means progressively increasing your exposure to fearful things, rather than jumping in over your head; that first rappel is a lot easier when it's on a slab and backed up with a belay instead of going off an overhang at night.

This knowledge base also includes preparing for emergencies by taking courses in self-rescue and advanced first aid; book knowledge doesn't cut it when the manure hits the fan. Learning from other people's mistakes is also an essential part of handling fear, since knowing what can go wrong is the first step in preventing calamity. Read *Accidents in North American Mountaineering* when it comes out every year, as well as accounts in articles and books. And remember, no form of climbing is completely safe.

Though you may have been working up to it for years, nothing quite prepares you for that initial glimpse of your first big wall or Himalayan peak. Nearly everyone wonders what they've gotten themselves into. But as a Laozi proverb goes, "A journey of a thousand miles begins with a single step." When you subdivide your goal into bite-size chunks, such as sections between bivis or camps, the overwhelming nature of the task becomes much less daunting.

Crises are inevitable if you climb long enough, and they come in all shapes and forms. You might be on a dicey lead when you look down to see your last piece has lifted out. Or a storm suddenly moves in while you are partway up a cliff. Or your partner might be severely injured in a fall. Handling your fears at these moments is essential—panic is not an option.

After the preliminary "oh shit," take a couple of deep breaths and will your pulse to slow; this is when those relaxation exercises pay off. Cleanse your mind of negative waves, Moriarty, and think positive thoughts. No matter how grim the situation, humor is an invaluable asset—smile—even a bad joke can be better than dour resolution. Sometimes gallows humor serves to reduce the tension, though this can also backfire with the wrong partners. As Jim Donini once quipped when asked about the team's chances while retreating in a storm from near the summit of Cerro Torre, "Survival is not assured."

During a crisis when you have a solid base of confidence, action becomes automatic. Hesitate only long enough to gather the required information that will help the circumstances. In most critical moments, time is the enemy.

GENDER AND FEAR

Men and women process fear differently. This fact is important to understand and accept when climbing with partners of the opposite sex in stressful situations. Expecting them to react the same as you will only make matters worse.

New research has revealed that this difference in coping with fear is actually hardwired into the brain. Scans show that the amygdala, an almond-shaped cluster of neurons that processes fear and other emotions (located deep in the temporal lobes), is more active on the right side in men and the left in women. For men, the amygdala communicates more with the visual cortex and an area that affects motor action, so we are more keyed into external influences. Women are better connected to internal sensations (heart rate, breathing, hormone levels, etc.).

Women often feel a need to get their fears out in the open. Particularly among themselves, such as an all-women team, just stating out loud that they are afraid of falling (or whatever) helps resolve the issue and allows them to carry on. In general, women are also better listeners and more respectful of each others' boundaries.

Men, on the other hand, tend to keep their fears bottled up and are loathe to admit them to others. By the time a man admits that the situation may be serious, the danger meter is likely already deep into the red zone.

Due to these gender differences in handling fear, women often state that climbing with other women is less stressful than climbing with men, even their significant other. This distinction is often lost on men, who feel no real difference in stress based upon the sex of their partner.

When a woman says "I'm worried" to a man, he may not understand that this is her way of coping. Men have an unfortunate tendency to write off these concerns as irrelevant or, worse, see them as a sign of weakness. All too often, men will be dismis-

sive when their female climbing partner voices anxiety, for example when they ask to rope up on a dicey section. Rather than say "oh, you'll do fine" or getting into an argument, it's better to de-stress the situation by pulling out the rope. Realize that her female partners would have replied "*we'll* do fine" as they roped up.

While it is always important to listen to your partner, mixed teams need to work at it a bit harder. Be mindful that everyone copes with fear in different ways. Men, especially, need to respect what their female partner is telling them about her confidence, capabilities, and comfort zone.

Of course, there are other ways for men to annoy female partners, often without even realizing they're doing something wrong. Charging up the trail and leaving them to hike on their own, or just tuning out with an iPod, is likely to put the guy in the doghouse; women never ditch other women and they actually enjoy conversations. Sandbagging a partner by putting her on a route that is way too difficult or scary is guaranteed to end badly for the man. And while well-timed, helpful advice can be a good thing, offering empty encouragement ("You got it," "C'mon, you can do it!") or endless beta ("left foot up, right hand to the hold") is decidedly irritating.

TRAINING INTUITION

Intuition is often what keeps climbers alive in the mountains, and like other aspects of the mind, it can be trained for better performance. On the battlefield, the U.S. Marine Corps includes "intuitive decision making" as a valuable attribute for a squad leader.

Intuition is that gut instinct that quickly rises in our consciousness and causes us to take action. Intuition has nothing to do with psychic ability nor is it a mental calculation. Rather, it is a feeling based upon prior experience and knowledge that we process at a level so deep we often do not realize where the thought comes from.

Developing our "sixth sense" is mostly a matter of paying greater attention and analyzing it rationally. It requires experience with both good and bad decisions to improve your intuition. Positively reinforcing the good decisions when you make them and downplaying the bad ones will help you trust your gut in the future.

ACCEPT FAILURE

When you talk with famous climbers about their achievements, most of them are quick to point out that they've had as many failures as successes. While admirers often forget these disappointments, the big names view them as essential elements of their careers. After all, if climbing were always a sure thing, few of us would even bother.

How you deal with failure will largely determine your climbing future. Temper tantrums, such as throwing shoes or loud cursing, do nobody any good—least of all those around you. It's important to put aside self-recrimination; shoulda-coulda-woulda doesn't help.

While some climbers strive for perfection from themselves, this is an exercise in futility. It is more fruitful to aim for an *optimal* performance. This subtle wordplay can have significant ramifications for future adventures.

Step back and examine the entire scenario from an outsider's perspective, looking for correctable faults. Then address the problems with action. Revise your game plan and possibly adjust your goals. Anyone reading this book will likely still be climbing years, perhaps decades, from now. Keep that long-term perspective when dealing with short-term failures.

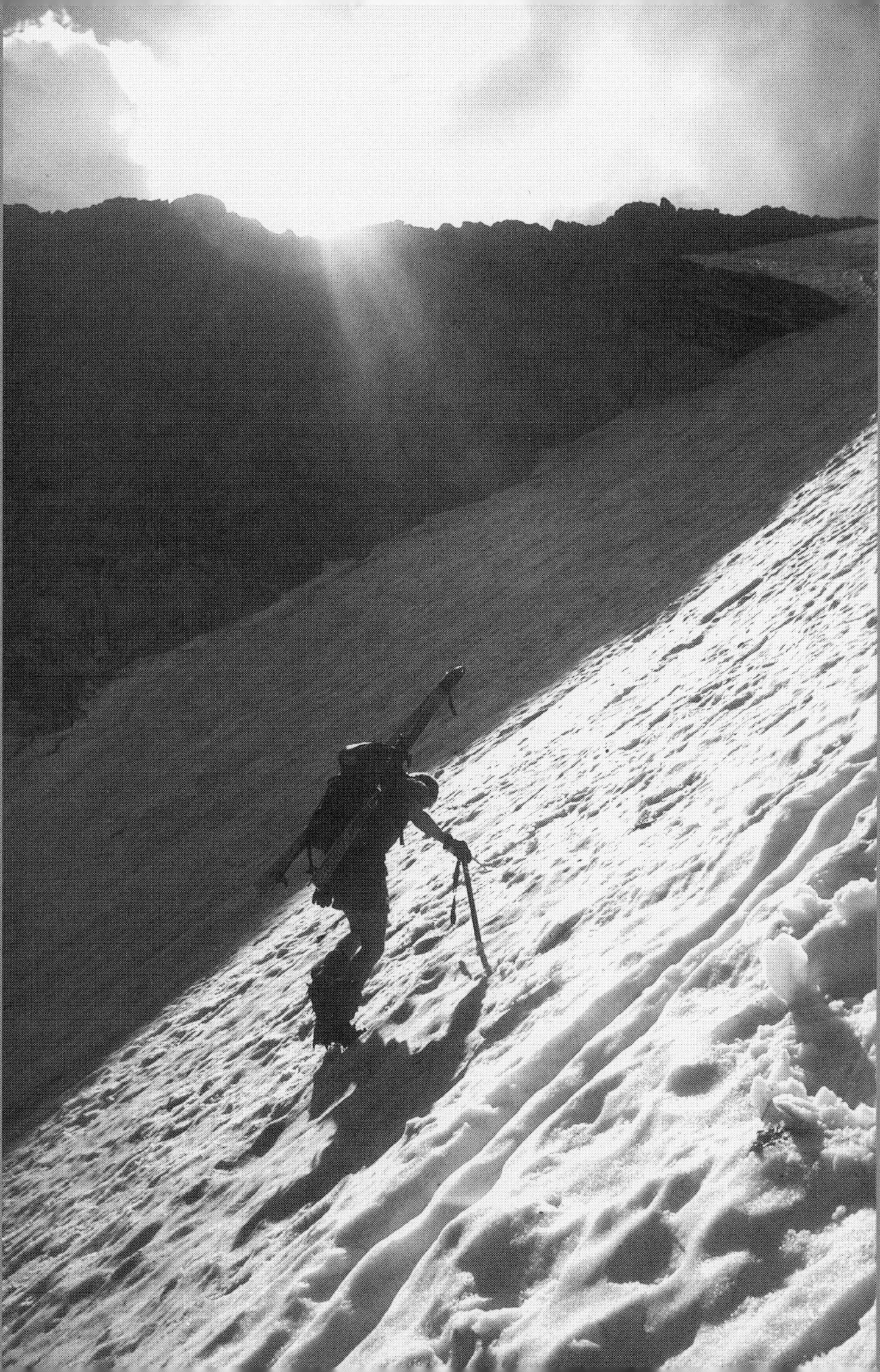

CHAPTER 4

Aerobic Conditioning

All climbers, no matter what aspect of the sport they are into, will benefit from improved fitness of heart and lungs. Those with the most to gain, obviously, are the alpinists and mountaineers who, by definition, breathe thin air while struggling uphill. Yet training for better utilization of oxygen—what aerobics is all about—will help other climbers improve overall stamina and control weight; you climb better when you aren't exhausted from the approach and aren't carrying excess baggage.

Aerobic training is any activity that gets your heart pumping between half speed and just short of full throttle for an extended duration. There are hundreds of ways to do this—a baker's dozen are presented here—so you aren't just limited to running. However, unless you are doing continuous laps or high-intensity circuits, gym climbing and resistance training have minimal aerobic benefit.

There are also long-term health benefits from superior cardiovascular function including decreased risk of heart attack, stroke, and diabetes. The well-known reduction in stress and improvement in sleep are all good reasons for regular aerobic exercise. A "runner's high," once attributed to the release of a natural cannaboid (anandamide) has recently been shown to result from the production of endorphins during exercise.

But the main reason to start aerobic conditioning—it can be a lot of fun!

AEROBIC FUNDAMENTALS

When it comes to making a movement, everything boils down to a little molecule called adenosine triphosphate (ATP), which energizes muscle cells but must constantly be recharged. The easiest way for our body to juice up is with the aid of oxygen; though relatively slow, it's pretty much an infinite system.

When going full-bore, we can't get enough oxygen and must rely on faster anaerobic processes to refresh that energy molecule. While these systems give you a quick turbo boost, they don't last long and tend to gunk up the works with by-products. How well we can handle these oxygenless demands is a major factor in athletic performance.

AEROBIC ADAPTATIONS

Among the many adaptations that result from an effective training program is increased aerobic capacity. This is the maximum volume of oxygen that you can utilize when working as hard as possible (VO_2max). By raising your VO_2max, you can do the same amount of work with less effort; your heart rate may be 20 to 40 beats lower per minute.

Depending upon the program, your current level of fitness, and inherent "trainability," VO_2max can be increased by about 10 to 15 percent. However, gains usually end after about eighteen months of training, and some people see no change. Nonetheless, VO_2max can be a good indicator of fitness and a benchmark for your own training. Since there are many variables that affect VO_2max, don't compare your result with someone else's unless the tests were done with the same lab protocol.

Although a high aerobic capacity is helpful when humping a pack up brutal hills, what matters even more in the mountains is your ability to sustain that output for a long time. When working very hard, you begin to breathe faster than your ability to consume oxygen (called the ventilatory threshold). At the same time, your body begins to rely more and more upon anaerobic energy production (see "Physiology of Strength" in chapter 6 for more details). Once you go anaerobic and are panting so hard you can't talk, you can only sustain a few minutes of output before you collapse, gasping for air.

One of the major goals of training is to raise the point at which your body enters the anaerobic realm. If you are out of shape, this may occur at about 50 percent of your VO_2max but it can rise to 80 percent or higher if you train appropriately. More accurately called the performance threshold (anaerobic threshold and lactate threshold are misnomers), a higher level allows a greater sustained peak output and faster recovery. In other words, you can go harder for longer. Even after you have maxed your VO_2max, you can still increase your performance threshold and power output.

With training, your maximum cardiac output increases considerably, which means at full effort your heart pumps much more blood. The heart itself becomes larger due to bigger chambers and thicker muscle walls. Even the electrocardiogram (ECG) of the "sports heart" is altered and may resemble a heart attack on the printout if the doctor doesn't realize you're an athlete.

Your heart rate also recovers significantly faster once you stop exercising. As fitness improves, your resting heart rate can decrease about 10 or more beats per minute. Both of these adaptations are good signs that all that work is paying off.

Other changes include a greater volume of blood plasma (fluid), which improves oxygen delivery because your blood is less viscous. After training, your body also produces more red blood cells—each of which carries over a billion oxygen molecules. This increase in oxygen-carrying capacity helps your muscles perform more efficiently.

Moderate and high-intensity endurance training actually causes your body to grow more capillaries within the muscles and expand the existing ones. These minute blood vessels allow a greater exchange of nutrients while more effectively removing waste and heat. Enhanced circulation may also translate to warmer fingers and toes in winter conditions.

Within the muscle cells, myoglobin (a protein that stores and transports oxygen), mitochondria (the powerhouses that produce energy), and the activity of oxidative enzymes (which break down fuels for use) all increase dramatically. Trained muscles store more glycogen, your primary aerobic energy source from carbohydrates, and triglyceride, the fuel form of fat.

Of major significance for mountaineers and other long-duration athletes, aerobic training enhances your ability to use fat as a source of fuel. This lipolysis effect, which can take years to fully develop, spares the limited amount of glycogen in the muscles and liver (only adequate for about 90 minutes) by tapping into the nearly infinite reserves of fat.

Both tendon and ligament repair are enhanced due to increased collagen activity within these connective tissues from aerobic activity. These tissues have relatively poor circulation and are normally very slow to heal, but low- to moderate-intensity exercise can speed the process.

TRAINING PRINCIPLES

The aerobic triumvirate rules an effective training program: frequency, duration, and intensity. If you don't go often enough, long enough, and hard enough, you will not get the desired results. Though not a complete waste of time—any exercise is better than none—haphazard workouts can leave you frustrated and out of breath. Train smart.

To make progress, you need to significantly elevate your heart rate at least three days per week for 30 minutes or more. Your workouts don't have to be in a single session (for example, having three 10-minute periods is fine), but most people find that more convenient. The goal is to elevate your heart rate to roughly 70 percent of maximum; lower levels of intensity can

have significant health benefits but do not improve aerobic capacity.

Forget about training in the mythical fat-burning zone. This falsehood, which continues to be promulgated by air-headed aerobics instructors and the mass media, is based upon a poor understanding of physiology. Although it is true that exercising at low intensity burns a greater percentage of fat versus carbohydrates, this is misleading. A higher level of intensity burns more total calories, including a greater amount of fat. And high intensity with intervals of rest produces slightly greater burning of fat after the exercise is over. Since few people have unlimited time or desire to train, make the most of every workout.

On the other hand, don't turn into a training junkie either. You can get health benefits with as little as 700 calories of aerobic exercise per week (roughly 5 to 8 miles of running). It takes more like 2,000 calories (15 to 25 miles) of effort to see significant fitness gains. Maximum aerobic results are achieved with 5,000 to 6,000 calories per week, which translates to 40 to 60 miles of running, although this depends upon body weight, intensity, and many other factors. Exceeding this volume may be necessary for long races (marathons and ultras) to prevent injury and train other components, but it won't enhance your lung power.

Many recreational athletes tend to train at a level of intensity that is too high for optimal gains. This is another case where more is not always better since some of the adaptations discussed previously are best achieved when you aren't going as hard.

You also run a greater risk of injuries and overtraining, which can set you back more than training less.

In the grand scheme of things, it makes absolutely no difference whether you exercise in the morning, afternoon, or evening. While some argue the pros and cons of minute differences in calorie burning at different times of day, what counts is that you establish a pattern that works for your schedule. Don't allow some perceived advantage of a certain time prevent you from working out.

If you are an early riser and prefer to exercise before breakfast, that's fine. However, be aware that you may not get as high a quality workout due to lower energy levels and dehydration. Conversely, elevating your heart rate late in the evening may make it difficult to fall asleep; don't sacrifice this vital nutrient.

Give yourself time to see results; heaping on too much, too fast will lead to injury. Remember, too, that what worked when you were a twenty-something may not apply later in life. It takes about two weeks for your body to adjust to a change and a full two months to fully adapt to a program. Increase only one component of the aerobic triumvirate at a time by no more than 10 percent, and don't expect overnight miracles.

ON THE RUN (OR BIKE, OR SKI)

As with all other forms of exercise, to prevent injury and increase flexibility, it is vital that you warm up properly prior to a hard effort. Always start with 5 to 10 minutes of gentle exercise to warm the muscles, increase blood flow, and lubricate the joints. This also gets you in the proper mind-set for what is to come.

No matter your endurance sport, hills are your friend. Don't fear them. Seek out hills and embrace them. They will reward you with better physical and mental conditioning. If you are a flatlander, try running up and down highway overpasses, stadium steps, or office building stairwells.

When it is safe to do so (no traffic), listening to music can be an excellent motivator during your workouts. With a portable MP3 player, you can easily customize the tunes to start you out with a gentle warm-up, psych you through the tough sections, and relax you during the cool-down. Of course, if music bugs you, then listen to your own rhythm.

Be sure to cool down gradually following your play—don't stop cold! Active recovery with a few minutes of light activity will leave you less sore the next day.

FOLLOW YOUR HEART

Your heart rate provides invaluable information for planning and carrying out an effective training program. There is a direct linear correlation between heart rate and training intensity. This fact allows us to monitor our level of exertion with greater accuracy than subjective interpretations of how we feel during a workout.

AT REST

At rest, the heart rates of those who are out of shape is typically around 70 to 80 beats per minute, though this depends upon age (it increases as you get older) and gender (women's hearts are slightly faster at rest). Following an endurance training program, resting heart rate (RHR) can drop into the 40 to 60 range. Although elite athletes often have a resting heart rate in the low 30s (some hearts may only beat 25 times a minute), a lower number does not necessarily indicate one is more fit than another.

Your heart rate is lowest in the middle of the night, but taking your pulse first thing in the morning before crawling out of bed is fairly close (averaging three mornings in a row is best). This number is useful as an indication that your training is paying off (RHR can decrease one beat per week) and for planning your program. If you notice that your RHR has increased by eight or more beats, it may be a warning sign of insufficient recovery, overtraining, or illness—time for a good rest. However, it could also mean you've just gone to a higher altitude, are jet-lagged (west to east is harder), or are dehydrated.

Another method for tracking progress is to monitor how quickly your heart rate slows down once you finish a workout. You can either see what your heart rate is after a set amount of time, say two minutes, or you can measure the time it takes for your heart rate to drop to a certain point. In both cases, lower is better and ideally the trend should be downward.

MAXED OUT

Contrary to popular belief, a high maximum heart rate (MHR) does not indicate superior fitness. This value is genetically determined, so you must play the cards you are dealt. No amount of training will increase your MHR; indeed, it can actually decrease by 3 or 4 beats as conditioning improves. However, maintaining a high level of fitness can slow the inevitable decrease of MHR that occurs with age.

If you are serious about improving fitness, it is very helpful to know your MHR with a high level of accuracy. This number serves as the basis for planning workouts at the proper intensity. Without this knowledge, you will be guessing—almost certainly incorrectly—and undermining your efforts. Don't waste time and energy; strive for quality.

The standard age-based formula for estimating MHR (220 – age) is a convenient method that is fraught with peril when it comes to developing a training program. The formula says a forty-year-old should have an MHR of about 180, but about two-thirds of this age group will have an MHR between 168 and 192. This prediction is even less accurate for those over forty who have been athletic most of their life since their MHR declines more slowly.

Several large studies have shown that a better estimate of maximum heart rate is provided by the formula MHR = 207 – (0.7 x age). This works reasonably well for men and women of all ages and histories of fitness. But it's still just an educated guess.

Maximum heart rate also depends upon the activity. Compared to running, using a rowing machine yields a MHR about 2 to 3 beats lower, biking will be 5 to 6 beats lower, and swimming can be about 14 beats lower.

The best method for finding MHR is via an all-out stress test using the American College of Sports Medicine (ACSM) guidelines under the supervision of a doctor. If you are over forty, have a family history of heart disease, or are starting up an exercise program after years of inactivity, this should be performed on a treadmill while being monitored by an ECG to detect abnormalities (and have the paddles ready). Many sports medicine clinics offer this test combined with a test to determine your VO$_2$max to give athletes a benchmark.

Those who are certain of their health and have no reason to be worried about pushing their heart can find their MHR with the aid of a heart rate monitor. Following a good warm-up, gradually increase your running or cycling pace so that, after 4 to 5 minutes, you cannot go any harder. Record the highest reading on the monitor. Be sure to warm down afterward. For greater accuracy, take a rest day and then repeat the test to get an average.

MONITORING PROGRESS

People who don't know how to use them routinely dismiss heart rate monitors (HRMs) as toys. Actually the feedback these devices offer can greatly enhance your training. But use a monitor intelligently and don't become a slave to the numbers.

One of the best aspects of using a heart rate monitor is that it teaches you to listen to your body. With practice, you will more accurately learn the feeling of different levels of intensity—of working at different percentages of your maximum heart rate. In other words: the more you use a monitor, the less you need one. After a while, you may only want to strap it on every couple of months to confirm your gut instincts.

A mid-priced heart rate monitor, such as the Suunto T3 (around $150), is fine for all but hard-core athletes and techies. The no-frills budget models are not worth the money because they typically lack features that help you train. Select a model that has a wireless chest strap and can record total duration of your aerobic activity, time spent within at least one heart rate zone (three zones is better), and maximum heart rate. If it records a minimum (many don't), obtaining your resting heart rate is easy: just sleep with the strap on.

Although the bells and whistles on the most sophisticated monitors, such as the Suunto T6 (about $400), add complexity, they can provide useful information to the serious mountain athlete seeking to top off their performance. Likely to be overwhelming for first-time HRM users, the top-end units often measure altitude as well as running and cycling speed (with optional attachments) and then upload all of the data to your computer for analysis.

When using a monitor, realize that in a hot environment, dehydration reduces the volume of your blood supply. This results in an upward creep in heart rate, even though the level of exertion remains the same (termed "cardiovascular drift"). Since it isn't always possible to drink enough fluid, keep this phenomenon in mind when the heat is on.

CARDIO PLANNING

Determining proper ranges, or zones, in which to keep your heart rate during an aerobic activity is the basis of smart aerobic training. This need not be complicated, but the more you put into it, the better the results.

Basing training zones upon percentages of VO_2max is the most common method of prescribing intensities (see the sidebar "Zone Play"). A simple percentage of MHR can also be used but leaves greater room for error at lower intensities; there is a straight-line relationship between MHR and VO_2max, but the slope varies with each individual and their level of conditioning.

Most recreational athletes do not care to visit a lab annually for VO_2max tests (low score on the fun meter). Fortunately, there is a good approximation available. Known as the Karvonen method, it uses what is called the heart rate reserve (HRR)—determined simply by subtracting resting heart rate from maximum heart rate (HRR = MHR – RHR).

Your target heart rate (THR) for training is then equal to the desired percentage of HRR—the percentage depending on how hard you want to work (see Zone Play)—plus your resting heart rate. (In formula form: THR = %HRR + RHR.)

ZONE PLAY

Zones 1 through 5 take you through increasingly tough aerobic training intensities at a target heart rate that is related to a desired percentage of your heart rate reserve (HRR). Remember that this is a continuum without hard-cut edges, that each of us is unique, and that our bodies are not static. Use this as a starting point and adjust accordingly.

Your Maximum Heart Rate (MHR): _____

Your Resting Heart Rate (RHR): _____

Your Heart Rate Reserve (HRR = MHR - RHR): _____

Your Target Heart Rate (THR) = (HRR x desired percentage) + RHR

Zone 1—Easy effort

Lower THR = (HRR _____ x 0.5) + RHR _____ = _____

Upper THR = (HRR _____ x 0.6) + RHR _____ = _____

Energy system: Extensive endurance zone; fully aerobic.

Feel: Can easily sing your favorite songs. Roughly 60% to 70% of MHR (36% to 51% of VO_2max).

Typical activity: Recovery workouts in the days after major exertions; 30 to 90 minutes of power hiking or easy spinning.

Comments: Modest aerobic benefit. Starting zone for beginners—soon to be surpassed.

Zone 2—Light effort

Lower THR = HRR _____ x 0.6 + RHR _____ = _____
Upper THR = HRR _____ x 0.7 + RHR _____ = _____

Energy system: Extensive endurance zone; mostly aerobic, some anaerobic.

Feel: Can hold a long conversation. Roughly 70% to 80% of MHR (51% to 67% of VO_2max).

Typical activity: Long, slow distance (LSD); 1 to 3 hours running or 2 to 6 hours cycling.

Comments: Seems too easy, but valuable for building a metabolic base; many important aerobic adaptations occur in this zone. Decent training for long uphill approaches and general mountaineering.

Zone 3—Moderate effort

Lower THR = HRR _____ x 0.7 + RHR _____ = _____
Upper THR = HRR _____ x 0.8 + RHR _____ = _____

Energy system: Intermediate endurance zone; both aerobic and anaerobic.

Feel: Can talk in short sentences. Roughly 80% to 87% of MHR (67% to 78% of VO_2max).

Typical activity: Runs of 1 to 2 hours at typical marathon pace, or rides of 2 to 4 hours.

Comments: Without guidance, most athletes spend too much time here when other zones can offer greater benefit. Good training for breaking trail, carrying heavy loads, and high-altitude climbing.

Zone 4—Hard effort

Lower THR = HRR _____ x 0.8 + RHR _____ = _____
Upper THR = HRR _____ x 0.9 + RHR _____ = _____

Energy system: Intensive endurance zone; performance threshold region.

Feel: Might be able to reply with a couple of words. Roughly 87% to 93% of MHR (78% to 87% of VO_2max).

Typical activity: Intervals, fartleks, and hills, oh my; race pace for 5K to half-marathon runs.

Comments: Where the real gains in aerobic performance are made. Good training for summit pushes and trying to outrun a thunderstorm.

Zone 5—Maximum effort

Lower THR = HRR _____ x 0.9 + RHR _____ = _____
Upper THR = HRR _____ x 1.0 + RHR _____ = _____

Energy system: Mostly anaerobic and downright painful; few climbers need go here.

Feel: All thoughts are on surviving, not talking. Roughly 93% to 100% of MHR (87% to 98% of VO_2max).

Typical activity: 60-second or shorter intervals, followed by 4 to 5 minutes of no exercise.

Comments: Short, intense bursts of speed. Good training for trying to outrun an avalanche or a grizzly bear.

For example: If your tested MHR is 180 and RHR is 50 (resulting in HRR of 130) and the desired percentage is 70, you'll want your heart pumping 141 beats per minute. You get this figure by adding your RHR (50) to 70 percent of your HRR (70 percent of 130 is 91) to arrive at 141. (In formula form: THR = $((180 - 50) \times 0.7) + 50 = 91 + 50 = 141$.)

Heart Sense

With this heart rate information, you can determine your own training zones that allow progress in the most time-efficient manner. For specific training programs, see chapter 9, but here are some general considerations to keep in mind.

If you are just starting out with a conditioning program, take it easy at first and permit your body to get used to the new sensations. Depending on how long you've been on the couch and how much excess poundage you're carrying, this means 15 to 30 minutes at the low end of Zone 1 every other day for six to eight weeks. If even that intensity is too hard, relax and do what you can—just don't give up!

Those with significant fat to lose should start with cycling, power hiking, or other low-impact activities; running is too hard on your joints. You'll be doing resistance training with weights, too, so it's important that you don't overdo it. Increase duration and intensity only 10 to 15 percent each week. Heck, if it takes twelve weeks, that's okay too—you're in it for the long haul.

When you can comfortably maintain 30 minutes at the low end of Zone 2, it's time to up the ante and build endurance. Despite the proclamations of fitness zealots, there is no need for more than four aerobic workouts per week; five to six days a week is overkill unless you plan to race. Just emphasize quality in each play session, and you'll continue to make good progress. Keep extending the duration until most are about an hour long and one bout each week goes well beyond that.

During the endurance stage, spend most of your time in Zone 2 with occasional forays into Zone 3 and even intervals of Zone 4. It can be tough for those who feel they're in pretty good shape to rein back, but the long-term rewards are worth it. Fear not, several hours of Zone 2 will whip your butt. Allow three to four months to build a solid endurance base.

Even when you're ready to work on speed, you should still spend a portion of your time in Zone 2. But now, when you're chomping at the bit, you get to push harder and suss out the anaerobic edge. While you're only spending a small percentage of your time in Zone 4, it is important to learn the feel of crossing over the threshold and intimately know the point just below it that can be maintained indefinitely. This phase of training lasts about two to three months.

For many climbers, this is a satisfactory end of the progression and they can enter a maintenance phase. This basically means go out and play hard aerobically a couple of days a week for the rest of your life. When something major comes up, such as an alpine climbing vacation or expedition, then it's fairly easy to fine-tune yourself in a short period of time. Starting all over from scratch sucks, so keep playing.

MAXIMIZING PERFORMANCE

Using heart rate, or even just feel, to guide training is probably sufficient for the vast majority of recreational athletes. But when you desire to perform at the highest levels, there are more tools available to enhance training: your performance threshold and intervals.

PERFORMANCE THRESHOLD

As exercise intensity increases into Zone 4 and we rely more upon anaerobic energy sources, lactate and hydrogen ions accumulate (by different processes) in the cells faster than they can be cleared. In addition, calcium leaks out of muscle cells, preventing them from relaxing. Eventually these hydrogen ions, which increase acidity and calcium leaks, interfere so much that cells can no longer contract and the muscles stop working (ouch!). Once implicated as the cause of fatigue, lactate is actually an energy source and its production may even delay acidosis.

Your performance threshold (PT) is the heart rate that corresponds with the maximum level of exertion that you can maintain for around 30 minutes. This maximal steady state value is a more useful measure than the amount of lactate in your blood (an indirect performance measurement affected by many factors), ventilatory threshold, or VO_2max.

Both the point of transition and our buffering capacity can be increased. For example, a person starting out may have a maximum heart rate of 180 with a performance threshold down around 130. But after a conditioning program, the PT might rise to 160. This greatly extends this person's aerobic range (140 is comfortable instead of painful), and it's now possible to hold out longer when at 165.

After a moderately high level of conditioning has been achieved (that PT of 160), climbers sincerely interested in the alpine world, or just playing really hard, may want to increase their PT even further (perhaps to 165 or higher). To be all that you can be, you'll need to find the heart rate corresponding to your PT and train accordingly.

Basing training upon your performance threshold—versus your maximum heart rate or your VO_2max—offers the advantage that it most accurately takes into account increasing (or decreasing) conditioning. Due to the complexity of the subject, an in-depth discussion of PT training plans is beyond the scope of this book. If you're in this sport for the money, consider hiring a coach. However, since the PT is the best benchmark of aerobic performance, it's a good way to track your progress even if you aren't that fanatical.

The ideal way to determine your PT is with a prolonged treadmill or bicycle ergometer test that correlates power output with heart rate—and again, few of us want to go there. If you are well attuned to your body, you can recognize when you've crossed over the threshold by a queasy feeling, breathlessness, and a burning sensation—you hurt.

For a more accurate estimate of your PT, here's a simple self-test that can be performed while running or cycling, given a flat course and a calm day (variable wind messes with you):

Warm up for at least 10 minutes, and then start the timer when your heart rate reaches 130. After 10 minutes, increase your speed until your heart rate is 140. Continue to increase heart rate by 10 beats every 10 minutes. When you can't (or can just barely) last a full 10-minute segment, subtract 5 beats from that rate for an estimated PT heart rate. You can use this as a starting point to find the highest heart rate that you can maintain with little variation for 30 to 60 minutes.

INTERVAL TRAINING

The standard approach for maximizing aerobic capacity is with intervals of relatively short and intense exercise bouts alternating with brief recovery periods. Recently, interval training has received attention for promoting fat loss, for which there is fairly good evidence, though the effect is weak.

Recent research has led many to tout high-intensity interval training (HIIT) as more time-efficient training than the traditional method of moderate-intensity steady-state workouts. While this sounds great in theory, and the fitness gains are real, it also ignores the other benefits of longer endurance training. And if you aren't in reasonable shape to start with, attempting high-intensity intervals is decidedly a bad idea; you can get hurt.

Particularly for alpinists and ski mountaineers, you still need to prepare yourself—physically and mentally—for long sessions of hard work. It is mere wishful thinking that interval training alone can

prepare you for that kind of effort.

Following hard exercise, particularly when it involves anaerobic efforts, your body consumes more oxygen than normal for several hours afterward. Known as excess post-exercise oxygen consumption (EPOC), this is your body consuming fuel to replenish energy stores, repair tissue damage, and build muscle.

There can be a measurable increase in metabolic rate that lasts as long as 38 hours following a hard workout. But the decay is fairly swift with as little as 13 percent difference after 3 hours and 4 percent after 16 hours.

The duration of the EPOC effect corresponds to the length of time that you train and the level of effort; you consume more calories while exercising aerobically but burn more after an anaerobic workout. Thus interval training is often touted because of the greater post-exercise burning of fuel. Although some research has suggested that EPOC comes from the burning of fat, a more rigorous study demonstrated that there is no greater fat oxidation than normal.

There are numerous forms of intervals (see the sidebar "Intervals" for a few options), and each is designed to elicit a different response from your body. Typically, the athlete trains with one type of interval for about three weeks. Some like to do different intervals within a week for greater variety.

The truly dedicated can follow precise interval workouts based upon times or heart rates; however, "fun" is never an operative word. Fortunately there are two good ways to get much of the gain from intervals without the anal-retentiveness: *fartleks* and hills.

Fartlek is the Swedish word for "speed play" and basically means add some short bursts of high intensity into your light to moderate workouts. You don't need a watch or monitor for fartleks: just go hard till that tree, surge up that hill ahead, or go full steam for the length of one song. Mix it up and have fun!

Hill repeats are also unstructured intervals dictated by the personality of your favorite hill. Run up it hard, then cruise down easy; do it again and again. Hills are especially good for climbers since they target the same muscles and teach mental toughness.

Remember that all forms of intervals are very taxing to your entire system, which is why they work. Be sure to warm down thoroughly and make the next day an easy one.

INTERVALS

Here are some options for interval exercises, at various percentages of the heart rate that corresponds to your performance threshold (PT). When designing intervals, keep in mind the specific energy systems that are to be targeted.

Endurance Intervals
Interval: 8–15 minutes at 97%–98% PT (about 85%–90% MHR)
Recovery: 5 minutes at 70% PT (about 60% MHR)
Repetitions: 4–5
System: Aerobic

Threshold Intervals
Interval: 2–8 minutes at 98%–102% PT (about 90%–95% MHR)
Recovery: 4–6 minutes at 60% PT (about 55% MHR)
Repetitions: 5–6
System: Lactate/Aerobic

Tolerance Intervals
Interval: 1–3 minutes at 101%–105% PT (about 95% MHR)
Recovery: 1 minute at 75% PT (about 65% MHR)
Repetitions: 5–10
System: Lactate

Sprint Intervals
Interval: 10–30 seconds at 105%–108% PT (about 95%–100% MHR)
Recovery: 3–5 minutes at full rest
Repetitions: 5–20
System: Phosphate

RESPIRATION TRAINING

Research is now starting to show that the muscles used for inhaling (external intercostals and diaphragm) and exhaling (internal intercostals and abdominals) can be trained with a resulting increase in breathing efficiency and endurance. Using a device called a PowerLung (about $110) that varies the resistance of inspiration and expiration, breathing can become easier. You simply breathe through the device about thirty times (three sets of 10 reps) several days per week.

Despite what you might think, this is not a fancy straw that you breathe through. The PowerLung allows you to dial in a specific resistance and won't let you cheat by changing the way you breathe. And unlike some devices, it works on exhalation in addition to inhalation.

In one study of elite rowers, the ones who trained with the device decreased their times by about 2 percent versus a control group. Not much to be sure, but every little bit helps. Other studies show some gains in endurance and significant gains in inhalation strength.

Respiration training may be particularly helpful to high-altitude climbers, although no studies have yet been performed. When you're sucking air at 8,000 meters, you'll appreciate any help you can get. Others who may benefit greatly are those with exercise-induced asthma.

CROSS-PLAY EXERCISES

Hardbody athletes have been talking about cross-training for decades—usually just referring to the triathlon sports: swimming, cycling, and running. Yet to many climbers, the term has onerous connotations that imply hard work with minimal benefit. The concept of cross-play, however, is to get 80 percent of the benefit while having 200 percent more fun.

Choosing your modes of aerobic play is largely a matter of personal preference, although some forms will be more directly applicable to climbing than others. The following selections are well suited to climbers but are by no means the only options. While specificity is nice, of far greater importance is selecting sports that you enjoy. The more you emphasize fun, the easier it is to get out the door to train.

Since aerobic training indoors can indeed be mind numbing, it helps greatly to psych yourself up with music. If you need additional inspiration, you can purchase commercial recordings to guide you through workouts.

The Cardio Coach series consists of eight different audio programs (about $15 each) designed for any indoor exercise machine. The well-designed 30- to 60-minute workouts are set to music and can be played on an MP3 or CD player.

For those who choose indoor cycling, the Spinerval series of DVDs (ranging from $30 to $40) offer excellent workouts where you can sweat along with a group of cyclists or go on "virtual reality" rides.

Don't just settle for one activity either. Having several options in your quiver will prevent burnout and allow "active rest" from your primary games. Another major reason to develop skills at other sports is coping with the inevitable injury. Sooner or later, it's bound to happen and few things are worse than a grumpy climber who can't climb. These one-track people are not only boring but they rarely allow adequate time for recuperation, which leads to a vicious cycle of repetitive injury.

Now get out and have fun!

TRAIL RUNNING

Pros. Arguably the king of aerobic exercises for climbers. It is the most physically demanding, and rewarding, form of running. Trails are lower impact than roads, and the irregular terrain offers greater variety for your joints and muscles. Trail running is also more mentally stimulating than running on roads, tracks, or treadmills. It provides an opportunity to recharge your batteries and connect with nature. If necessary, it is worth driving to a trail instead of pounding pavement.

Cons. Trail running can be addictive. Beginners, and those weaning from roads, run a greater risk of ankle or knee injuries. The progression to more rugged trails and longer distances is much like that to harder climbs—it takes time.

Form. The key to injury-free running is landing softly; strive to move gently through the countryside, not plod along. Use either a mid-foot or heel landing, depending on the terrain and your natural gait. Look at the trail well out in front of you, not down at your feet.

Keep your head upright, your shoulders relaxed, and your spine erect. Do not bend at the waist. Instead, lean forward slightly from the ankles so that you need to place the next foot in front to prevent falling on your face: this momentum makes running smooth and effortless. Allow your arms to swing naturally back and forth, without crossing your midline, and keep your hands relaxed.

When running downhill, commit to the descent and, depending on the angle, either lean forward or remain upright; knees should be slightly bent, never extended, when landing. If you tense up or lose focus, disaster may be around the next corner.

Gear. When starting out on dirt roads and bridle paths, road-running shoes are more than adequate. But once you're ready for single-track trails in mountainous terrain, real trail-running shoes make the sport safer and more enjoyable. These offer better traction, particularly on downhills, and more lateral support; both are needed for safe descents at speed. For sloppy winter runs, trail shoes with waterproof/breathable linings keep your feet dry (unless you have stream crossings) and encourage you to run through puddles, which is better for the trails.

Well-designed clothing is important in the mountains and on long runs. Avoid cotton. Modern synthetics offer greater comfort and faster drying, while merino is the runner-up.

Wear a hydration fanny pack on longer runs to carry clothes and accessories. Never wear ankle or hand weights when running (too much joint stress); increase intensity or add weight to the fanny pack if you want a harder workout.

ROAD RUNNING

Pros. The most readily accessible aerobic workout for many people: just head out the door. There are many clubs and countless races throughout the country that can help psych you to run and improve your technique. Comparing your race times is a good measure of fitness.

Cons. Inferior to trail running with the possible exception of availability. Concrete is the hardest running surface, something you can feel in your body after a while. Asphalt is noticeably softer, but always running on one side of a cambered road can create imbalances in your body. The most

challenging aspect of a marathon isn't the distance—average runners are only on the road for four to five hours—it's the boredom of such repetitive pounding.

Form. The same as with trail running. Run softly and land mid-foot, weight over the bent knee at touchdown, followed by a quick bounce off the heel. Heel striking can be a symptom of overstriding, which slows you down and increases impact forces. If you are new to mid-foot landing, transition gradually to give your calves time to adjust.

Some people will find a gentle heel landing is preferable: just don't plod.

As with cycling, a faster cadence is superior to long strides/lower gearing. Overstriding results in your center of gravity behind your forward leg so you are constantly applying the brakes. There should be no vertical component to your movements; distant objects shouldn't bob up and down as you run.

Try to vary your course frequently to avoid a rut. If possible, run in parks where you will breathe less air pollution and enjoy a modicum of nature. Running on a sandy beach, just above the water's edge, is a very demanding yet energizing workout (wear shoes unless you're sure there is no broken glass or sharp shells). Because of the cross-slope, it's best to run out and back to avoid imbalances.

Gear. Due to the very regular surface, good shoes with biomechanics suited to your feet are critical to prevent injury. Go to a specialty running store where the employees can give knowledgeable advice. Look for a model with good forefoot cushioning, but you probably don't need the fanciest models. Shoes with excessive heel cushioning do not prevent injuries or improve performance.

Depending on your weight, among other factors, expect the cushioning to wear out after 300 to 500 miles—long before the uppers. Continuing to run on shoes that are worn out is the leading cause of injury in roadrunners. The change is subtle, so many runners keep two or more pairs of shoes (one a bit fresher) in rotation.

INDOOR RUNNING

Pros. The lowest impact forms of running are also independent of weather and time of day. The better machines can change their angle during the workout to allow more variety. In a gym, you can switch machines to prevent boredom.

Cons. You're inside. Good treadmills and elliptical trainers can be very expensive; cheap ones ensure a lousy experience and tend to break. The footpads on many elliptical machines are wider than your normal stride, placing greater load on the outside of the feet and legs. The calories-burned estimations on most machines are

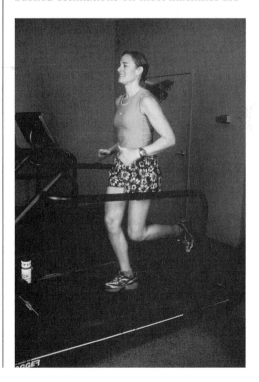

worthless and some perpetuate the fat-burning zone myth.

Form. Your form is the same as road running; emphasize a smooth gait instead of heavy plodding. On a treadmill, the angle needs to be set at about 1 degree to compensate for the lack of a headwind. Vary the angle between or during workouts to better challenge your muscles.

When using an elliptical trainer, never rest your hands on the side rails; this significantly reduces the quality of your workout. If the machine has moving arms, you must actively resist their motion; don't just go along for the ride. Set the program to vary the angles as you run, and occasionally run backwards (reverse direction), to work muscles differently.

Gear. The cheapest home treadmills have a harsh ride, are noisy, and break quickly—most are intended for walking, not running. Better models, which start around $2,000, use higher quality motors (minimum two horsepower continuous-duty) and have a two-ply belt at least 57 inches long and 18 inches wide (shorter than that is inadequate for running, particularly if you have long legs). A thicker deck (¼ inch or more) will offer lower impact to prevent shin splints and back aggravation. The top speed should be at least eight mph and the incline should adjust up to 15 degrees for plenty of workout options. Commercial models have all of these features and are built for heavy traffic, so they cost upward of $5,000.

Elliptical trainers are more complicated machines with a greater likelihood to require expensive maintenance. Rear-drive models offer a more natural elliptical motion than front-drive, plus they have a smoother ride and allow longer strides. The better machines have adjustable inclines (12 to 25 degrees), variable resistance, and allow a stride of at least 17 inches.

Cross-country ski machines are poor simulations of what is done on snow, and the motion is very different from running or hiking, but they can provide a serious workout. These machines are okay for gyms but a poor choice for home use. No matter which indoor machine you get, check the warranty to get an idea of quality; some are only ninety days on parts while good ones are covered for two to five years. A small fan to keep you cool is a good idea.

POWER HIKING/NORDIC WALKING

Pros. This is the most specific form of training for mountaineering and a good all-around workout. Performed with trekking poles, this is basically aggressive hiking with the goal of keeping the heart rate up—it is not a casual walk in the park. Although hilly terrain is ideal, power hiking can be effective even on relatively flat ground. On long downhills, the use of poles can remove a huge amount of stress from your knees.

Cons. Almost none. You won't develop the speed that you can with running, and you may have trouble performing higher-intensity intervals. There also isn't the adrenaline rush of flying down a hill, but descending with poles is safer. The frequent "where are your skis?" question from hikers gets old.

Form. Using trekking poles properly requires a bit of skill. Adjust the length so that your elbows form right angles. Use the straps as you would with cross-country, not alpine, poles; your hand enters the loop from below and the straps run between thumb and forefinger. Adjust the straps for a snug fit with the pivot point near the grip. The point of all this is that most of the weight from your arms is suspended by the strap—you shouldn't grasp the pole tightly.

When going uphill, raise the pole well in front of you and plant the tip near your feet. You are almost pulling your way upward, using significant upper body strength. On the descent, plant the pole below you and lower yourself downward. Throughout the entire workout, try to get a smooth, powerful rhythm going. Focus on higher speed instead of more weight in a pack.

Gear. If you've never tried trekking poles, you can start off with some old alpine poles sans baskets. However, poles specifically made for hiking have a more comfortable grip (often made of rubberized cork) when used with sweaty bare hands. The small baskets give flotation in sand without snagging on every bush, and the poles collapse for easier transport. The better trekking poles have shock absorbers built in to reduce elbow stress; some models allow this to be locked out, too.

Footwear is whatever is appropriate for the terrain; this is also an ideal way to break in mountaineering boots. To increase intensity, you can wear a pack. If you will be doing steep training climbs, consider weighting the pack with water and dumping some before descending to reduce knee strain.

STAIRS AND STAIR-STEPPERS

Pros. Passable options for flatlanders preparing for the hills. Running up and walking down long flights of stairs is a good interval workout. The stair-stepper machines (also called step machines or stair-climbers) take up less space than most other indoor options (treadmills, rowers, etc.).

Cons. Not even close to the real thing. Stadium steps are usually concrete so there may be greater impact forces. Although low-impact, stair-steppers place a lot of stress behind the kneecap, and they do nothing to simulate going downhill, which is also important. Though commonly recommended by the misinformed, wearing a pack while using a stair-stepper or climbing stairs is a terrible idea. It does not give you a better workout or prepare you for the mountains; a heavy pack just trains you to go slow (wrong) and increases the chance of knee problems.

Form. Mix it up when running stairs: skip one or two steps, zigzag from side to side, bound upward—anything you can think of to vary the workout.

When using a stair-stepper, never rest your hands on the side rails—this bad habit reduces intensity by over 20 percent and

won't improve your balance. Be sure to use a full range of motion while keeping your feet flat on the platforms (don't push with your toes). Stand up straight. Use a high cadence (around 100 steps per minute) so you don't train to be a plodder; set the resistance to achieve your desired heart rate without taking baby steps.

Gear. Stadium steps are popular since they tend to be long and have walkways that break up the repetitiveness. Old staircases in parks are often more uneven (a good thing) and offer better scenery. Those who live or work in a high-rise building might investigate the stairwells, but they aren't exactly cheery places.

The better step machines feature independent stepping for a more natural feel. Cheaper non-motorized models have dependent stepping so that pressing down on one side pushes the other side up. The inexpensive mini steppers lack a handrail so they are compact for storage but they also tend to have a limited range of motion (only 8 inches) and are difficult to adjust resistance.

ROAD BIKING

Pros. Cycling is superb aerobic training because you can go for 6 hours without feeling too beat up afterward. With good technique, road biking works nearly all the muscles below the sternum and is not stressful on the knees. In addition to a good physical workout, the mental aspect of road biking has much to offer. The mind-set of riding up a long, steep mountain is much the same as when slogging up a snow slope at high altitude. And the concentration required while screaming downhill at 50 mph is much the same as what keeps you alive when climbing. A rich history permeates the racing world, with legends and heroes as great as any in mountaineering.

Cons. Traffic is a serious danger in many areas. Not an exact simulation of climbing. Less time-efficient than running. The upper body gets a minimal workout unless there are steep hills. Can be hard

on your knees, back, and neck if the bike doesn't fit or you don't learn good form.

Form. Concentrate on smooth, fast pedaling (90 to 110 rpm) with a quiet upper body (no bobbing). Try to apply power throughout the pedal circle by pulling at the back of your stroke as well as pushing at the front; it's no faster, but it balances the leg muscles.

On moderate hills, slide back in the saddle a bit and push more as you spin along. Stand up out of the saddle on steep hills and let the bike rock naturally back and forth beneath you (don't exaggerate the motion) but maintain a high rpm. Pull up on one side of the handlebar while pushing down with the opposite foot, directing your body weight directly into the pedal.

Unless you are in a full tuck (head to the bars, knees on top tube) on a steep grade, you should be pedaling hard down hills—this ain't no free ride! For a long, gradual descent off a pass or down a canyon, get in the drops of the handlebar and push down that hill.

Gear. Decent road bikes cost around $1,500, though you can easily blow many times that. Fortunately there are great deals available on the used market. The advantage of buying new at a specialty shop is that the bike will be tuned and properly fit to you. A poor-fitting bike is more painful than the wrong-size hiking boots! With a used bike, you may need to upgrade parts (handlebar, stem, seat post) and overhaul the components. However, with basic maintenance, a quality bike will last indefinitely, so a used high-end bike can be a better value than an inexpensive new one.

For your riding pleasure, spend top dollar on the contact points: anatomic handlebars with good, padded tape; bike gloves with shock-absorbing foam; comfortable saddle that fits your derriere; eight-panel bike shorts with contoured padding; totally rigid road shoes with floating cleats; comfortable helmet with good ventilation. It's advisable to get a triple crankset if you ride in the mountains.

A cyclocross bike is a fun alternative, or supplement, to a road bike. These resemble road frames with knobby tires but there are other differences that make them a blast for zooming along on dirt roads. Depending on where you live, a cyclocross bike can open up a new world on roads too rough for your road bike and too boring for a mountain bike.

MOUNTAIN BIKING

Pros. While road biking offers great endurance workouts, mountain biking tends to give superb interval fun. The nature of the terrain dictates the workout—long and easy, short and fierce, or somewhere in between—but you often ride in spectacular country. Sometimes the rides include weight training (read: hike-a-bike).

Cons. Finding suitable trails can be difficult, depending on where you live. Long stretches of flat road are tedious at best; sections with sand are evil torture. Probably draws more blood than any other sport offered in this book.

Form. As with road biking, a smooth and quiet riding style offers the best performance gains. There is a much greater emphasis on balance and body position;

in many ways, mountain biking is akin to telemark skiing. On steep hills, standing out of the saddle requires more finesse than with a road bike; to maintain traction and prevent spinning out the rear wheel, lean forward sharply at the waist.

Good form also includes being polite to hikers and horseback riders by stopping to allow them to pass. Access is no less of a concern in the mountain-bike world than the climbing world—don't screw it up for others!

Gear. At the very least, you will want a mountain bike with front suspension. However, full suspension is the way to go if you plan to ride a lot. The current generation of cross-country soft-tail bikes (about 4 inches of travel) climb well, descend great, and won't leave you feeling beat up at the end of a long, hard ride. Downhill bikes with 6 inches of travel are the all the rage now but these tanks are so heavy they aren't much fun without a car shuttle to the top of the hill. If you are 5 feet 10 inches or taller, consider getting a 29-er (a mountain bike with 29-inch wheels instead of the standard 26-inch wheels) for a smoother ride.

The best values are the mid-price bikes (around $1,000 to $1,500) that you can upgrade later to reduce weight. The cheaper bikes rarely can be turned into good rides, while the more expensive machines often sport lots of jewelry but don't necessarily perform better. Sad to say, you should also consider how the bike carries over your shoulder; some designs look cool but are very awkward on long uphill hikes. Unfortunately, purchasing a used mountain bike is a risky proposition since, by definition,

they get hammered and many early full-suspension designs were quite poor.

If you are serious about training, you may also want a single-speed bike. As the name implies, the bike only has one gear and the rear wheel can coast on the downhills. This actually gives you three speeds (sitting, standing, and walking) and can be a brutally effective workout.

Comfortable shorts, well-padded gloves, and stiff shoes with aggressive treads for hiking are essential. Only idiots mountain bike without a helmet.

INDOOR CYCLING

Pros. Among the best indoor aerobic workouts around—high quality and time efficient. Indoor cycling, often called spinning, is somewhat of a cross between road and mountain biking, with an instructor who will push you hard. Although it is a group exercise, there is little peer pressure since nobody else knows how hard you are working. While emphasizing the lower body, there is substantial involvement of the upper body too.

Cons. Need to find a gym that offers

spinning classes. The quality of the instructors varies and this greatly affects the workout. Trying to spin at home requires a lot of mental fortitude and will probably be less effective unless you use music or videos to provide motivation.

Form. Though it bears many similarities to outdoor cycling, there are significant differences. The hand positions are unlike those on either a road or mountain bike, which changes your form somewhat. On a normal bike, you generally strive for a quiet upper body and allow the bike to move underneath you. When spinning, however, the bike is fixed solidly to the ground, so you should emphasize upper body movement to release energy and avoid back problems.

As with other forms of cycling, a faster cadence (over 90 rpm) is most efficient. When you apply power throughout the entire stroke, the bike offers positive feedback as a vibration you can feel.

Gear. Plan on spending 40 to 60 minutes on the bike and sweating profusely. Cycling shorts and a synthetic top are a good idea. Bring a towel and a large water bottle. You can use running shoes, but it's best to wear stiff cycling shoes; many bikes have Shimano pedals.

Spinning bikes use a 45-pound flywheel that is fixed to the pedals; unlike normal bikes, coasting is not possible. The resistance is adjusted by turning a dial to squeeze the flywheel with felt pads. With practice, you can dial in your heart rate to within a beat or two. Many classes require a heart rate monitor, and it's a good idea to use one for all of them—you can learn a lot about yourself.

At present, the best indoor cycle for those interested in maximizing their performance is the CycleOps Pro 3000PT (close to $2,000). What separates this from all the others is a special hub that measures power output and a sophisticated computer that allows detailed analysis of your workouts. It is a well-designed bike that is fully adjustable and comes with a good warranty (one year electronics, three years parts, lifetime frame).

If you have a road bike, you can use it to work out at home with an indoor trainer that uses fluid resistance (best feel), magnetic resistance (reasonable compromise for feel and price), or wind resistance (noisy but cheap). Rollers are another option but require more skill and are best for committed racers. It is worth spending $35 for a rear tire designed for trainers since they heat up more than when out on the road.

Of the many trainers on the market, the Kurt Kinetic Road Machine (around $350) is widely considered the best. This fluid trainer has a smooth, realistic feel and will never leak or wear out (unconditional lifetime warranty). A new version, called the Rock and Roll (about $560), has a frame that allows your bike to pivot side to side for a very natural feel when climbing out of the saddle. This means you are also getting a better core and upper body workout. An optional Power Computer (at $50 or so) is a worthwhile accessory for planning workouts.

You'll probably want a fan to cool yourself down and a drip guard if you have a nice bike. Since motivation is often a problem, a television and DVD player can help with boredom; the Spinerval DVDs are excellent.

INLINE SKATING

Pros. A very good aerobic workout that also helps prepare you for ski season. Really works the legs, abdomen, and lower back.

Cons. Not practical unless your city has a good bike trail system. If you go down, it's always painful.

Form. This is speed skating, not the trick stuff. The emphasis is on a strong push-off and a long glide on the opposite leg. As speed increases, you will crouch into a lower, more aerodynamic position. Arm swing may be used to help propel you forward until you reach cruising speed, then tuck them behind you. Keep your eyes on the path well out in front of you, which means craning your neck.

Gear. Choose either four-wheel skates with a long wheelbase and no rocker or five-wheelers. Brakes are optional but recommended for beginners and those who have hilly bike trails; use a drag stop if you don't have brakes. The uppers should be comfortable (many aren't), well ventilated, and have decent ankle support. Hold off on the low-cut racing boots until you've been at it for a while.

When inline skating, always wear a bike helmet! You can be moving at 20 mph or more, with your head fairly close to the ground, and go down in a nanosecond if a stick, dog, or crack in the path suddenly appears. Wrist guards are another essential that can mean the difference between a minor mishap and weeks of infirmity. Beginners should consider elbow and knee pads as well.

CROSS-COUNTRY SKIING

Pros. The absolute top of the aerobic pyramid. Both skating and classic techniques will work your entire body like no other sport. Skating is particularly suited to climbers because the powerful upper body movements are similar to pulling down. The peaceful feeling of gliding quietly over the snow is like no other—Zen-like at times. There is an active racing scene, especially in Europe, where some events resemble moving cities.

Cons. Requires groomed ski trails; these days it can be harder to find quality grooming for classic skiing. Both styles require a fair level of skill, though classic can take years to refine. You will also need to learn the fine art of waxing, though this is now greatly simplified. Can be difficult to stay sub-anaerobic, particularly when skating on hilly courses. For people susceptible to exercise-induced asthma, the very dry air can induce attacks (low temperature, no matter how cold, is not a factor).

Form. Herein lies a book. The smartest thing you can do is take lessons. For either style, work on full weight shift from the hips and emphasize gliding on one ski. Poling is intrinsically connected with breathing—track skiing is all about rhythm. As with rock climbing, where women who lack tremendous upper-body strength can often out-climb burly dudes, technique is more important than raw power.

Gear. If you are starting out, choose skating equipment and select the best that you can afford. You will get a better, more enjoyable workout with the lightest-weight gear that is designed for performance. A state-of-the-art cross-country ski package (either style) costs less than a decent road bike and should last for years. Don't waste your money on "combo" gear; none of it is any good at either style. Used equipment is often a bad buy unless you really know what you're shopping for; the technology changes significantly every few years.

Dressing properly can be tricky. Even though it may be well below freezing, you will be working up a good sweat, so effective moisture management is important. Since you are moving fairly fast, the wind is also an issue. A lot of cross-country ski clothing has wind panels on the front (men absolutely need windproof briefs!); however, quality multisport apparel also works well. Good gloves are important since your hands are often above heart level and may not receive the best circulation.

Due to the intense demands of this sport, staying well fueled and hydrated is vital. Many people bonk because the cold weather fools them into underestimating output. If your Nordic center does not have trails that loop back to the lodge, you may want to use a winterized hydration pack.

BACKCOUNTRY SKIING

Pros. Excellent preparation for ski mountaineering. Whether on telemark or alpine touring (AT) equipment, breaking trail uphill with a pack on your back is a serious aerobic workout. The descent can be a supremely fun interval session. The early days of climbing and skiing are closely related—great reading.

Cons. Requires a high level of skill and fitness, more so for free-heel, which is best acquired at downhill resorts (more vertical per day). Significant risk of avalanches. Rather expensive to assemble a complete package including the required accessories.

Form. On the ascents, there is no difference between the two forms of skiing; set the steepest track that your skins will climb. On flat or rolling terrain, telemark gear has a slight advantage since a more extended stride is possible—true kick-and-glide works best on packed trails with lighter gear. When it's time to go down, telemark and parallel techniques are very similar above the waist. Keep your upper body quiet and facing down the fall line with hands out in front of you. Your poling, breathing, and turns are all interrelated. Learn to fall properly; slow rearward, twisting falls are the knee killers.

Gear. Telemark has the most graceful of turns and modern gear has made it far easier. However, the lack of a fixed heel makes

mountaineering and ice climbing.

With either setup, select the lightest gear that is practical for your needs. Used equipment is somewhat risky since older stuff is often heavy and prone to breakage. You will also need ski poles, climbing skins, heel elevators (if not provided), a snow shovel, an avalanche probe, and an avalanche beacon.

SNOWSHOEING

Pros. Good winter workout that requires almost no skill. Very low risk of injury. More options for training grounds than with skiing. Less expensive, too.

Cons. Running with snowshoes requires specialized models and packed trails, though you can pack down your own course after a couple of laps. Arguably not as much fun as cross-country skiing.

Form. For an aerobic workout, snowshoeing is more than just plodding along through the woods. Since this can be either power hiking or trail running with paddles on your feet, many of the concepts are the same. Pacing yourself requires attention to the terrain and snow conditions.

Gear. Running snowshoes are quite different from those made for walking or mountaineering. They are lighter, smaller, and have an asymmetric design that allows for a more natural gait. The binding pivots on a strap so that the tail snaps back to your foot to keep it from dragging in the snow. These characteristics limit them to packed trails—they are lousy in the backcountry.

Most people wear running shoes or hiking boots, though they should be large enough to accommodate heavier socks for warmth.

the equipment more tiring on long descents in difficult snow, and the old-style boots are rather poor for climbing on snow and rock due to the duckbill toe. New telemark norm (NTN) boots are better for mountaineering and also can be used in AT bindings.

For mountaineering, alpine touring equipment is more practical because it is less tiring when skiing in less than ideal snow or with a heavy pack. When the goal is climbing, some bindings will accept mountaineering boots, although the lack of support makes these boots quite poor for descents. You can also use alpine touring boots for pure skiing fun; these are acceptable for moderate

Shoes with waterproof/breathable uppers will keep your feet dry from melting snow.

Because running snowshoes kick up a rooster tail, your backside will be covered with snow. Therefore wear tops and bottoms with a smooth outer surface; fleece is a bad choice. Even in cold weather, the intensity can be quite high, so moisture management in your clothing is also important.

INDOOR ROWING

Pros. Provides excellent cardio workouts that involve all the major muscle groups in the body. Generally, the best value for indoor aerobic equipment.

Cons. The machine can take up quite a bit of space unless you select a folding model. Since climbers already tend to use their back muscles heavily, a rowing machine can exacerbate imbalances.

Form. Although the upper back gets used heavily, rowing also works the legs, core, and arms. A good rate is around 20 to 24 strokes per minute, while emphasizing a full range of motion. Do not overreach and allow your back to round. Keep your arms straight until the legs are fully extended, then pull the handle to your navel with elbows down by your side and leaning back slightly.

Gear. Expect to spend anywhere from

$800 to $2,700 for a good rowing machine. The better indoor rowers use air, water, or magnets for resistance; these provide a realistic simulation of the real thing. Air rowers provide cooling as you work out but are very noisy, while water rowers look great and are quieter but difficult to move and expensive. Both air and water rowers require you to manually adjust the resistance, which can disrupt your workout.

Rowers that only use magnets are nearly silent and can easily vary resistance but do not provide a realistic feel or any cooling. The cheapest and most compact rowers use pistons; they can give you a workout but are not very smooth and lack many useful features. If you are tall, be sure to look for a full-size frame with a rail at least 54 inches long since the compact models may limit your extension. Folding rowers can save space but the cheaper ones tend to be less sturdy than non-folding designs.

The LifeCORE Fitness R100 rower (about $1,500) is a state-of-the-art air/magnetic rower that starts off using a fan for resistance but switches to smooth and relatively quiet magnets once you are up to speed. This exceptional machine features sixteen levels of resistance that automatically adjust according to one of fifteen programs. It also has a heart rate function and can automatically adjust resistance to keep you within a desired zone. Other niceties include an adjustable vent to direct the cooling breeze, a recovery program that monitors your heart rate following a workout to gauge fitness, a sturdy full-size frame that folds without disassembly, and a five-year warranty for parts and a lifetime warranty on the frame.

CHAPTER 5

Climbing at Altitude

Altitude adds a whole new dimension to the climbing realm, one that armchair mountaineers seldom comprehend. Although it is impossible to predict how severely altitude will affect you, there are measures you can take to minimize its effect.

Planetwide, the percentage of oxygen in the atmosphere remains a constant 20.93 percent. At sea level, the atmospheric pressure is 760 millimeters of mercury (mmHg), which means the oxygen content is 159 mmHg. However, at the summit of Everest, the oxygen content is just one-third of sea level; 53 mmHg in June (51.5 mm in January, a potentially critical difference for climbers). On the plus side, a 70 mph wind at that extreme altitude has the force of only a 40 mph wind at sea level.

Many climbers are cavalier with terminology in discussions concerning altitude, yet from a physiological viewpoint, the definitions are more specific. Elevations between 5,000 and 11,500 feet (1,500 to 3,500 meters) are labeled "high altitude" and most people can adapt well given sufficient time. The range between 11,500 and 18,000 feet (5,500 meters) is termed "very high altitude" and is where individual factors determine performance; more than 10 million people throughout the world live at this altitude.

Above 18,000 feet is properly called "extreme altitude" where the lack of oxygen (less than half of sea level) is the major issue. Nobody can live at extreme altitude on a year-round basis, and performance severely declines. The so-called Death Zone, often claimed to start at 26,000 feet (8,000 meters), has no scientific basis; there is no cut-off altitude at which digestion and acclimatization stop or the body shuts down.

CHANGE OF ALTITUDE

In as little as 3 hours after moving to a higher altitude, our bodies begin to adapt to the thinner air. But everyone's rate of change is different, and it takes over a year to fully acclimatize.

Because we must suck in more air to make up for the reduction in oxygen, both the rate and depth of respirations increases. This hyperventilation messes with the blood chemistry, making it more alkaline until bicarbonate compensates. Even after eight weeks at 12,500 feet (3,800 meters), ventilation remains slightly elevated.

Another consequence of faster, deeper breathing is increased dehydration from the drier air, even when you're sitting around in camp. As if working hard in dry air weren't enough to dry you out, altitude induces diuresis (you pee more), and cold weather suppresses thirst. Thus few trekkers or climbers are adequately hydrated when in the high country.

This dehydration during the first two days reduces the volume of blood plasma, causing a sudden "false" increase in the percentage of oxygen-carrying red blood cells (a higher hematocrit). But as your hydration status improves, the hematocrit returns to the previous level and you are still easily winded since there aren't enough blood cells yet to compensate for the thinner air.

The reduced oxygen levels at higher altitudes triggers greater output of erythropoietin (EPO), the hormone that stimulates production of red blood cells (erythrocytes). It takes a week for an increase in EPO to have a noticeable effect on performance, from more oxygen reaching your muscles, but around a month to reach your maximum hematocrit and athletic potential.

Though elite endurance athletes sometimes use it, much to the chagrin of authorities, supplemental EPO would be a very bad idea for high-altitude climbers. Normally, the hematocrit of adults at low elevations is 36 to 46 percent (women are on the lower end). But after living in thin air for several weeks, this can safely rise to about 54 percent; almost one-fourth of high-altitude natives are in this range. But a hematocrit that is too high raises health risks and decreases performance because the blood turns to thick sludge that perfuses muscles poorly.

To compensate for the temporary reduction in plasma volume, your heart rate at rest and submaximal efforts will dramatically elevate during the first week of exposure to altitude. As the plasma volume restores, your heart rate should soon return to normal; it may even go lower as red blood cells boost total blood volume. However, your maximum heart rate continues to decrease the higher you go, and it won't improve until you drop lower. Even after

six weeks at Everest base camp (17,600 feet; 5,400 meters), the average MHR is about 17 percent lower than at sea level.

VERY HIGH CONSIDERATIONS

Above 5,000 feet (about 1,500 meters), every additional 1,000 feet (about 300 meters) of elevation gain will decrease your VO_2max by about 3 percent, though this response is highly individual. The bad news is that those with the biggest aerobic capacity tend to experience the greatest losses. According to the physiologists, "altitude is the great equalizer."

On one Everest expedition, the average VO_2max of climbers declined from 62 ml/kg/min at sea level (way above average) to about 15 ml/kg/min near the summit. Considering that your minimum oxygen requirement at rest is about 5 ml/kg/min, that doesn't leave much room to perform without bottled gas. The good news is that Reinhold Messner, the only person so far to solo Everest without supplemental oxygen, had a sea-level VO_2max only on the high end of average.

Short-term (three- to five-week) studies at very high altitude indicate that VO_2max shows little, if any, improvement during this time. However, endurance (measured by time to exhaustion at sub-maximal levels) can improve by 40 to 60 percent. This is likely because you just can't go hard for long when up high, so the training that would improve maximal aerobic capacity is compromised but not the intensity that helps endurance. For the first couple of weeks, you are pretty much reduced to light to moderate exercise, with lots of brief anaerobic episodes.

Just about everyone loses weight on expeditions to extreme altitude (men more so than women), sometimes dramatically, though a good portion of this is from chronic dehydration. Besides all the work you are doing, your basal metabolic rate (minimum energy requirement) increases by about 10 percent and fat utilization is lower. Plus your appetite changes; you feel full faster and turn from a gorger to a nibbler. Even without altitude sickness, forcing down enough food is difficult up high. Something that you love at base camp may be nauseating on the mountain.

Unfortunately, you aren't losing just water and fat. Muscle mass is also decreasing (cell diameter reduces) and you become weaker. This is due to less activity of enzymes within the muscles and a negative nitrogen balance. Plus much of the endurance work involved with high-altitude climbing is muscle-eating (catabolic).

Everybody has trouble sleeping at extreme altitude, especially above 23,000 feet (7,000 meters), and bizarre dreams are common. Even at much lower elevations, some people's breathing pattern really gets out of whack. While sleeping, they breathe faster and faster, then slower and slower—stopping for a scarily long time—then starting the cycle all over again. This phenomenon, called a Cheyne-Stokes pattern, is uncomfortable for the victim and distressing for their tent mates; sleeping pills can exacerbate the problem.

Women should note that there is an increase in maternal and fetal complications at altitude. It's best to make babies at lower elevations. There does not appear to be any problem with the use of oral contraceptives at altitude. If you are on the pill, you can safely delay menstruation by not skipping a week.

At very high altitude, many climbers exhibit slight bleeding in the retina (back of the eyeball) and it's pretty much universal above 22,000 feet (6,700 meters), though this is generally considered harmless. Complications from eye surgery, such as LASIK, appear mostly related to incomplete healing; it's best to wait at least a year after surgery before going high.

Unfortunately, brain scans reveal that high altitude climbing causes permanent damage. Even three years after expeditions, most climbers who have been above 6,000 meters showed cortical atrophy or enlargement of Virchow-Robin spaces. . . . umm, what were we talking about here?

GOING LOW

After acclimatization to high altitude, you will temporarily retain some benefits after returning to the lowlands. You can expect your best aerobic performances about seven to ten days after arrival. This should taper off gradually for over a month, since those mature red blood cells carrying extra oxygen last for about 120 days. However, some of this gain is offset by the noticeably thicker air and higher humidity.

Although you may still have an elevated red blood cell count, it appears that you lose your resistance to altitude sickness, pulmonary edema in particular, within days of going low. So flying from Everest Base Camp to Kathmandu for a few days and then back again may not be a hot idea.

Training and sleeping high is not a formula for success because workout intensity is necessarily reduced. Athletes who both train and sleep high perform only marginally better than those who train and sleep low. The real winners are those who sleep high and train low.

IMPROVING ALTITUDE PERFORMANCE

Countless hours of training cannot prevent acute mountain sickness (AMS) or other altitude illnesses (pulmonary and cerebral edema). Indeed, superb conditioning may underlie some of the problems. Young, healthy men are the mostly likely to experience difficulties at altitude due to testosterone-induced stupidity; because they are very fit and think they're invincible, they push too hard too fast. Best advice: start slow and taper.

In addition to wisdom, age appears to confer other benefits for high-altitude travel, not the least of which is increased stamina. There is very little research on this, but old geezers frequently kick young pups' butts when mountaineering and in ultra-endurance events.

Still, going to the high mountains unprepared is foolish (see "High Mountain Expedition: Four Months" in chapter 9 for a training program). It's pretty much a given that you will be working hard for 6 to 8 hours a day, perhaps more, day after day. If you haven't worked up to this amount of stress beforehand, life is gonna suck.

When mountaineering, the rule of thumb is to drink enough to pee "clear and copious." You should feel a need to pee almost hourly, and your urine should be pale yellow (barring mega-doses of vitamins that you don't need). If you are hydrating well, you will need to wake up at least once during the night to urinate, which is why most mountaineers carry a pee bottle.

To achieve proper hydration requires consuming at least 1 gallon (4 liters) on mellow days (cool temps, moderate exertion) and over 2 gallons (8 liters) on intense days (sweltering heat, mega-work). Severe dehydration can shut down your summit bid faster than any snowstorm.

Emphasizing carbohydrates in the diet has numerous advantages when climbing at high altitudes. Although fat packs more calories per gram than carbohydrates, which makes it weight-efficient in your pack, it also requires more oxygen to burn. Furthermore, one study has shown that a diet of more than 70 percent carbohydrates decreased AMS by 30 percent after a fast ascent to 14,000 feet (4,300 meters).

Anticipate a lot of knee strain from carrying a heavy pack up and, especially, down hills that seem to last forever (trekking poles are a good idea). You want to reach the mountains with a high performance threshold and sufficient muscle mass that you won't wither away. Use the approach trek to help prepare for what is to come. If you have a choice between a long or short route (such as hiking from Jiri or flying to Lukla to reach the Khumbu), take the extended option.

Some climbers wonder if they can get a head start by spending a few days on local intermediate (14,000 feet) summits before heading to a high (20,000+ feet) peak thousands of miles away. Alas, this works only with massive logistical support. Most of us have to spend too much time down low while in transit to benefit from this form of pre-acclimatization.

Those with a large disposable income can get a head start on the hills by purchasing or renting an altitude tent; cost is somewhere in the range of $6,000 to $20,000. These are airtight sleeping enclosures with a molecular sieve, a sophisticated machine that removes oxygen to simulate higher altitudes (approximately 12,000 feet, though some go a bit higher).

Used by many elite endurance athletes as a "natural" alternative to EPO injections, an altitude tent might reduce acclimatization time for climbers. While the companies selling the equipment are quick to offer testimonials, the tents have never been shown to actually improve acclimatization time in controlled studies. And there is reason to believe that the 16 to 18 hours per day that you spend outside of them will largely mitigate any effects.

Some guides advocate "pressure breathing" at high altitude. The concept is that exhaling forcefully through pursed lips will increase pressure in the alveoli (air sacks in the lungs) and aid oxygen uptake. While the theory sounds plausible, the reality is that the technique does not increase blood oxygen levels for healthy climbers. Research has shown that pressure breathing only helps people with compromised lungs (emphysema patients and victims of pulmonary edema) and fighter pilots breathing 100 percent oxygen in non-pressurized planes above 40,000 feet. The primary reason

guides advocate loud huffing and puffing is to take clients' minds off how miserable they are from a fast ascent.

EXPEDITION NUTRITION

Maximizing your chances of success on big peaks, when you are away for weeks or months, requires a lot of planning. Even smaller objectives in remote corners of the world have considerable logistical challenges. Often, ensuring an adequate and nutritious diet is one of the biggest dilemmas. (See my book *Climbing: Expedition Planning* [Mountaineers Books, 2003] for more details.)

Anytime you are away from civilization for more than a few weeks, food becomes the number one topic of conversation. If you've done your homework and planned well, the banter is about how great the meals taste and getting fat. When you've gone with the low bidder for a trekking agency, the talk is about the first meal you'll get to enjoy back home and losing weight. At the base camps on big mountains, it's easy to spot the expeditions that skimped by the empty dining tents at mealtime.

Do not underestimate the importance of the cook. After your *sirdar*, who runs the show, he is the most important asset of the team; the expedition leader and liaison officer are less significant. You would do well to seek out recommendations for a cook from previous Western expeditions to the area (someone favored by Asians may not serve your particular taste). Both the cook and his staff must be well schooled on the importance of cleanliness (always washing hands and utensils, using clean water sources, boiling water); don't assume they have already been taught.

The food for the trek and while in base camp are usually the domain of the trekking agency, though you should check their menus and make requests ahead of time. Be sure there is a lot of variety and abundant quantities. It's also a good idea to bring some favorite treats for base camp (good coffee and a non-breakable French press, hot chocolate, drink mixes, hot sauces, popcorn, Scotch whiskey, etc.) to enhance appetites and morale. For a successful expedition, base camp must be a place to look forward to when the weather deteriorates or when it's time to recoup before the summit bid.

Many climbers unwittingly set themselves up for disaster by not paying attention to their health before they reach the trailhead; once the trek starts, you're relatively safe. The moment your flight leaves home, if not a few days earlier from the last-minute packing frenzy, stress hormones in your blood rise significantly. Since you'll be in a small box with a lot of other people, consider taking echinacea for a few days prior to a long flight to boost immune protection.

After flying to the opposite side of the planet, it takes about five days to recuperate from jet lag (going north or south has minimal effect). The cities where you typically spend that time preparing for departure often have significant air pollution (carbon monoxide, nitrogen and sulfur oxides, and particulates) and noise that add to your stress. Be sure to get an air-conditioned hotel room (this is not a luxury) and take your antioxidants. If you must do a training run,

do so early in the morning and try to find a park away from traffic.

Of course, be careful of what you eat and drink: before the expedition departs is not the time to sample the local street cuisine! You can indulge to your stomach's content upon your return. It's safest (but no guarantee) to dine at three- and four-star hotels, even if you don't stay there, or well-established restaurants frequented by many tourists. Stick with mainstream dishes that are sure to be made fresh daily; more exotic requests are likely many days old. No matter how bad your craving, do not eat salads, fruit you can't peel, or ice cream; it just isn't worth the risk. However, fresh yogurt can be a good, safe choice. Especially during monsoon season, be careful to avoid drinking the water when you shower; use bottled or treated water to brush your teeth.

Should you get a bout of diarrhea, it's best to knock it out early with a full course of antibiotics such as ciprofloxacin (consult your doctor). For the trek in, when the risk is highest, some climbers bring acidophilus tablets—the good bacteria found in yogurt—to help the digestive system recover after the antibiotics are finished. These tablets can be found at health food stores, but check the expiration date and avoid heat or freezing to keep the critters alive.

MOUNTAIN FUEL

Most of the food you'll eat above base camp must be brought from home. Do not count on finding edible mountain food in Kathmandu or Islamabad; what's available are the leftovers that nobody liked. Whether on a private or commercial expedition, do not assume that your tastes will be accounted for. Food is what gets you to the top. If you leave this critical element up to somebody else, no matter how extensive the questionnaire you may have filled out, blame yourself for a growling stomach. Those with food allergies must pay extra-special attention to what will go up on the mountain.

For high-altitude mountaineering, the climbers who eat and drink the most have the best chance to succeed. There are a lot of changes occurring within your body that conspire against adequate nutrition, but much of it is a question of willpower: you must force yourself to fuel even when you aren't hungry or feel sick.

Simply living in below-freezing temperatures raises your basic energy requirement by about 1,000 food calories (more for lean people when clothing is inadequate). The extra weight, resistance to movement, and interlayer friction of clothing also increase caloric demand. Underfeeding yourself not only threatens your own chances but also that of your team—and possibly everyone's safety.

You will probably need 30 to 35 calories per day for each pound of body weight (a 180-pound climber will consume 5,400 to 6,300 calories a day); some days will be less, some more. Ideally, two-thirds of that intake should come from carbohydrates. Though the taste has improved in recent years, few of the freeze-dried meals on the market provide nearly enough calories; adding olive oil or squeeze-on margarine is a weight-efficient way to boost calories. Despite some claims to the contrary, many climbers crave nuts, sausages, and other fatty treats at high altitudes.

Bring anything that sounds appealing—there are no bad calories above 6,000 meters—but anticipate that your tastes will change the higher you go.

Although they aren't ideal for optimal hydration, high-carbohydrate drink powders can be a good source of extra calories that are reasonably lightweight and compact. Some of these offer 150 to 200 calories of carbs per cup and they may also contain 30 to 50 calories of protein. There are at least a half dozen brands to choose from, but it's vital that everyone on the expedition test the candidates at home to see which taste good and stay down. Beware sponsorship from a product that only one or two people can stomach! Consume these drinks in camp, not while climbing, and keep pumping down the fluids (tea, hot chocolate, soup).

SUPPLEMENTS FOR ALTITUDE

Given sufficient water, nutrition, and time, there is rarely a need for any supplements or drugs to aid climbing at extreme altitude, let alone lower elevations. The problems start occurring only when you skimp on one or all of these key ingredients. It is infinitely better to avoid altitude illness than to rely on drugs.

Inadequate time for acclimatization is the primary evil when it comes to AMS. Keeping your ascents between camps to less than 2,000 feet (600 meters) per day is a well-proven tactic for fending off acute mountain sickness. Pushing too hard during the first days at altitude may also make things worse; stay at a light to moderate intensity.

It's also possible that some cases of AMS really are misdiagnosed cases of infection, because many symptoms are similar. Since your body is heavily stressed when climbing at altitude, it's probably wise to boost immune protection with antioxidants—particularly when traveling in foreign lands.

Here's a look at some of the supplements occasionally used in high-altitude mountaineering:

Multivitamins. Since diet is often out of your control once the trip starts, it's wise to take a daily multivitamin/mineral supplement just to ensure your needs are covered. There is no justification for mega-doses (see "Supplements" in chapter 2).

Antioxidants. Due to the stress of exercise and altitude, antioxidants can help bolster your immune system for increased protection. One study of trekkers going to Everest base camp reported that supplementing the diet with 1,000 mg vitamin C, 400 IU vitamin E, and 600 mg alpha-lipoic acid (half with breakfast, the rest with dinner) gave a significant increase in blood oxygen saturation and a decrease in AMS. However, vitamin C combined with excess iron turns to a pro-oxidant, which can be dangerous—even fatal. Do not take high dosages of iron along with antioxidants.

Amino acids. Both BCAAs and glutamine have been suggested as aids for acclimatization, and one study lends some credence to the theory. These amino acids are associated with improved recovery and immune protection, so supplementation might help, but more research is needed.

Aspirin. For over a century, mountaineers have been taking aspirin to combat headaches at altitude. Other over-the-counter painkillers, such as ibuprofen and naproxen, work as well. However, aspirin also helps thin the blood, so it might help performance at very high altitude. Do not take aspirin with ginkgo biloba or high doses of garlic because they can increase the tendency to bleed.

Acetazolamide. When all else fails, you may need to resort to Diamox (acetazolamide), a prescription drug in many countries. This diuretic causes the kidneys to excrete carbon dioxide in the form of bicarbonate. This in turn re-acidifies the blood, which stimulates your body to increase the breathing rate, particularly at night.

Diamox has proven very effective in speeding acclimatization and it greatly improves sleep (alleviates Cheyne-Stokes breathing). It does not mask symptoms, so if more severe altitude problems are present they can still be detected. Diamox will not, however, prevent AMS from worsening if the ascent continues—don't continue upward until symptoms subside!

Most people get substantial relief with two 125-mg doses (half a tablet) per day with minimal side effects. Start the course a day before a fast ascent is anticipated and discontinue after your second night at your high point; symptoms will not worsen once you stop taking it, your body just returns to its normal rate of acclimatization. It's best to avoid taking aspirin and Diamox at the same time since complications may arise.

Diamox will cause frequent urination, therefore dehydration becomes an even bigger concern. It can also cause tingling in fingers, toes, and lips (paraesthesia), ruin the taste of carbonated beverages, and blur vision. Because this is a sulfa drug, people with allergies to those medications must refrain. If you've never tried Diamox before, do so before you get to a remote location to avoid any nasty surprise.

Dexamethasone. Some climbers also carry dexamethasone, a powerful steroid that reduces brain swelling. The oral form is used to treat AMS; however, it should only be used once severe symptoms have appeared, not prophylactically during the ascent. The treatment lasts three days, but AMS may rebound after it has been discontinued; some people report depression afterward too. Dexamethasone is also used to treat cerebral edema, given as an intramuscular injection.

Other drugs. While it may sound like a joke, sildenafil (Viagra) may actually decrease the chance of getting high altitude pulmonary edema (HAPE) by suppressing the pulmonary artery pressure increase that normally occurs with hypoxia. However, it currently isn't available in low, long-acting dosages and much more research is needed. Another drug recently implicated in preventing HAPE is salmeterol (Serevent), a bronchodilator for asthmatics, but the jury is still out.

Nifedipine (Procardia) is often used in the treatment of HAPE because it dilates blood vessels by blocking calcium from entering them. For those susceptible to this condition, nifedipine may prevent recurrence. Whenever HAPE is suspected, descent is imperative; a Gamow bag can buy the victim some time. Be smart, ascend slowly; better yet, don't get sick in the first place.

Though its use may stir an ethical debate over cheating, modafinil (Provigil) is a new drug that can keep you awake for several days without the nasty effects associated with amphetamines.

Folk remedies. Garlic has been used for millennia to help thin the blood. Four large cloves of raw garlic per day, or 2 grams of garlic powder, might improve blood flow in the lungs by reducing pulmonary vasoconstriction. It's been shown effective in rats, but no human studies have confirmed the results. Unfortunately, cooking deactivates the active ingredient (allicin), though other compounds are released that may also be beneficial.

Ginkgo biloba is another folk remedy for AMS that several studies have now shown as ineffective compared to a placebo. Numerous other herbs, such as reishi, are marketed for preventing or treating AMS, yet none have proven themselves in controlled studies.

Supplementary oxygen. The least desirable supplement for mountaineering is oxygen. Due to physiological and logistical reasons, if you need supplemental oxygen for summits below 8,500 meters, you probably don't belong there. It is far better to acclimatize properly or attempt a peak within your capabilities. If you are concerned about possible brain damage, stick to lower peaks.

Even when a higher summit is the goal, you must seriously weigh the pros and cons of oxygen. When you rely on this gaseous crutch, you may be safer but you're also placing many other people at risk. The rich climbers using oxygen always need low-paid porters to make extra trips through icefalls and avalanche terrain with the heavy cylinders. Should the supply run out during the ascent or descent, you will turn into a useless blob and other climbers may be endangered by your mistake.

CHAPTER 6

Resistance Training

As the great philosopher Pogo eloquently stated, "We have met the enemy and he is us." In our case, climbers have been hampering themselves for decades with The Big Lie: climbing is the only training you need. This oft-repeated claim sounds logical yet it ignores a multitude of truths.

No matter the sport, if you practice it to the exclusion of everything else, muscle imbalances are created that can lead to decreased overall performance and chronic injuries. In climbers, the muscles prone to underdevelopment include hamstrings, mid to lower trapezius, pectorals, deltoids, rotator cuff, triceps, and wrist extensors. A program of resistance training, often called weight lifting though there is a subtle distinction, is the most effective and efficient way of tuning the body.

Although climbing gyms have revolutionized the sport, most of us tend to work our strengths since that's more fun. Even with the use of campus and system boards, it can be difficult to target weaknesses because it's rarely possible to isolate muscles when climbing. It is also difficult to maximally train muscles because you fall first.

STRENGTH BASICS

Lest there be any doubt: resistance training will *not* make you a better climber! It can make you stronger, safer, and less prone to injury—hence increasing your performance—but technique can only be learned by climbing when the nervous system is trained and economy of movement is developed. Weight lifting is a supplement, not a substitute, for climbing. The proper balance depends upon you and your goals.

BENEFITS OF RESISTANCE TRAINING

For those who don't have unlimited time to work out, a primary advantage of resistance training is efficiency. With just 45 to 90 minutes of lifting weights, you can fully work every major muscle group in the body. And if you do it with minimal rests, you can improve cardiovascular capacity as well. Even if it were possible to get a total body workout while climbing, it would take many times longer to achieve the same results.

Prevention of injuries is another major reason for systematic resistance training. Repeated mechanical loading beyond a minimal threshold stimulates bone growth. Without sufficient force, bone density and mass decrease: "use it or lose it" applies to bones as well as muscles. Both stress fractures (an overuse injury) and osteoporosis (a degenerative disease) may be prevented with training. And stronger bones will be less likely to break in a fall.

While aerobic endurance exercise

speeds the repair of connective tissue through increased collagen metabolism, high-intensity loading (heavy resistance) makes your tendons and ligaments thicker and stronger. Tendon stiffness also increases so they transfer energy more efficiently. Even the sheaths that surround muscles and groups of muscles adapt to resistance training, helping with tensile strength and elasticity. Bone mass also increases where the tendons attach and injuries are less likely to occur here.

Should the unfortunate happen and an accident lay you up, resistance training combined with physical therapy is the shortest route back to the rock. Even when one limb is out of action, you can maintain the rest of your body and keep from going stir-crazy.

Yet another, subtler, advantage of lifting weights is increased body awareness. When you isolate muscles, you learn their function (and names) and feel how they affect other parts of your body. The goal of resistance training is moving the muscles; for weight lifting, moving the mass is the emphasis and the body is secondary.

While resistance training will benefit people of all ages, seniors perhaps have the most to gain, or regain: vitality. Unless you are a dedicated masters athlete, you have probably lost significant muscle mass and bone density. Resistance training is unquestionably the best way to reverse the aging process.

RESISTANCE TRAINING MYTHS

The number one myth about weight lifting is that you will get "too big." Since climbing is a sport where the strength-to-mass ratio plays a significant role in performance, the fear is understandable albeit misguided. This notion of overbulking is fostered by climbers who have a poor understanding of physiology and assiduously avoid the weight room.

Some who put down resistance training will point to the photos of the rather grotesque bodies in the muscle magazines as an example of what will happen if you heft a chunk of steel. Look further, beyond the pictures, and read the articles and advertisements. The extremes of lifting (15+ hours per week is common) and chemical supplementation (both legal and illegal) are scary: those body builders are desperate for anything that will make them more "ripped."

The truth is that more than 80 percent of men and nearly all women are "hardgainers." Without a volume of work far in excess of what any climber would consider, we simply lack the genetic predisposition to look like the Incredible Hulk (or Hulkess). Although moderate-intensity resistance training causes muscles to get bigger (hypertrophy), endurance training is catabolic (breaks down muscle). With a moderate amount of aerobic play and a normal diet, most people find it is virtually impossible to gain excess muscle.

Another falsehood is that weight lifting creates "dumb" inflexible muscles; this can only result from dumb training. When done properly, resistance training actually increases flexibility. It is also easier to educate (recruit and coordinate) muscle cells that are developed than to raise them from infancy.

A related myth is that certain exercises can alter the shape of muscles, making them "short and bulky" or "long and lean." This was predetermined nine months before you were born and there is nothing you can do to change where tendons attach or the length of the muscle belly.

On the other hand, there is also a myth that muscle burns ten times more calories than fat (50 versus 5), so building muscle raises the resting metabolism. Typically it's stated in grandiose terms like "adding a pound of muscle will burn five pounds of fat over the course of a year." Unfortunately, a more careful analysis reveals that fat burns about 2 calories per pound and muscle at rest consumes just 6 calories; an insignificant difference. There are many reasons to build muscles but burning fat isn't one of them.

Many people claim that weight lifting is boring and, frankly, it can be—if you approach it mindlessly. This boredom is most often the result of poor teaching that frequently occurs in school and commercial gyms; many coaches and trainers are not good educators. In reality, there is so much to think about while lifting that there rarely should be a dull moment—it is an intellectually stimulating, even fun, activity. When you are resistance training, your focus should be on your body, not the weight you are moving (or that cutie across the gym). With all the exercises, intensities, and rest periods to choose from, there is no reason to fall into a rut.

The most blatant lie regarding resistance training is that abdominal exercises will give you a "six-pack" like those bulging abs on dehydrated fitness models (they drink almost no fluids for several days prior to a photo shoot in order to look ripped). There is no such thing as spot reduction! Those damnable TV infomercials are scams: it is physiologically impossible to selectively remove fat from one area of the body (sans liposuction). Like it or not, men tend to put on fat in the upper body (apples), while women store it in the lower body (pears). Since this is the first place fat is laid down, it is also the last place that it comes off. While proper training does build the abdominal muscles, only after the excess fat is gone will they become visible.

Girls, what your mother and women's magazines may have told you is wrong: when it comes to training muscles, you are the same as boys. The structure and trainability of muscles is identical between the sexes. Both genders should use the same exercises and intensity. Since you have much lower levels of testosterone than men, lifting heavy will not turn you into a freak; gorgeous yes, overmuscular no. Feel free to slap anyone upside the head who claims that women should only use light weights for "toning," "sculpting," or "shaping"; they need some sense knocked into them. These nonsensical programs and terms have been hampering women's athletic progress for far too long. Women (and men) who want to climb hard need to be hard.

ANATOMY 101

There is a lot of loose talk around gyms and in popular magazines about body parts that don't really exist. Likewise, gym talk frequently includes references to muscle groups that can be trained in sections when the evidence is to the contrary; EMG (electromyograph) studies show equal activation of fibers.

No such thing:

- Inner and outer pecs
- Inner and outer delts
- Upper and lower lats
- Upper and lower biceps
- Upper and lower quads
- Upper and lower abs
- Upper and lower obliques

For real:

- Upper and lower pectoralis major (clavicular and sternal)
- Front, middle, and rear deltoids (anterior, medial, posterior)
- Upper, middle, and lower trapezius
- Inner and outer biceps (short and long heads)
- Inner and outer triceps (long and lateral heads)
- Inner and outer quadriceps (vastus medialis, vastus lateralis)
- Inner and outer abdominals (transversus and rectus abdominis)
- Abdominal segments (all sections contract but some more than others)
- Side abdominals (internal and external obliques)

PHYSIOLOGY OF STRENGTH

Think of a muscle as a winch and a tendon as a cable that connects to a moveable object. Both the tendon and cable can pull but cannot push. The only way to move the bone (object) away is to relax the muscle (winch) and pull from the opposite direction.

When a muscle contracts (the agonist) to move a limb, its counterpart muscle (the antagonist) must actively relax to control and stabilize the movement; for example, the biceps are stabilized by the triceps and vice versa. In addition to the prime moving muscles, other muscles like the brachioradialis are synergists that help refine the direction of motions. If the antagonists and synergists are underdeveloped, you will lose fine motor control as fatigue sets in.

Strength is simply the maximum force that your muscles can generate, no matter the velocity. If a movement can be performed more quickly, then greater power is generated: power = (force x distance) ÷ time. When training for power, you are

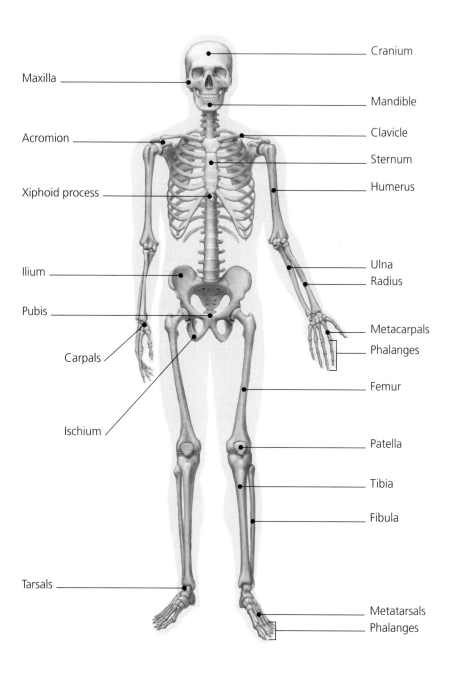

Cranium

Maxilla

Mandible

Acromion

Clavicle

Sternum

Humerus

Xiphoid process

Ulna

Ilium

Radius

Pubis

Metacarpals

Carpals

Phalanges

Femur

Ischium

Patella

Tibia

Fibula

Tarsals

Metatarsals

Phalanges

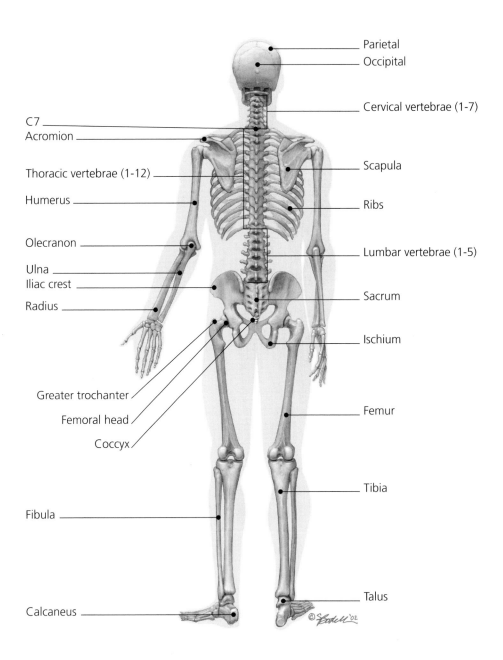

Parietal
Occipital
Cervical vertebrae (1-7)
C7
Acromion
Scapula
Thoracic vertebrae (1-12)
Humerus
Ribs
Olecranon
Lumbar vertebrae (1-5)
Ulna
Iliac crest
Radius
Sacrum
Ischium
Greater trochanter
Femoral head
Femur
Coccyx
Tibia
Fibula
Talus
Calcaneus

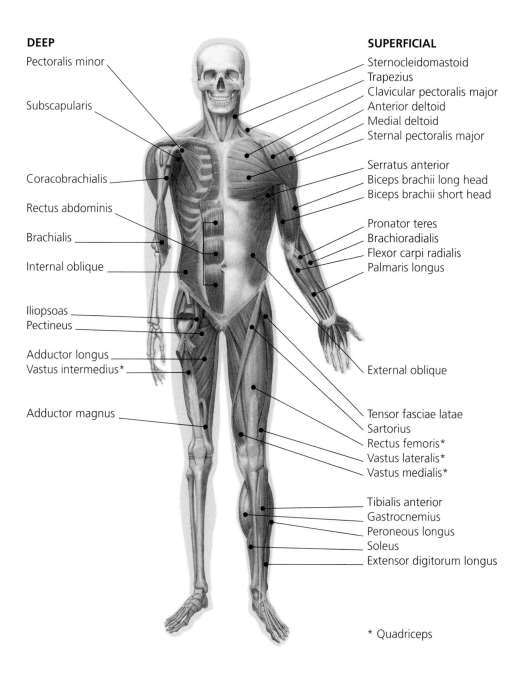

DEEP

Pectoralis minor

Subscapularis

Coracobrachialis

Rectus abdominis

Brachialis

Internal oblique

Iliopsoas
Pectineus

Adductor longus
Vastus intermedius*

Adductor magnus

SUPERFICIAL

Sternocleidomastoid
Trapezius
Clavicular pectoralis major
Anterior deltoid
Medial deltoid
Sternal pectoralis major

Serratus anterior
Biceps brachii long head
Biceps brachii short head

Pronator teres
Brachioradialis
Flexor carpi radialis
Palmaris longus

External oblique

Tensor fasciae latae
Sartorius
Rectus femoris*
Vastus lateralis*
Vastus medialis*

Tibialis anterior
Gastrocnemius
Peroneous longus
Soleus
Extensor digitorum longus

* Quadriceps

DEEP

SUPERFICIAL

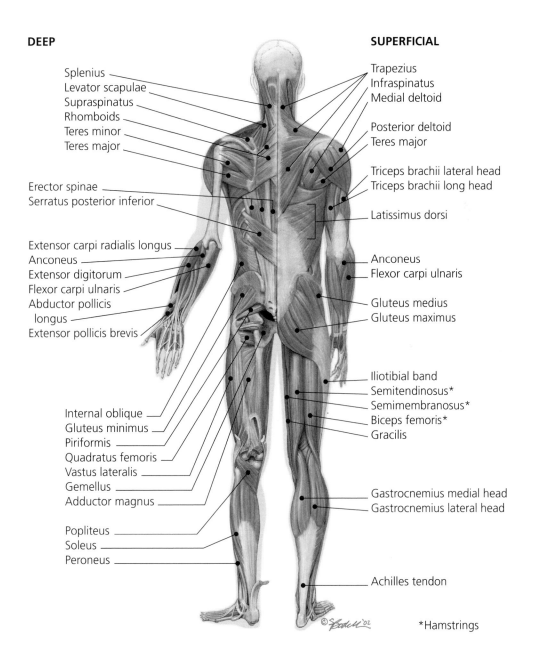

Splenius
Levator scapulae
Supraspinatus
Rhomboids
Teres minor
Teres major

Erector spinae
Serratus posterior inferior

Extensor carpi radialis longus
Anconeus
Extensor digitorum
Flexor carpi ulnaris
Abductor pollicis
  longus
Extensor pollicis brevis

Internal oblique
Gluteus minimus
Piriformis
Quadratus femoris
Vastus lateralis
Gemellus
Adductor magnus

Popliteus
Soleus
Peroneus

Trapezius
Infraspinatus
Medial deltoid

Posterior deltoid
Teres major

Triceps brachii lateral head
Triceps brachii long head

Latissimus dorsi

Anconeus
Flexor carpi ulnaris

Gluteus medius
Gluteus maximus

Iliotibial band
Semitendinosus*
Semimembranosus*
Biceps femoris*
Gracilis

Gastrocnemius medial head
Gastrocnemius lateral head

Achilles tendon

*Hamstrings

127

increasing high-speed strength. The primary energy source for both maximal strength and power is the phosphocreatine (phosphate) system.

Endurance is the ability of muscles to either repeat an action many times or to sustain an action for a long time. Aerobic energy sources—the oxidation of carbohydrate and fat—provide most of the ATP (the cellular form of energy).

In between these two extremes of strength/power and endurance is a full continuum in which fast (anaerobic) glycolysis—the breakdown of blood glucose and muscle glycogen without oxygen—is a significant energy source. Since the end product of this anaerobic process is lactate (lactic acid is a precursor), it is also called the lactate system. Lactate can either be used as an energy source directly or converted back to glucose in the liver. Rather than an enemy, lactate is our friend.

Many people believe that lactic acid causes fatigue, but that theory has been disproved. During the anaerobic release of chemical energy (hydrolysis of ATP), a hydrogen ion is also released that lowers muscle pH when it accumulates. This increased acidity has been suspected of impeding cellular function until buffers restore pH from a low of 6.4 to the normal 7.1. However, recent research implicates the accumulation of phosphate as well as the loss of potassium and calcium from within a cell as factors in fatigue.

While the high-intensity phosphate system will last 6 to 8 seconds, the moderate-intensity lactate system burns for about 2 to 3 minutes, and the low-intensity aerobic system is long term (depends upon glycogen stores and fat utilization). However, it is never all-or-nothing—your body is always using all three energy systems, just in different proportions. (See the sidebar "Muscle Magic.")

Attempts to describe this spectrum have led to a confusing array of terms that are sometimes used incorrectly (or imprecisely). Intensive power endurance, high-level power endurance, high-intensity endurance, and anaerobic endurance all mean that phosphate and lactate energy systems predominate. Extensive power endurance, low-level power endurance, and low-intensity endurance all imply that lactate and aerobic systems are the main energy sources. Local endurance, SACC (specific aerobic capacity and capillarity), and muscular endurance all refer to aerobic systems as the primary source. Finally, there are aerobic endurance and general endurance, which refer to the body's overall capacity of exercise, not certain muscle groups.

The practical aspect of this energy continuum comes when describing the intensity of training and even the character of a climb. The number of sets (a group of repetitions) of an exercise and the number of repetitions (reps) within a set determine the changes within the muscles. But again, there is no hard threshold where one aspect, such as strength, stops and another begins. The human body is far too complex for such simple distinctions.

Climbers have developed their own terminology not recognized by other sports, such as contact strength (ability to apply power to holds and sustain it) and lock-off strength (ability to pull into a high position for a long reach and hold); both are isometric (static) muscle actions. While we generally know what we mean, the definitions are rather vague since they really are describing strength and endurance simultaneously.

MUSCLE ADAPTATIONS

While it is universally accepted that resistance training increases muscle strength, the jury is still out on the mechanisms. Everyone agrees that the long, skinny muscle cells (fibers) become thicker in cross-section (hypertrophy). But a great way to start an argument with sport scientists is to ask whether heavy resistance training causes muscle fibers to split in two (hyper-

plasia); possible but unproven in humans.

We are all born with a predetermined percentage of Type I (red or slow-twitch) and Type II (white or fast-twitch) muscle fibers. The overall average is about 45 percent Type I and 55 percent Type II, but this varies widely within the population. Successful sprinters, for example, tend to have more Type II fibers, while marathoners have more Type I. However, the differences are not great enough to predict performance based on fiber composition alone.

The distribution of fiber types within your major muscles (the primary movers) is about equal. But postural and stability muscles tend to be higher in Type I; the soleus, a small calf muscle used for standing, has the most Type I fibers (88 percent)

CHARACTERISTICS OF MUSCLE FIBERS

Fiber Type	Type I	Type IIa	Type IIb
Activity	Aerobic	Long-term anaerobic	Short-term anaerobic
Contraction time	Slow	Fast	Very Fast
Force production	Low	High	Very High
Resistance to fatigue	High	Intermediate	Low
Fiber diameter	Small	Large	Very Large
Mitochondrial density	High	High	Low
Capillary density	High	Intermediate	Low
Oxidative capacity	High	High	Low
Glycolytic capacity	Low	High	High
Major fuel storage	Triglycerides	Phosphate, Glycogen	Phosphate, Glycogen

while the muscle that closes your eyelid has the most fast-twitch fibers (87 percent).

You probably cannot change the basic fiber ratio you were given, though debate continues. However, training can significantly increase the ability of fiber types to use oxygen; they can become more aerobic. There are two subcategories of Type II (the more oxidative IIa and less oxidative IIb) that can transform back and forth. Strength training turns those IIb fibers into oxygen-rich IIa—but the process can reverse when you lay off the weights. There are also Type III fibers that are a hybrid between I and IIb, as well as IIc fibers that are more oxidative than IIa or IIb; neither of these is common.

When exercising at low intensity, your body will use mostly Type I fibers. But as the intensity or speed increases, greater numbers of Type II fibers are called into action, termed recruitment. One of the major goals of resistance training is to stimulate more of these Type II fibers so that they will get stronger. This can only be done with high-intensity levels.

In addition to muscle fibers, we are also developing the nervous system that stimulates the muscles. During the first six to ten weeks of a program, neural training has a more significant effect on strength gains than muscle growth. Much of long-term training, and better climbing, is about enhancing neural factors.

Greater force can be applied at the origin or insertion of some muscles, which changes the recruitment pattern of the motor units (the nerve cell and the fibers it activates). Our muscles are also very particular about the movement pattern required to recruit different fibers. This is where specificity comes in and why it's important to train a muscle from different angles.

Another adaptation to endurance exercise is an increase in the size and number of capillaries, the micro-vessels that carry blood and remove waste. While this helps us overall with aerobic conditioning, increasing muscle-specific capillarity is also important for climbers. Due to enhanced blood flow the major climbing muscles of the arms and back will be more resistant to fatigue.

While many climbers focus on grip endurance (such as squeezing a gripper hundreds of times), they should also think about maximum strength training for their forearms. When you are gripping a hold, the pressure of your muscles begins to squeeze the blood vessels shut. The tighter you grip, the more plasma builds up in the space between the cells—the dreaded forearm pump we feel—and the time-till-failure clock is ticking faster.

The goal is to raise the performance threshold for specific muscle groups. Increasing your maximum grip strength will allow you to exert the same amount of force while using less muscle pressure so you can hang on longer.

PRINCIPLES OF RESISTANCE TRAINING

All climbers need a combination of strength, power, and endurance; the ideal balance depends upon your goals. If your emphasis is on endurance climbing (multi-pitch and alpine routes), strength training will not harm your performance; indeed, it can help. However, if your climbing is strength-oriented (high-level bouldering or sport climbs), too much endurance training can make you weaker.

To increase strength or endurance, your muscles must be stressed to ever-increasing levels. This concept isn't exactly new: around 540 BC, Milo of Croton trained for wrestling by carrying a newborn ox every day until it grew to full size (then he supposedly ate it in one day). Milo won six consecutive Olympics.

Termed "progressive overload," this means that you should always strive for more weight, duration, or frequency. Never be content with the status quo. More subtly, progress can also come from performing an exercise with better technique, control, or range of motion. Aim for perfection.

Resistance exercises generally consist of a concentric phase, in which the active muscles shorten, and an eccentric phase, where they lengthen. For climbing, both phases are important and should be trained equally; that is, it should take as long to lower the weight as to lift it.

Isometric training involves holding a static position for an extended period of time. This is a situation that climbers often encounter; however, our bodies are very specific regarding joint angles—just a small change makes a big difference. Because of this specificity, isometric training is not usually recommended for conditioning programs.

Some programs emphasize the eccentric phase (negative failure), such as doing a pull-up with two arms and lowering with one. The eccentric contraction generates higher force, so there is potential for greater strength gains; debate rages on this subject. However, it also results in greater delayed-onset muscular soreness (DOMS), those aches that set in two or three days later. Often used for rehabilitation, eccentric exercises may help you break out of a plateau or overcome a weakness. But climbers need to be well rounded in their strengths, and your training should reflect that concept.

In regard to climbing, the least effective weight training is for muscular endurance because of the time involved. It is better to do this form of low-intensity workout in a climbing gym or on real rock where you will also improve technique and efficiency. If climbing is not an option, keep the endurance workouts to a couple of primary multijoint exercises, such as squats and lat pulls.

STARTING OUT

Those who are new to resistance training, even veteran climbers, are likely to make significant gains in the first six months. The results will be noticeable in the mirror and you'll feel better. If you've been thoughtful, you should be climbing better too. Enjoy it: never again will it be that easy to improve so much, so quickly.

Don't force the gains, either; it takes your tendons about twice as long to match the strength improvements of muscles. There is a fine line between training to failure—when you can just barely finish a movement with full control—and training till it hurts. While that last rep should strain the entire muscle, there should never be sharp pain; especially in a joint. Think: No pain, all gain.

Do not fear heavy weights; with good form, they are perfectly safe for healthy individuals. As you will see, lifting heavy potentially has the most to offer climbers. However, those who are new to lifting will need to work up to this level of stress, otherwise injury is sure to follow. Due to spinal or knee problems, some people will have to settle for lighter loads, but you can still make progress.

Every time you pick up a weight or sit at a machine, keep in mind that the ultimate purpose is to improve your climbing performance. With this focus, you won't waste time on things that have minimal benefit. Whenever possible, simulate movements made while climbing. For example, vary hand positions and lean back while doing lat pulls to mimic climbing an overhang. This will speed the recruitment of those muscles once you get on the rock, ice, or snow.

KIDS AND TRAINING

Climbing is a great activity for kids! But they are susceptible to the same overuse injuries and muscle imbalances as adults. Starting at about age eight to ten, children can safely start resistance training with light weights. They can benefit from increased strength, enhanced bone development, fewer injuries, and better self-image. Prior to that age, let the monkeys scamper.

However, it is important that progress be slow and gradual—and form perfect— because the bones of children do not fully ossify until after puberty. Damage to growth cartilage in the joints or to the growth plate on bones, as well as the lumbar region of the spine, can have lasting consequences. Keep your young'uns at lower resistance and higher reps (no less than eight) and allow adequate time for rest.

Pushing children and adolescents too hard can result in overuse injuries—not to mention the risk of turning them off the sport entirely. Several studies have shown that 30 to 50 percent of all pediatric sports injuries are related to overuse. Those most at risk are kids that specialize in one sport and train obsessively year-round.

Because kids grow so fast, a layoff from resistance training and climbing over summer break will basically nullify any gains. In addition, boys aged twelve to fourteen and girls aged ten to thirteen (before the growth spurt) run a greater risk of bone fractures and need to be reined in somewhat.

During the pubertal growth spurt, teens' relative strength declines somewhat because muscle mass cannot keep up with the increase in height. This is often accompanied by a decrease in skill performance as they adjust to their new bodies—not to mention a number of other awkward embarrassments associated with puberty. After about sixteen, they're good to go.

MACHINES

Most gyms are very proud of their weight machines—largely because they cost huge amounts of money—and will often start beginners off using them. This isn't necessarily bad, because the newer machines do have their advantages.

Those who are new to resistance training are usually less intimidated by machines, in part because all those people with bulging muscles are over in the free-weight section of the gym. Machines also appear to be safer, since a weight won't come crashing down on you, but that is an illusion because they permit bad form at higher loads.

If you are of average height (5'4" to 6'2", 160 to 190 cm) with average proportions of arm, thigh, and torso length, you can get a good workout on machines fairly quickly. Not having to rack and de-rack your weights can save a significant amount of time. Selecting a load from a weight stack or manually loading plates adjusts the resistance on most machines. Some machines use pneumatic pressure or electric motors, which allows a computer to vary the resistance more accurately.

In general, machines fall into two categories: variable resistance and constant resistance. Through the use of eccentric cams or air pressure, variable-resistance machines try to match the mechanics of the body by increasing resistance at strong points and decreasing resistance at weaker areas of the movement (isokinetic). While this sounds good in theory, the reality is that many people do not move with the velocity and movement pattern required by the machine.

Constant-resistance machines use a round pivot point or pulley so they act more like free weights; the load being moved does not change (isotonic). With constant resistance, however, only the weakest portion of your range of motion is fully taxed because the angle of your limb changes.

The recent trend in resistance machines is to emulate free weights by allowing multiaxial and unilateral (left and right side don't assist each other) movement—often called functional trainers. While a step in the right direction, most climbers will be better served by free weights if time permits.

One device to strictly avoid is the Smith Machine, which holds a barbell on a vertical track. A favorite of lazy personal trainers, the Smith offers the worst of both worlds—neither variable resistance nor activation of stabilizer muscles. The linear motion has value for rehabilitation of injuries and advanced bodybuilders, since very specific areas can be targeted. But multisport athletes are better off with free weights, even if lighter loads must be used.

FREE WEIGHTS

Although machines can be effective for training when used intelligently, it's still hard to beat the old-fashioned picking up of heavy objects. Dumbbells, barbells, and kettlebells have been the foundation of many high-quality resistance training programs for more than a century.

The major drawback to early-generation resistance machines is their linear movement pattern. With free weights (and machines designed to simulate them), you must draw upon small stabilizer muscles to control the weight. This provides an efficient workout that promotes joint stability and is a better simulation of real life activities. Some of the exercises can also improve your balance. Another big advantage of free weights is they truly are one size fits all.

Dumbbells and kettlebells allow greater movement so the body must work more to control them than with a barbell. Thus you can usually lift heavier loads with a bar. But the increased freedom of motion with the smaller weights tends to transfer better to sports so they're more useful.

Most barbells and dumbbells have a similar grip diameter (between 1 and 1½ inches, 25 to 32mm). However, a thicker grip (2- to 3-inch diameter, 50 to 75 mm) wickedly targets the hands, wrists, and forearms for greater strength development. This also applies to pull-up bars, which get significantly harder to use as the diameter increases.

Another way to enhance a barbell workout is by using chains or resistance bands to stimulate maximum muscular contraction throughout the entire range of motion. By hanging long, heavy steel chains off the bar for exercises such as the bench press and squat, the resistance increases as the bar gets higher off the floor. Bands can be employed similarly for this form of accommodating resistance by anchoring them to the floor and attaching to the bar.

Although some trainers advocate the Olympic lifts—the "snatch" and the "clean and jerk"—for developing power, they can also be a fast way to the emergency room. These ballistic barbell exercises require careful coaching through a progression of exercises with a long learning curve. Even the slightest slip of form can result in serious injury.

While Olympic lifts can be effective, there are generally safer ways to achieve the same goals: squats, deadlifts, and swings. Should you decide to try these explosive movements, consider using a dumbbell and doing them with one arm. This is both safer and allows your joints to move naturally, enhancing the benefit.

BODY WEIGHT

The old standbys of pushups, pull-ups, and other common body weight exercises have the advantage of affordability and portability. Although they can be performed without any equipment, this makes it somewhat difficult to vary the amount and direction of resistance. Some simple props, described in "Home Gym," will allow you to get superior results with minimal cost.

GYM CONSIDERATIONS

Among the top factors in a successful resistance-training program are the accessibility and quality of your gym. The sad reality is that most people who start a program at fitness clubs will end up dropping out after a few months, largely due to a lack of motivation. If your gym is too far away or depressing to visit, it becomes all that much harder to keep yourself psyched.

While a home gym is supremely convenient, it can be difficult to block out a period of time without distractions (phone calls, kids, etc.). Many people thrive on working out with a partner or in a class. For whatever reasons, some people have a harder time getting motivated to work out at home than going to a gym. And it can be cheaper to join a commercial gym for a few years than to outfit your home.

FITNESS CLUBS

In most cases, commercial gyms and fitness clubs offer far greater variety of equipment than what you might assemble at home. The atmosphere of like-minded people helps you stay psyched to work out. There are trainers available who can correct your form and show you new techniques. Many gyms at colleges, city recreation centers, and nonprofits (such as the YMCA) have good facilities at reasonable prices.

Before signing a contract, some of which can be very difficult to break, it pays to shop around. The first consideration is distance. Ideally your gym should be no more than 15 minutes from home or work. While taking a tour, try to get a sense of the friendliness of the staff and attention to maintenance.

Beware the hard sell—some of these people, particularly at chains, are slimier than your stereotypical used car dealer. The best deals on membership rates can usually be achieved in the off-season (May to September). Registration fees are nearly always negotiable and can often be waived entirely if you don't appear too eager to join. Make sure they don't hit you with extra fees for things you don't intend to use such as ten-

nis courts, swimming pool, towel service, or saunas. And don't sign any contract without a very clear understanding of how and when you can cancel.

When inspecting the facilities, be sure there are a lot of free weights and benches, with at least two power cages. The free weight area should have plenty of floor space and mirrored walls for watching your form (not posing). Look for a good assortment of modern weight machines, but these are less important than the free weights. Gyms rarely have a hangboard, but you may be able to convince the management that this inexpensive item is worthwhile.

Since aerobic areas tend to get clogged at peak times, be sure there are plenty of treadmills, elliptical trainers, bikes, and rowers. Some gyms put a 30-minute time limit on aerobic equipment, which may not be enough if that's your primary training.

A spinning studio, with a full schedule of classes, is a real plus. Most gyms also offer yoga and stretching classes as part of the membership. The less froufrou stuff (juice bars, step classes, Tae Bo, etc.) the better, since they indicate a trendy social club instead of a serious place to work out.

Many rock gyms have an area with free weights and aerobic machines that receives little traffic. Unfortunately this fitness section is usually thrown in as an afterthought and is not conducive to a good workout, so it becomes a self-fulfilling prophecy: a poorly designed training facility discourages users so management decides against improving their gym.

For a rock gym to be a viable alternative

to a regular gym, the workout area requires a mirrored wall, rubber floor mats, good lighting (75 to 100 foot-candles), temperature regulation (72°F to 78°F), and ventilation (twelve to fifteen air exchanges per hour). There should be a number of well-maintained, good-quality aerobic machines, a full assortment of dumbbells and Olympic weight bars, several multi-angle benches, and at least one power cage.

THE FITNESS CLUB SCENE

If you've never been to a fitness club, it can be intimidating at first. There will likely be guys in there who could squash you like a bug and gals who might be supermodels. Relax. They don't bite, and half don't know what they're doing (but act like they do).

Your membership may include a free session with a personal trainer—be sure to use it. Have them show you how to operate all of the machines and the proper form with each. This is important because there will be times when a machine you want is occupied, and it will be expedient to simply use a different exercise for the same muscle group. Plus, variety is the spice of fitness.

Most gyms are packed on weekdays from 7:00 AM to 9:00 AM and even worse from 5:00 PM to 7:00 PM (except Friday). If you can arrange your schedule to avoid those peak times, you'll be able to finish your sessions faster. Try to establish a weekly routine and you'll soon recognize familiar faces.

Don't hesitate to ask one of the regulars how to use a machine, to check your form, or for a spot. If they aren't in the middle of a set, the vast majority will be happy to help (and the rest are just jerks). However, some posers who work out religiously have atrocious form, often accompanied by loud grunting and clanking of weights, and should be avoided. Be leery of anyone who lifts tiny weights a thousand times.

Some gyms enforce a time limit on aerobic machines during peak times. Even without a limit, it's a good idea to try a different motion after a while if you need a long workout. If the gym is crowded, it's okay to "work in" by asking to do a set while someone is resting. But don't disturb someone if a similar exercise is available elsewhere. It's rude to hog a machine or bench by jabbering away unless you truly are resting between sets. Never use a power cage for anything but squats and other heavy lifts; performing bicep curls in a cage is proof positive of dweebdom.

Although some people use the gym as a meat market and social club, especially at peak hours, most are there to get a workout without wasting time. Don't be perturbed if someone puts on a game face (or headphones) and is not interested in idle conversation; they may be more willing to talk after they're done. Holding a conversation during a heavy set isn't possible—it takes too much focus—so don't bother someone while they are lifting.

Not that it really matters, but the best way to earn respect from gym regulars is to keep showing up: attendance counts much more than appearance or how much you can lift. There is always an influx of soon-to-be dropouts who clog the gym after New Year's and the start of school.

The worst breach of gym etiquette is failure to re-rack weights where they belong (10-pound plate on the 10-pound pin, etc.). Pick up after yourself! Avoid blocking someone else's view of the mirror; it actually is a tool. It's common courtesy to wipe down the machine or bench when finished, especially during flu season. (Rags and spray bottles are scattered around most gyms.)

Wear clean workout clothes and deodorant (but not perfume); if you notice the gym clearing out around you, there's a reason. For liability reasons, many gyms require shoes (old running shoes are fine) and will not allow sandals. Leave your cell phone in the locker; don't let the outside world intrude upon your training or people nearby. To save time making trips to the water fountain, carry a water bottle as you move through the gym.

Do not wear a weightlifting belt, because it will prevent strength gains in your abdomen and back—key muscles for climbing. It is better to work your way up to loads that you can safely handle. Similarly, gloves will prevent calluses and improve your grip but they reduce the training effect, so you are better off barehanded.

TRAINERS

From time to time, it can be an excellent idea to hire a personal trainer who will correct your form and push you harder, safely. Unfortunately, quite a few trainers are fountains of bad advice, giving information that is outdated or simply wrong. Currently there are no state or federal requirements for calling oneself a personal trainer, so it's caveat emptor.

The lack of standards has resulted in an industry with more than seventy personal trainer organizations, some of which sell certifications with virtually no requirements. In the United States and Canada, the ACSM (American College of Sports Medicine) and NSCA (National Strength and Conditioning Association) are the most respected certifying agencies. Both require certified trainers to pass a demanding written exam and keep themselves up to date with continuing education. With certification comes membership in a professional organization, journal and newsletter subscriptions, and liability protection.

Many trainers get certified in the latest fitness fad by paying money and taking a course: Spinning, kettlebells, CrossFit, Indian clubs, etc. This isn't a bad thing, but it does lead to a bit of, um, over-enthusiasm and exaggeration of their particular routines. If the trainer is really good, he will give you an honest appraisal of the pros and cons as well as have a working knowledge of the alternatives. Beware the axiomatic trainer who gushes about how his method is superior to all others.

No matter their certification, few trainers at fitness gyms understand the demands of climbing so you may need to educate them; they can still be of great help. While you are performing an exercise, the trainer may gently touch the active muscles to help you notice the contractions and improve technique. This "cueing" provides biofeedback and improves your self-awareness.

Many rock gyms have climbing coaches available, but there is no national standard or formalized training at all for this title (yet). Often these folks only know about sport climbing and have a limited understanding of physiology, nutrition, or mountaineering. Which is not to say that all climbing coaches are bad, just that you have to be extra careful before hiring one.

With any trainer, your best bet is to watch her in action with other clients before committing your wallet and body. Make sure her style and knowledge match your needs. It is advisable to get several references and talk to them. The hallmark of a good trainer is that she will push and educate you by pointing out areas for improvement and correcting technique.

HOME GYM

If you have a spare room available, a decent gym can be created for only a couple hundred dollars. But investing a bit more will give you more workout options to keep things fresh.

If possible, try to spruce up your home gym with good lighting, adequate ventilation, a music system, and motivational posters. Rubber mats can muffle noise as well as protect your floors and equipment; you can save a bundle by purchasing it from a tack shop (horse supply) instead of a fitness store. It is also helpful to have a dry-erase board so you can use colored pens to write your workouts and training goals.

Those with significant disposable incomes may wish to consider a modular home gym that has selectorized weight stacks. Much of the equipment at sporting-good stores is poor quality that will be uncomfortable to use and will wear out quickly. Go to a fitness specialty store if you are serious.

By today's standards, the universal machine, with a half dozen stations and fixed movements, is obsolete. Likewise, most of the exergadgets sold on TV and in department stores are junk. Don't waste money on the Bowflex or Total Gym; they are overpriced and too limiting.

If your budget permits $2,000 to $4,000, the best choice is one of the new generation "functional machines," which offer nearly unlimited options for resistance training. Some models to look at include the Lamar Vertical Function Trainer or TechTower T4, Life Fitness CM3 or G5, Torque Fitness F5 or TQ3, Vectra VFT100 and Vision Fitness ST200. These all take up relatively little space yet allow you exceptional workout opportunities.

Fortunately, you don't need to spend that kind of money to assemble a great home gym. If you start with some basics (dumbbells, stability ball, hangboard), you can train every muscle quite effectively. Then as your budget allows, you can expand your gym to intensify your workouts.

Dumbbells. The starting point of any home gym should be a set of dumbbells because the number of exercises is only limited by your imagination. Since these can take up a lot of space, the adjustable dumbbells are a great option. PowerBlocks are the original, and still arguably the best, but several other

Dumbbells

Power Cage and Weights. Although you can do a lot with dumbbells and kettlebells, it is hard to beat a good power rack and Olympic barbell set for serious training. It pays to spend the money for quality products since they never wear out.

A power cage (aka power or squat rack) is the steel-framed box found in any good gym that is used for lifting safely. When choosing a power cage, it needs to be a minimum of 7 feet tall, 5 feet deep, and 4 feet wide or you won't have enough room to train. The upper, front cross bar should be knurled for chin-ups. The spacing of the holes for the bar hooks and spotting rods should be no greater than 2 inches. It is helpful to have two sets of bar hooks to rest the bar inside or outside the cage. Pins to hold your weights up off the floor are nice too. Some cages have the option of attaching dip bars or a lat pull-down attachment. A basic power cage runs about $300, but they can go up to well over $1,000 for better ones with accessories.

An Olympic weight set typically features a 7-foot-long, 45-pound bar that takes plates with 2-inch diameter holes. Standard bars are shorter (5 to 6 feet), have narrower grips (25mm versus 28mm) and take plates with 1-inch diameter holes. For squats, it's worth investing in an Olympic bar and a set of weights. A basic set, including 300 pounds of weights, costs about $400 and will handle most people's needs. If you can afford them (roughly double), rubber-coated weights, are a nice option to reduce clanking.

companies offer adjustable dumbbells as well. It is worth the money for the optional stand so that the dumbbells are easily reached. A standard PowerBlock set goes from 5 to 45 pounds in 5-pound increments (nine pairs), takes up only 3 square feet, and costs about $400 with the stand.

Whether you get conventional or adjustable dumbbells, you may wish to fine tune the increments at the lighter loads. Particularly when rehabbing after an injury, the jump from 5 to 10 pounds, or 10 to 15, may be too much. PlateMates are magnetic weights that attach to your equipment when needed. They come in a variety of sizes and weights (around $30 per pair) and you need one pair per dumbbell for best balance.

Adjustable Bench. An adjustable weight bench can also come in handy since you can use it for a wide range of upper body and core exercises. Look for a model that can lie flat and has several angles of incline; decline is a nice option but not vital. Beware that the cheap benches are made with foam and vinyl padding that wears out quickly; a bargain they are not. Expect to spend $150 to $250 for a bench that will last a long time. Most of the optional attachments are not needed.

Kettlebells. What is old is new again; these simple devices likely originated in ancient Scotland (not Tsarist Russia). Over a century ago, kettlebells were standard equipment in gyms worldwide. But they fell out of favor as new equipment was invented. Now, these balls with a handle attached are making a comeback as one of the latest fitness fads, albeit one with some heft.

While some of the kettlebell exercises are more novelty than truly productive, others provide a serious workout with good crossover for climbers. Compared to a dumb-

Kettlebells

bell, a kettlebell of the same weight will feel heavier due to greater distance of the center of gravity from the hand. The shape of the handle is also better for two-handed grasps and allows a few other moves.

Overall, kettlebells are a reasonable adjunct to other training methods, but it's best to start with dumbbells for your home gym. Using kettlebells exclusively is a bad idea because they impart additional strain on your wrists and connective tissues of elbows and shoulders due to the nature of the exercises.

To train effectively with kettlebells requires at least two: a lighter one (18 to 26 pounds, 8 to 12 kg) for upper body presses and a heavy one (35 to 53 pounds, 16 to 24 kg) for lower body swings; ideally you would have at least four to allow good progression. However, these low-tech chunks of cast iron are surprisingly expensive (over $200 for a set of four) and shipping can jack that up even more.

For all but diehard enthusiasts, a better option is a pair of adjustable Kettlestacks ($55 each), which are well-designed handles for which you provide the weight (standard plates available at any sporting good store, another $50 to $70). The advantage is you can easily fine-tune each kettlebell to the amount of resistance that you need; plus they take up less space than a selection of standard kettlebells. Once assembled, these have a solid feel and a nicer grip than most traditional bells, but don't use them for tosses.

Resistance Tubing. Stretchy tubing with handles on the end are almost too simple

Resistance Tubing

to believe they can be useful for a serious workout. Yet they offer a wide range of options for resistance and rehabilitation, are highly portable, and very affordable. The tubing is particularly useful for strengthening the rotator cuff of the shoulder. The cheaper resistance bands made of sheets of colored elastic are similar but they lack handles and deteriorate rather quickly.

One of the key differences from free weights is that the resistance curve of tubing is the opposite. With many free weight exercises, the resistance starts high but decreases as the angles change. Tubing, on the other hand, starts off easy and gets progressively harder toward the end of the motion. Tubing can also be used with free weights to increase resistance at the top of the lift, where the load normally decreases.

Among the nicest resistance tubes are the Slastix, which have a nylon webbing covering that increases comfort and durability. There are four levels of resistance (12, 19, 26, and 33 pounds) and an optional Fit-Stik that tubing handles slip into to create a barbell; the entire set sells for about $75.

Suspended Resistance. Many climbers have certainly marveled at male gymnasts performing on the rings in the Summer Olympics. Rings can be an excellent training device for the upper body and core, take up little space, and are relatively inexpensive. Because the rings are not stationary, the motions are very natural and your small stabilizing muscles are forced to work.

Elite Rings (less than $100 for a pair) are designed specifically for fitness training so they are easily adjustable, have a good texture, and can be hung from any solid support, such as a ceiling beam. The optional DVD shows a full progression of forty exercises from basic push-ups all the way to the Iron Cross (if you dare).

Taking rings to the next level is the TRX Suspension Trainer (around $150) with even more options for body weight workouts in a very compact package. This is arguably the best portable gym available—fits into a small stuff sack and only needs a single anchor point (even a door will work)—and it can deliver a serious full-body workout. A variety of DVDs are available to give you

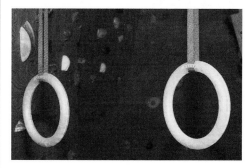

Rings

workout ideas. The less expensive Metolius Rock Rings (about $30) are a cross between rings and a hangboard; they are suitable for pulling and hanging but not pushing.

Parallettes. Another item borrowed from the gymnastic world, these compact and inexpensive devices allow a wide range of body weight workouts that can be as gentle or as brutal as you desire. A parallette is simply a sturdy bar about 24 inches long that is held up about 8 inches off the ground by a stable base on each end; you need two of them. It's very easy to make your own parallettes from 1¼-inch PVC pipe and plumbing parts for a cost of about $30. Or you can purchase a pair of wooden parallettes from a gymnastic supply for about $70.

Another option is the Lebert Equalizer, a pair of parallettes made of 1½-inch steel tubing that cost about $100 (a workout poster and DVD are included). The main difference is the bars are about 28 inches off the ground, plus they can be laid sideways for grips about 7 inches from the ground, so the Equalizer increases versatility. Sturdily built (each one weighs almost 9 pounds), the Equalizer takes up little storage space but offers a lot of workout options. The slight heft and large leverage also create opportunities for forearm exercises to train grip and alleviate elbow problems.

Stability Ball. There probably isn't a gym in the country that doesn't have a pile of stability balls in a corner. These inexpensive (about $25) inflatable balls (sometimes called exercise, fitness, or Swiss balls) are excellent for core exercises and can even serve as a weight bench or desk chair.

Surprisingly, after years on the market, somebody figured out how to improve on the concept by adding 2½ pounds of sand inside. The Ballast Ball (about $60) creates dynamic

Parallettes

Stability Ball

resistance during many lifting and shifting exercises. Another key advantage is the ball will not roll away when you stand up.

Hangboard. One of the best additions to any rock climber's house (or dorm room) is a hangboard for finger training. Sometimes called a fingerboard, this is a small panel, about 24 inches (63 cm) wide and 6 inches (15 cm) high that is used to increase grip strength.

There are numerous commercial hangboards available (around $50 to $100) that have a selection of large and small in-cut holds, slopers, and some wide grips for pull-ups. However, many have a texture that is too coarse for extended hangs. It's also fairly easy to make your own from wood since all you really need is a ledge about 1 inch (25mm) deep with a rounded edge. For installing over a doorway, it is often best to mount the hangboard to a larger sheet of plywood, which is then screwed into studs of the wall.

Forearm Trainer. The forearms are, of course, vital to train for nearly all types of climbing (mountaineering being the main exception). While bouldering and training on a hangboard are good for grip strength, specifically targeting the forearms can also help. It's true that building forearm strength by repetitive squeezing does not directly translate to climbing better since we often rely on isometric strength with an open hand. But the fact that you can do it anywhere and while doing something else makes grip training useful.

Most of the squeeze-type gadgets, rubber donuts, and gyro toys sold in stores are woefully inadequate with just 30 to 50 pounds of resistance; if you can do 50 or 100 squeezes in a set, the training value is minimal. As with the major muscles of

Hangboard

Grippers

the body, building strength requires heavy resistance and progressive overload. For climbing, holding a partial squeeze (like an open-handed grip) for an extended time is more important than fully closing the hand.

Among the best hand tools are the Iron-Mind grippers (about $20 each), which come in two styles. The traditional size Captains of Crush grippers have knurled aluminum grips and are available in ten levels of resistance, starting at 60 pounds and going up to 365 pounds. The two-finger IMTUG grippers have larger diameter grips and come in seven levels of resistance; these are particularly handy for working on pinch strength.

Though not as compact, the Ivanko Super Gripper (around $32) offers more than forty levels of resistance (45 to 345 pounds) in one device. This allows fine tuning the resistance in small increments. The design also accommodates a variety of hand sizes and can be used pivot down (normal) or pivot up for variety. You may want to wrap it with friction tape for better texture.

Plyometric Box. Just a very sturdy box that is used for stepping and jumping to build power. They come in different heights but you likely only need one about 20 inches tall. Plyo boxes are surprisingly expensive (starting around $100) considering how simple they are.

If you are handy, you can build your own from ¾-inch plywood, 1¼-inch screws, and glue. For a 20-inch-tall box, the landing deck should be about 24 inches square to give the box sufficient stability (tipping over when you jump is decidedly not good). Tapering the base to an 18-inch deck is even better but greatly complicates construction since cuts must be at angles. Be sure to add a slip-resistant surface (rubber mat is ideal for a bit of cushion) and bevel the top edge to prevent scarred shins from a missed jump.

Lateral Leg Trainer. If you are one of those climbers who considers skiing a major part of your lifestyle, then a lateral leg trainer can give you a head start on the season and help prepare you for major ski mountaineering excursions. Combining variable resistance with sideways movement and quick reaction is also valuable for alpinists, trail runners, and anyone who is susceptible to knee injury.

The Pro Fitter 3D Cross Trainer ($600)

Leg Trainer

is a superb ski simulator for increasing strength and power while improving reaction skills. The foot sled moves across rails with a natural rocking motion and resistance is easily adjusted by varying the number of elastic cords. Twenty to thirty minutes on the Pro Fitter provides a serious yet fun workout. This is highly specific to alpine skiing but also crosses over well for telemark and skate skiing. The device can also be used for core muscle training and is excellent for rehabbing knee injuries.

Specialty Devices. Things that can spice up your workouts: medicine balls, manila climbing rope, sand bags, Indian clubs, and heavy sleds. Without question, all of these can be great adjuncts to your training programs. Each device has some vocal advocates that exhort the superiority of their favored product. But start with the basics described here before spending time or money on these training products.

Worthless Devices. Electrical stimulation machines are widely used in physical therapy for retraining muscles that have forgotten how to fire properly. But as far as a method for actually training athletes, they are a waste of money. There is no research that even hints that these gizmos are useful.

Another category of overpriced, underperforming products are whole-body vibration (WBV) machines. As usual, the claims are extravagant ("Complete workout in 10 minutes!" Blah, blah, blah.) but the science is weak. Perhaps useful for geriatrics with osteoporosis, when you look at the actual research that applies to athletes, these boneshakers don't do much of anything.

HOME WALL

A home climbing wall can provide an excellent, highly specific workout for rock climbers—now ice climbers can train in the off-season too. Even if you join a rock gym, a home wall allows you to train when you don't feel like a drive across town to vie with the hordes for a pump. If you have a lot of room and money, then go for it and build your own Fontainebleau!

However, a wall need not be elaborate to be effective. An 8-by-8-foot wall made from two sheets of half-inch marine plywood can provide sufficient variety that you won't become instantly bored. If possible, design it so the angle may be adjusted between 15 degrees and 45 degrees to work your muscles differently and allow for improvement. For a wall this size, plan on at least 250 climbing holds of all sizes and shapes, though you can get by with half that amount at first.

Two very effective options are a system wall and a campus board. A system wall is about 10 feet high overhung about 30 to 50 degrees past vertical. It has a set of identical holds designed to elicit specific combinations of hand and arm positions. With a system wall, you can focus on pockets, side pulls, slopes, crimps, monos, and underclings in a systematic fashion rather than at random as with bouldering.

A campus board is about 15 feet tall and overhung at 15 degrees, thus it's harder to find a suitable location in many homes. It

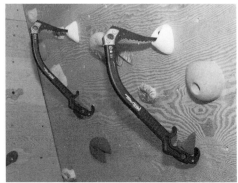

Dry Tooling Holds

Campus Board

has a series of rungs ¾- to 1½-inch deep that are used for plyometric training to develop power. Since they are relatively cheap, it is best to purchase commercial rungs instead of making your own. If you have the space, a campus board allows you to work on dynos and lock-offs for brutal yet effective workouts.

Ice climbers have the option of training indoors as well, thanks to the availability of bolt-on holds designed for dry tooling. Although you can use normal climbing holds, the steel picks tend to chew them up, making them unpleasant for fingers.

Currently, two companies offer holds for dry tooling: Dry Ice Cubes from Woody's Holds and the Ice and Hook holds from MR Climbing. These holds have indents that will accept picks but not fingers and are beefed up for durability. A selection of about twenty holds will allow climbers to get a good head start on ice season.

The key to success with a small home wall is a cheery atmosphere; otherwise it will have the appeal of a dungeon. Make sure the room is properly lit so you can see the footholds and the overhead light isn't shining in your eyes. Ensure a safe landing zone (old mattresses and futons are popular), adequate ventilation, and good tunes.

As your training progresses, trad and alpine climbers might consider a scuba diver's belt with the soft lead shot weights (distributes the load evenly around your waist) to simulate the gear you will wear in the field. However, sport climbers and boulderers will actually decrease their performance by climbing with weights because it teaches your muscles to fire differently than they will on a route or problem.

WEIGHTY CONCEPTS

When you are about to embark on a resistance workout, it is a good idea to start with a 5- to 10-minute warm-up. Use any form of aerobic exercise you wish and go at a moderate pace until you just break a light sweat. The point is to increase circulation, warm the muscles, and lubricate the joints so that you can train harder and safer. If you choose a lower-body warm-up, such as running or cycling, then precede an upper-body workout with a light endurance set.

FUNCTIONAL TRAINING

In recent years, "functional exercises" that combine balance and twisting motions with resistance have become popular. Theoretically these more accurately simulate real-life movement patterns, which often involve three planes of motion: frontal (side to side), sagital (forward-backward and up-down), and transverse (rotational). Standard resistance exercises generally have a specific movement pattern in one or two planes of motion. When used for physical therapy, functional training is superb for rehabbing patients that have lost motor function due to injury.

However, in healthy individuals, most functional exercises demand less resistance than can be achieved with specific training, thus the muscles are not fully taxed. Additionally, many of these exercises do not optimally challenge the muscles since the direction of force changes relative to the orientation of fibers. Performing exercises on balance boards has been shown to actually decrease performance because the movements don't translate to the real world.

Frequently, the terms "open chain" and "closed chain" are brought up in training discussions, usually to the derision of the former. An open-chain exercise is one in which the distal end of a limb (farthest from the body) is free to move (bench press, bicep curl, knee extension, etc.). With a closed-chain exercise, the hands or feet are fixed and the proximal joints (closer to the body) move, as in the push-up, pull-up, and squat.

While useful for academic purposes and physical therapy prescriptions, these terms become problematic in the real world. For example, a push-up off the ground is closed chain but is open chain when performed using rings so the hands are free to move.

When considering exercises, it's important to ask: functional for what? Just because something is performed on an unstable platform or with a piece of "functional" equipment doesn't mean that it will actually help your own performance. Consider how the movement pattern approximates what your activities involve. If the pattern isn't specific to what you will do, then it's better to spend the training time getting strong. Many of the high-velocity rotational exercises also create greater opportunity for injury, which shuts your functionality right down.

For maximal strength gains, keep your exercises pure and use high resistance. Nearly all standard free weight and body weight exercises are highly functional—even when performed in one plane of motion, stabilizer muscles are called in that keep the resistance from going into other planes. The primary exceptions are single-joint isolation exercises, which are used to target specific muscles that need help. By mixing up the routines, your body is constantly challenged, and your training will be functional and fruitful.

PROPER FORM

The prime directive for every repetition of every exercise is: form, control, precision. It really helps to repeat this to yourself during a set. If possible, use a mirror to watch yourself while performing the movement to ensure that you are doing it perfectly. Each repetition should work the full, biomechanically correct range of muscle movement. Use less resistance instead of partial reps.

For maximum muscle stimulus, a set should take about 30 to 90 seconds. This may be slower than what you'll see others doing at the gym, but it's a speed where the best gains are made for both slow- and fast-twitch fibers. Thus a full rep might include: 2 seconds pulling the weight toward you, 1-second pause, 2 seconds controlling the weight back, and a 1-second pause before starting again. A faster tempo, however, is more sport specific; training for power requires explosive bursts.

Never cheat a repetition by swinging the weight to gain momentum, springing at the bottom of a movement, or bouncing a barbell off your chest. This places greater peak forces upon your joints while reducing the training benefit for the muscles. When you can no longer maintain proper form, the set is over.

To prevent injury, always maintain a natural (lordotic) arch in the spine for upper and lower body exercises. You should not flatten your back against a bench or pad (tilts the pelvis), nor should you round your back (strains the lumbar region). Tighten your abdomen before lifting heavy to "block" your torso.

The neutral position is strongest when you pull your shoulder blades together and slightly raise your chest, like a soldier standing at attention. Performing all heavy exercises in this retracted shoulder blade position will strengthen your core and improve posture. With lighter loads (over 15 reps), you can "unlock" the shoulder blades for a full range of movement.

When performing an exercise, your breathing is part of the rhythm. Inhale during the first half, exhale gradually during the second half, or vice versa; whatever comes naturally. The transition from the eccentric to the concentric part of the motion is often a sticking point, and it may help to exhale forcefully (for example, blow out as you are pushing up from the bottom position of a squat or bench press). Most of all, do not hold your breath during either phase as this spikes your blood pressure, which in turn makes your heart work harder (pushing the blood around becomes more difficult).

WEAK LINKS

Blindly jumping into a resistance program is a good way to ensure mediocre results. Climbers often state that they must "get stronger" to improve their performance. Yet you need to be specific in your goals or you will merely train your strengths. Your time will be much more productive by working on weaknesses.

In some cases, your body type may be indicative of a natural weakness. While there are plenty of exceptions, climbers who are long and lean tend to have relatively good finger strength and poor upper body strength. Conversely, those who are muscular and stocky will often have a powerful back and arms yet relatively weak fingers.

Relative to total body weight, women frequently have two-thirds the upper body strength and power of men (the disparity is less in the lower body). Part of this is because females have a higher body fat percentage and greater fat-free mass below the waist. Society, however, is also at fault for discouraging girls and women from proper training.

Since it can be difficult to honestly evaluate oneself, seeking comments from climbing partners is useful—assuming you can elicit more than, "Dude, you suck!" For those who are serious about maximizing their performance, good feedback is among the most valuable paybacks from hiring a coach or personal trainer.

If outside help isn't forthcoming, you may want to develop some self-tests for the aspects of strength that are important to your climbing; these could be either key exercises or climbs of a particular type. Many people find it useful to carry a small notebook and jot down details of their workouts. This information can be useful to monitor your progress, or lack thereof, and it can aid you, or a personal trainer, in developing a better program for yourself.

STRUCTURING THE WORKOUT

The emphasis of your training program should be on primary exercises that use multiple joints, instead of a single joint, in one plane of motion (no twisting or rotation). For example, a squat flexes the ankle, knee, and hip joints while a leg extension just bends the knee. "Compound" exercises tend to be more sport specific and they save time as well.

Use the "simple" single-joint exercises—such as the biceps curl and leg extension—for isolating and improving weak links. The spine and shoulder are considered single joints when training, though this is not literally the case.

In general, it is best to first exercise the big muscle groups most important to your climbing, then work your way to progressively smaller muscles. Thus you might start with the back, then work the arms, and finish with the core (torso) and fingers. This way you are hitting the major muscles, and performing the exercises that require the most coordination, while you are fresh. Training smaller muscles at the end of a session also serves as a cool-down period.

After you are well trained, you can try reversing the order to pre-exhaust the small stabilizing muscles before working the big muscles. However, it's more important to finish the session with easy aerobic activity to flush metabolites from the muscles. There is also greater risk of injury since controlling the weight is more difficult.

A common routine involves doing all the sets of a pull exercise for one body part, followed by all the sets of a push exercise for the same body part, for example, three lat pull sets followed by two bench press sets. This way you are ensconced at one machine or station until you are done and, if you are doing another exercise on that muscle group, it gets a good rest before the next session. If this is too demanding when you are starting out, you can alternate upper- and lower-body exercises (say, lat pulls followed by leg presses) to increase the rests further.

When time is an issue, and the gym isn't crowded, you can perform supersets and get out of there in a hurry. This involves doing a set on the agonists and then, without taking a rest, doing a set on the antagonists of the same body part—for example, going straight from a set of lat pulls to a set of dips, or leg extensions to hamstring curls. Repeat this until the desired number of pushes and pulls are completed. Supersetting a routine can increase your endurance and will get your heart pumping since you don't stop the entire time; it's been a popular training method long before anyone trademarked the word CrossFit.

Once you are ready to really tax a muscle group, you can start using compound sets. For these, you do two similar exercises in a row, alternating between sets with only a short rest. Try lat pulls followed by seated rows, going back and forth until the desired number of sets is complete, then moving on to the next body part. This type of workout is very demanding so plan on a day off afterward.

The logical extension of this is a split routine, where you do upper-body exercises one day and lower-body the next, then repeat the cycle. Normally, splits are unwarranted for climbers but they may be used to make rapid progress for a major goal, such as an upcoming expedition. There are other variations of split routines, but they usually require more training time than most of us should consider.

FREQUENCY

How often you resistance train depends upon several factors, not the least of which is how much climbing you are doing. During the prime climbing season, if you have achieved a good level of fitness, you may want to suspend your gym membership for a couple of months. It's better, however, if you continue to get in one or two days a week of lifting to maintain the underutilized muscles that climbing doesn't hit.

For those who are starting a resistance program to build muscle, try for three days per week with a rest day in between (Monday, Wednesday, Friday works well for many). Two days is the bare minimum required by your body to make strength gains. You can, and should, climb on the days that you aren't lifting, but work on endurance and avoid very pumpy routes—this is "active rest" and you don't want to overdo it. Make one day per week a complete recovery day: no liftin', no climbin', no runnin', no nothin'.

After you have built a solid strength base, you can increase the frequency to four days per week if you are working toward a demanding goal. Before you do, read, mark, and inwardly digest chapter 8 on recovery. Climbers should only go to four days of lifting when their bodies are prepared for this level of stress and they have a clearly defined reason for pushing so hard. Use a split routine to ensure adequate rest. Remember that you are also climbing and aerobic conditioning during this time: if you aren't careful, you may be sidelined by injury.

There is very rarely, if ever, a reason for climbers to resistance train five days per week. Six is right out. And seven will turn you into a bodybuilding gym freak. That much lifting places you at a high risk of overtraining and means that you aren't climbing enough—your performance *will* decrease.

INTENSITY

Selecting the proper intensity—the load lifted and number of repetitions—is at the very heart of resistance training. At first, it may be hard to decide how much you can handle, but it won't take long to get a good feel for what is appropriate. Never attempt lifts with more load than you can control; you should be able to stop at any point during the motion.

There are two methods for specifying the intensity of a set: the right way and the wrong way. The proper method is to state the maximum repetitions (RM) in which muscular failure occurs. When a set is 10 RM, there is little room for doubt: if you can only do 8 reps, the weight is too much, and if you can do 12, you need to add more. With a little practice, it becomes easy to dial in your load with a high degree of accuracy.

Unfortunately, the wrong way—basing the load on a percentage of your one repetition maximum—is still very common. Based on meathead mentality, this method assumes that if you can lift 150 pounds one time, then you should be able to lift 90 percent of that (135 pounds) four times, and 80 percent of that (120 pounds) eight times. The problem is that all the charts assume a linear relationship between the load and reps, which is never the case. This also does not take into account your level of conditioning unless you actually test your 1 RM weekly—a rather dangerous and nonproductive procedure. Sometimes they test the 10 RM and then estimate the 1 RM from that, but this bassackwards approach still leaves a lot of room for error.

If you are new to resistance training, start out with 12 to 18 reps per set for the first couple of weeks to get used to the equipment and motions. Then work your way into the 8- to 12-rep range for a couple of months to build a solid foundation. Once you are solid, then it's time to maximize your strength and power.

When counting reps, it may help to go backward: 5-4-3-2-1. This little trick helps you stay focused and makes the set seem easier. Instead of worrying if you'll make it to rep X, your mental image is positive and you can get all the way through the set.

Because you must keep upping the ante if you want a bigger reward, the resistance must also increase over time. When you first start out at a particular load, you may be able to do 10 reps on the first set, 9 on the second set, and only 7 on the third set. After a couple of weeks, you should be able to max out on all three sets at 10 reps. When you can do this two training days in a row, it's time to add more weight.

MUSCLE MAGIC

Adjusting the intensity and rests for any exercise will yield different results. Higher intensity brings more muscle cells into play (greater recruitment) and emphasizes anaerobic energy sources. The "maximum load" is the amount of resistance required so that you cannot complete one more repetition with proper form.

Power

- 2–5 reps at moderate/high loads and maximum speed.
- 2- to 5-minute rest between each set.
- Fibers recruited: Nearly all Type I, all IIa, all IIb.
- Energy system: Mostly phosphate, minimal aerobic, and lactate.
- Maximum recruitment and neural training.
- No effect on muscle growth or endurance.
- Develops explosive power for short, intense problems, but greater risk of injury.

Strength

- 3–6 reps at maximum loads.
- 2- to 5-minute rest between each set.
- Fibers recruited: All Type I, all IIa, all IIb.
- Energy system: Mostly phosphate, some lactate, minimal aerobic.
- Maximum recruitment and neural training.
- No effect on muscle growth or endurance.
- Develops raw strength for hard climbs without adding bulk.

Strength and High-Intensity Power Endurance

- 6–8 reps at maximum loads.
- 1- to 2-minute rest between each set.
- Fibers recruited: Nearly all Type I, nearly all IIa, many IIb.
- Energy system: Mostly lactate and phosphate, minimal aerobic.
- Moderate recruitment.
- Moderate muscle growth and power gains.
- Good gains, but training above or below this range may have more pronounced effects.

High-Intensity Power Endurance

- 8–12 reps at maximum loads.
- 45- to 90-second rest between each set.
- Fibers recruited: Most Type I, most IIa, some IIb.
- Energy system: Mostly lactate, some aerobic and phosphate.
- Maximum muscle growth.
- Significant strength, power, and low-intensity endurance gains.
- Good all-around training range when combined with aerobic conditioning.

High- and Low-Intensity Power Endurance

- 12–18 reps at maximum loads.
- 30- to 60-second rest between each set.
- Fibers recruited: Many Type I, some IIa, minimal IIb.
- Energy system: Both lactate and aerobic, minimal phosphate.
- Modest muscle growth.
- Minimal effect on strength and power.
- Best range to start a resistance program.

Low-Intensity Power Endurance

- 15–25 reps at maximum loads.
- 15- to 30-second rest between each set.
- Fibers recruited: Many Type I, some IIa, minimal IIb.
- Energy system: Mostly aerobic and some lactate, minimal phosphate.
- No effect on strength, power, or muscle growth.
- Good range for warming up prior to hard sets.
- Useful, but climbing is superior to this for training endurance of major muscles.

Muscular Endurance

- 20–30 reps at maximum loads.
- 15-second rest between each set.
- Fibers recruited: Less than half of Type I and very minor II.
- Energy system: Mostly aerobic, minimal lactate and phosphate.
- Improves capillarity and increases enzyme activity.
- Useful training for deep, minor muscles such as rotator cuff.
- Ineffective use of time for major muscles—go climb.

The amount you increase the load will depend on your conditioning and the body part (err on the side of less with shoulder exercises). For the upper body, a beginner should add 2.5 pounds, an intermediate might add 5 pounds, and an advanced lifter could go up by 10 pounds. For lower body exercises, a beginner can try adding 5 pounds, an intermediate will put on 10 pounds, and the burly can go for 15 pounds or more. Try the new load for a set and see how many reps you can bust out, then adjust accordingly. Don't overdo it or try to impress anyone!

VOLUME

Just as intensity affects the results of your training, so does the volume, which is the number of sets that a particular exercise is performed. When starting out, an untrained person can make significant gains by performing only a single set (but doing it really well). However, after a few months, this volume is often inadequate for continued improvement.

For most routines and intensity levels, a total of three sets per exercise provides superior stimulus for muscle development. This is a matter of rapidly diminishing returns: you get roughly 60 percent of the benefit from the first set, 20 percent more from the second, an extra 10 percent from the third, and even less in subsequent sets. So if time is short, it's generally better to do one set of all the exercises in a routine than to leave some out in favor of more sets.

When training in the hypertrophy range where most growth occurs (8 to 12 reps),

most climbers should stick with two or three sets; rarely four if a particular muscle group is lagging. This won't bulk you up overnight but will prepare you for bigger strength gains.

Working on power and strength is a different matter. After a thorough warm-up of several lower-intensity sets (not counted), many athletes will go for five to six sets. Beware that these may not seem too taxing at the time, because it's just a few reps per set, but you'd better plan on taking the next day (or two) off.

Try to do your muscular endurance training on the rock (real or plastic). If for some reason you can't climb, endurance routines are typically just two to three sets.

REST PERIODS

The period between sets is more important than many people realize since it determines how much recovery occurs. Don't just gab between sets; time the rest periods (a watch or wall clock is helpful) so they are neither too long nor too short.

For endurance sets, the rest break is only 15 to 30 seconds long to get the most gains. The highest level of fatigue occurs in hypertrophy sets with short rest periods (30 to 90 seconds). By going with shorter breaks, you will eventually build your resistance to wearing out.

Even though power and strength workouts are high intensity, the duration is fairly short so lactate remains at low levels. These sets normally call for 2- to 5-minute rests to allow sufficient recovery of the phosphate system for maximal efforts.

DANGEROUS EXERCISES

Many exercises performed in gyms are holdovers from the old days before biomechanical science: some myths die hard. Although these exercises don't guarantee injury, they offer greater risk with little additional muscle gain. We punish our joints enough while climbing—don't exacerbate problems while training.

Behind-the-neck exercises: Both lat pulls and overhead presses in this position stress the shoulder joint in its weakest position. To make matters worse, and to the delight of chiropractors, the cervical spine is often strained as people crane their necks. Always keep your hands where you can see them.

Upright rows: When your hands are close together, this barbell exercise creates a bone-on-bone arm position that can result in shoulder impingement problems. A wide grip is better, but still can overly stress the rotators.

Excessive shoulder range: The Pec Deck is a common chest machine, where you squeeze two forearm pads together in front of you, which can place a lot of stress on the shoulder joints. When using this machine, or doing dumbbell flies, never let your arms move behind your centerline or allow your shoulder to rotate. Likewise, with a bench press, don't drop your elbows below chest level; there is no benefit.

Excessive knee range: Controversy rages over the safety of deep squats. Some cite greatly increased force on the patellar cruciate ligament and others point to the billions of people who squat deep every day without knee problems. When weight lifting, it's prudent to bend the knee no more than at a right angle unless you have strong reasons for going lower.

Excessive spine range: Chronic back injuries are grim. Hyperextending (arching backward) or hyperflexing (curling forward) the spine places a great deal of force upon the ligaments, muscles, and discs between the vertebrae. Only for body core exercises do you flex your spine, and those are within a controlled range. Even when climbing, you should protect your spine from severe stress.

Anything that causes sharp pain: Either modify the exercise or avoid it. There are other ways to achieve a goal.

Any exercise in this book that isn't performed correctly!

PERIODIZATION

Too much of the same thing leads to stagnation: you call this boring, your body calls it a plateau. The way to stay out of a rut and continue making gains is through cycles, or periods, where your training program varies in intensity, volume, and frequency over the course of weeks, months, or the year.

Many climbers do not need to schedule their training because the seasons do it for us: the shorter days and nastier weather of late fall and winter encourage strength training in the gyms; by spring, we are going stir-crazy and start getting out for aerobic play and early climbing, but variable weather still keeps us at the gyms a fair amount; when we finally get the long days and good weather of summer and early fall, we're out climbing and aerobic playing as much as possible, so the gyms are a matter of willpower.

However, those with a one-track mind—for example, preparing for a major climb or only interested in sport climbing and bouldering—should consider using periodization to maximize performance during a key period. This typically means subdividing three or four months into phases in which only one aspect of strength is trained. This level of structure does not suit everyone but can be effective for those who stick with the program. Although the peaks in performance can be higher, the valleys will also be deeper; without sufficient recovery, overtraining will result.

For intermediate to advanced athletes, a good way to break up the monotony of training is with one-week cycles. Thus you could make Monday a light day with lower weights so that you can do sets of 12 to 15 reps before reaching muscular fatigue; Wednesday a heavy day (3 to 5 RM); and Friday a moderate day (8 to 10 RM). In addition to working different energy systems, this also helps to protect against overtraining.

When doing a maintenance routine just one or two days per week, you might use a training pyramid for the primary exercises. This could start with a set of 15 RM, then increase the load for a set of 10 RM, then 5, then 10, then finish with 15. Or if time is short, you might do half a pyramid starting with 10 reps, then 8, then 6, then 4. Using machines makes pyramids and descending sets very time-effective since you only have to move a pin to adjust the resistance.

RESISTANCE EXERCISES

With all the options at your disposal—exercises, loads, sets, repetitions, and cycles—there is no reason to ever get bored in a gym. Use your creativity and always maintain good form. Keep your eye on the prize: it's all about climbing more and better.

UPPER BODY EXERCISES

1 Lat Pull

Why? This multi-joint exercise is the next best thing to real climbing. Lat pulls are superior to pull-ups because you can lean back to simulate the angle of overhangs and better target the muscles. The lats originate at the spine and insert into the upper arm at several angles; a vertical orientation makes the resistance less efficient.

Muscles. Latissimus dorsi, teres major, middle and lower trapezius, rhomboids, posterior deltoid, biceps group.

Form
- Position the seat and knee pad so that your hips and knees are at right angles, thighs are snug under the pad, and feet flat on the floor.

- Stand up and grab the bar with your palms facing away and hands wider than your elbows. If the angled part of the bar is too wide, just grab where it's comfortable or select a different bar.
- Sit down and tuck your knees under the pad. Elbows should be slightly bent.
- Lean back at a 15- to 45-degree angle, keeping your spine and neck straight. Press your shoulder blades down and together and keep them in that position throughout the set.
- In a smooth motion, pull the bar down to almost touch your chest.

- Then control the speed of the bar as it rises. Don't just let it be lifted!
- Back at the starting position, maintain the tension in your shoulder blades and pull down again. Don't let your elbows lock out straight. Repeat.

Tips. Concentrate on your back muscles, not your arms, and do not rock back and forth. Don't jerk the motion. Avoid overgripping with your hands; this isn't a forearm exercise.

Variations

- When the resistance is less than body weight, raise the knee pad so that you can't use it. These lat pulls require more work from your core muscles.

- Vary your hand position: narrow, wide, palms facing you, parallel grip.
- Practice lock-offs at various angles by stopping the ascent of the bar for several seconds.
- Try one-arm pulls while sitting on a stability ball.
- The plate-loaded, unilateral machines allow a full range of motion to waist level and require each arm to work independently.

Precautions. Do not perform lat pulls behind the neck; the motion has nothing to do with climbing, the direction is suboptimal for the muscles, and it places stress on your cervical spine and rotator cuff. Those with shoulder impingement problems or a torn rotator cuff should be cautious with lat pulls. Try using a narrow, parallel grip instead (makes this a lat row).

2 Pull-up

Why? This multi-joint exercise has long been a favorite among climbers for barroom bragging rights even though it has little to do with climbing ability. Pull-ups require very little to no equipment—having a bar conveniently located at home or work allows you to pop off sets throughout the day.

Muscles. Latissimus dorsi, teres major, middle and lower trapezius, rhomboids, posterior deltoid, biceps group.

Form

- Use a bar approximately 1½ inches in diameter that is far enough off the floor

for you to hang vertically. Bending your knees to fit is less desirable since you lose concentration.

- Grab the bar with your palms facing away and hands wider than your shoulders.
- Squeeze your shoulder blades down and together and keep them in that retracted position throughout the set.
- In a smooth motion, pull yourself up until your nose is at bar level. Exhale as you pull.
- Then lower yourself in a controlled movement. Repeat.

Tips. Try ascending 1:1 sets (do 1 rep, wait that time, do 2 reps, wait that time, do 3 . . . but stop 1 to 2 reps before your limit and start over) a couple of times a day. If you have trouble with pull-ups, start with chin-ups (palms facing you). The assisted pull-up machines at gyms are excellent for those who lack the upper-body strength to perform many reps. At home, you can simulate these by attaching elastic resistance tubing to the pull-up bar and standing in loops.

Variations

- Place a stool several feet forward of the bar and rest your heels on it while keeping your back straight; by varying the height and distance, you can change the angle of resistance.
- When you are ready, increase resistance by adding weights to a waist pack or hanging them from a harness.
- While lowering, lock off at various angles and hold for as long as possible.
- Use gymnastic rings to do pull-ups but stagger their height to force one arm to work harder, then switch.

Precautions. Do not dead hang; keep some tension in shoulders and elbows between reps. Avoid pull-ups on a door molding; this is very stressful on finger joints and detracts from quality pull-ups. Those with shoulder impingement problems or a torn rotator cuff should be cautious with pull-ups.

3 Bent-over Row

Why? A multi-joint exercise that allows you to focus on each side of the back, particularly the lower trapezius, without straining the lumbar region. This helps ward off shoul-der impingement problems by promoting scapular stability.

Muscles. Latissimus dorsi, teres major, lower trapezius, rhomboids, posterior del-toid, biceps group.

Form

- Prop yourself with one hand and one knee on a padded bench and the other leg standing on the floor, knee slightly bent; your back is flat. Also may be done standing with one hand resting on a table or chair.
- Grasp the dumbbell and allow your arm to hang straight down. The wrist is

3a

3b

neutral, the elbow slightly bent, shoulder blades retracted, and your back is neutral.

- Starting with your back muscles, pull the weight toward your chest until your elbow is at a right angle. Your upper arm just brushes the ribs.
- Hold the contraction for a moment, then slowly lower the weight. Do not let gravity just pull it down. Repeat.

Tips. Emphasize the pull from your back, not the biceps. Keep your torso parallel to the floor; don't rotate your chest to the ceiling or allow your shoulder to drop downward.

Variations

- Instead of a bench, kneel on a stability ball to discover some tiny muscles you didn't know were there.
- Vary the angle of your back from horizontal to as much as 45 degrees; this works well with a cable machine and a pulley near the floor.
- The barbell bent-over row is essentially the same, but you can't brace yourself so it requires more balance. The wide grip provides good variety.
- A renegade row involves using a pair of dumbbells (flat-bottomed so they don't roll) or kettlebells and getting in a pushup position with arms straight. Alternate picking up the weights to waist level and throw in some pushups if you really want to max out.

Precautions. An unsupported bent-over row places significant shear force on the lower back. Instead, do one side at a time or rest your chest on a bench or ball and use a pair of dumbbells.

4   Seated Row

Why? Since the back muscles are vital for all types of climbing, they need a good repertoire of exercises. This multi-joint exercise is excellent for improving posture and can be a good simulation of an undercling.

Muscles. Latissimus dorsi, teres major, middle trapezius, rhomboids, posterior deltoid, biceps group.

Form

- Sit at the machine with your feet firmly braced against the platform or floor. Knees are slightly bent.

- Bending at the hips, reach forward and grasp the handle. Then sit up until your back is vertical; this is the start and finish position.
- Starting with your back muscles, pull the handle toward your abdomen. The elbows stay at your side and point behind you. The shoulder blades move back and together.
- Hold the contraction for a moment, then slowly reverse the motion, allowing the shoulder blades to move forward. Do not let gravity just pull the handle back. Repeat.

Tips. Use a variety of grips and hand positions to mix up the stimulus.

Variations

- Most gyms have several machines that perform essentially the same operation—try them all.
- Use a straight bar and grasp it with an undercling (palms up).

Precautions. Rocking forward from your hips can strain your lower back; there are better ways to train and stretch these muscles. Don't allow your shoulders to be pulled forward or your elbows to hyperextend. If you find yourself leaning back, reduce the resistance slightly.

5 Rear Delt Row

Why? This multi-joint exercise develops shoulder and arm muscles that are often used when climbing. It's similar to a bent-over row except your elbows are away from your side.

Muscles. Posterior deltoid, middle and upper trapezius, rhomboids, biceps group.

Form

- Prop yourself with one hand and one knee on a padded bench and the other leg standing on the floor, knee slightly bent; your back is flat. Also may be done standing with one hand resting on a table or chair.
- Grasp the dumbbell and allow your arm to hang straight down. The wrist is neutral, the elbow slightly bent, and shoulder blades are retracted.
- Starting with your back muscles, pull the weight upward until your elbow is at a right angle. Your upper arm is extended straight out to the side.

5a

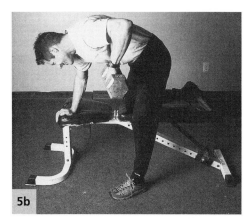

5b

- Hold the contraction for a moment, then slowly lower the weight. Do not let gravity just pull it down. Repeat.

Tips. Don't let your shoulder be pulled all the way to the floor at the bottom of the movement; keep a flat back.

Variations

- Instead of a bench, kneel on a stability ball to improve balance.
- Use a split rope with a cable machine, either sitting or standing.

Precautions. An unsupported rear delt row places significant shear force on the lower back. Instead, rest your chest on a bench or ball and use a pair of dumbbells.

6 Bench Press

Why? This multi-joint exercise directly targets antagonist muscles that are often underdeveloped in climbers. While climbers tend to think it's all about pulling strength, there are actually many pushing and pull-down moves that involve the pecs. A primary exercise in any well-rounded program—don't leave the gym without it.

Muscles. Pectoralis major, anterior deltoid, triceps.

Form

- Sit on a flat bench with the dumbbells on either side of you and your feet planted flat on the floor.
- Pick the weights up and bend your elbows about 90 degrees. As you lean back, push the weights straight up.
- Take a moment to get comfortable. Your arms are straight up, elbows out and slightly bent, thumbs pointed at each other. This is the start/finish position.
- Bending the elbows, slowly lower the weights in an arc until your upper arms are parallel to the floor—no lower!
- With a squeeze of the chest, straighten your arms. Do not lock out your elbows or bang the weights at the top. Repeat.

Tips. Avoid the barbell bench press if you want performance instead of bragging rights. The bar makes the exercise easier since range of motion is limited and fewer stabilizer muscles are needed so you can lift heavier weights than with dumbbells. At the same time, the muscles of the rotator cuff that are used receive greater stress. Most of the machines are sorry imitations of the real thing (better ones follow an arc and allow a squeeze of the chest at the end).

Variations

- Raise the angle of the bench between 45 and 60 degrees to emphasize the upper pectorals and anterior deltoid (incline bench press).
- Lower the angle of the bench about 10 to 30 degrees to emphasize the lower

portion of the pectoralis major (decline bench press).

- Use a stability ball instead of a bench for flat or inclined presses to involve more core muscles.
- Do alternating one-arm presses so that one is raising while the other is lowering to involve the obliques.

Precautions. Start off with lighter weights than macho-ness dictates. Increase the load only when you can fully control the weight. It's bad form to drop the dumbbells—but getting hurt is worse.

7 Push-ups

Why? This multi-joint exercise has nearly all the advantages of the bench press, plus you can mix it up with a variety of props. The only drawback is that it can be some-what more difficult to accurately judge the amount of resistance.

Muscles. Pectoralis major, anterior deltoid, triceps.

Form

- You know what to do. Keep your body straight and go down until your elbows are at a 90-degree angle. The upper arms can be either close to your rib cage (hands shoulder-width apart) or out away from your body (hands about double shoulder width).

Tips. If doing a full set of push-ups is too difficult, you can use your knees instead of your feet for support. Or do push-ups against a chair or table. To increase the challenge, prop your legs up on a chair, low table, or stability ball so that your head ends up downhill at the bottom of the press.

7a

7b

7c

Variations

■ Use an upside down BOSU Trainer with your hands resting on the outer rim to involve more stabilizer muscles.

■ Select an object about 4 to 12 inches (10 to 30 cm) high that can support one hand. Do a push-up with your right hand on the floor and left hand elevated, then switch hands; keep alternating throughout the set.

■ The ultimate push-up exercise is performed with gymnastic rings (or TRX Trainer). Because of their free-moving nature, there is no point that you are truly at rest since you must constantly stabilize your position. Raising or lowering the grips, as well as where you locate your feet, allows a huge continuum of resistance possibilities.

Precautions. As with the other shoulder exercises, do not exceed right angle bends of the shoulders and elbows. All of the gain is achieved in this range and exceeding it merely stresses the joints.

8   Fly

Why? This single-joint motion works the chest to the fullest extent; greater contraction of the pecs is possible than with most other chest exercises. This is a good one to include for protecting the shoulders from injury.

Muscles. Pectoralis major, anterior deltoid.

Form

■ Place a bench in the center of a cable crossover machine so that your shoulders will be aligned with the pulleys.

- Sit on the bench and grab one low handle and then the other.
- Lie back while raising your arms straight overhead.
- Take a moment to get comfortable. Your arms are straight up, elbows out and slightly bent, palms facing each other. This is the start/finish position.
- Keeping your arms straight, slowly lower the weights until your upper arms are parallel to the floor—no lower!
- Contract the chest and bring your arms together. Repeat.

Tips. Be sure to get the last squeeze at the end for full benefit; there is no advantage to your arms crossing past midline. Dumbbell

flies are less effective than cable flies since resistance decreases as your hands come together. The straight-arm fly machines allow you to superset with a reverse fly that works the midtrapezius and posterior deltoid.

Variations

- Substitute a stability ball for the bench to work your core muscles.
- Incline the bench to target the upper pecs.
- Instead of a bench, stand at the crossover machine with a 30-degree bend at the waist and use the high grips; this targets the lower pecs.

Precautions. A potentially dangerous exercise when performed with heavy resistance; stick to lighter weights or bench press instead. Never let your arms reach behind your body. Fly machines that bend your elbow 90 degrees, a "pec deck," may cause elbow and shoulder pain yet are no better for chest development.

9 Dips

Why? A multi-joint exercise that can help on mantle moves. This also balances the major climbing muscles. Dip machines reduce your body weight to allow more reps than might otherwise be possible.

Muscles. Pectoralis major, triceps.

Form

- Set the handles on the narrower width if the machine has that option.
- Stand on the foot bar and lean forward at the waist slightly. Elbows are slightly bent, back straight.
- Lower yourself until your upper arms are parallel to the floor—no lower!

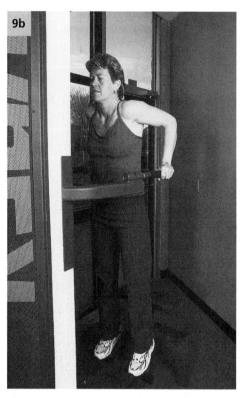

- Contracting your chest, push back to the top. Repeat.

Tips. A vertical body alignment emphasizes the triceps, while leaning forward emphasizes the pecs (but stresses the front of the shoulder joint). Treat dips as a hypertrophy or endurance exercise with sets that are no less than 8 reps. Because these machines often double for assisted pull-ups, this makes a great superset.

Variations

- You can use two parallel chair backs for assisted dips at home or when traveling.

Face them away from each other and just over shoulder-width apart and balance on your toes.

- Dips performed on rings are especially challenging. As with push-ups, vary the height of the grips to change resistance.

Precautions. Dips can be very stressful on the elbows and shoulders—some people just shouldn't do them. Avoid going lower than a right-angle bend of the elbow and do not use heavy loads. Beware of pain on top of the shoulder when you are in the start position.

10 Shoulder Press

Why? This multi-joint exercise is the opposite of just about everything you do while climbing—a good reason to do it.

Muscles. Anterior deltoid, medial deltoid, triceps.

Form

- Sit on a stability ball or bench; knees and hips are bent at a right angle and the spine is erect the entire time.
- Hold a dumbbell in each hand at shoulder level, elbows bent and pointed down, palms facing forward.
- Press the dumbbells upward in a natural arc until your arms are almost straight.
- Lower the weights to the starting position. Repeat.

Tips. Keep the dumbbells in the same plane throughout the motion. For higher resistance, use an incline bench set about 15 degrees back from vertical to target the muscles without stressing the shoulder joints.

Variations

- Called a military press when performed with a barbell; you can lift more but don't get as much benefit (fewer stabilizers are used) and risk rotator cuff problems.
- Many machines attempt to replicate the dumbbell shoulder press. If you try them, look for machines with multiple joints and hand positions.

- When you progress to heavier loads, you can do one arm at a time while using the other hand to help get the dumbbell into the starting position. This one-armed press is well suited to a kettlebell and is great for engaging core muscles.

Precautions. Many machines can create problems with shoulder impingement. Strictly avoid the behind-the-neck barbell press unless you enjoy shoulder problems. If you want to target the posterior deltoid, some of the machines are a safer choice.

11 Internal Shoulder Rotation

Why? Those who have been through shoulder rehabilitation will recognize this as a standard exercise. It's better done before injury as prevention, rather than after you've torn a rotator cuff.

Muscles. Subscapularis.

Form

- Attach a resistance tube to a solid post at elbow height.
- Stand sideways next to the post and put your hand in a loop of the band. Your elbow is next to your side and bent at a right angle.
- Adjust your position so that your forearm is partially rotated toward the post—don't force it—just to one o'clock.
- Without allowing the elbow to move, in a smooth motion, pull your hand across your body as far as it will go.
- Hold the contraction for a moment, then return to the start position. Repeat for a full set, then do the other side.

Tips. Do not rotate your torso. Some people

attempt this exercise while standing with dumbbells; however, the resistance is not optimal for the muscles so it's ineffective. Occasionally perform sets with less resistance and higher reps for greater endurance.

Variations

- The best alignment is with the elbow slightly farther away from your body than the shoulder. Reach across with your other hand and tuck it between the upper arm and chest or use a folded towel.
- Lie on your side and hold a dumbbell in the hand next to the floor, then raise and lower the weight.
- May also be performed on a cable machine with the pulley at waist level. Some gyms have a machine designed for rotator cuff rotations at various angles: use it.

Precautions. You may be sorry if you don't do this one regularly.

12 External Shoulder Rotation

Why? The counterpart to the internal rotator motion to promote shoulder stability; the external rotators are often the weakest muscles in the shoulder. The two exercises aren't "either-or"—they're "both or suffer."

Muscles. Infraspinatus, teres minor.

Form

- Attach a resistance tube to a solid post at elbow height.
- Stand sideways next to the post and put your hand on the opposite side in a loop of the band. Your elbow is next to your side and bent at a right angle.
- Adjust your position so that your forearm is rotated toward the post as far as it will go while keeping your elbow in position.
- Without allowing the elbow to move, pull your hand across your body and smoothly rotate outward as far as it comfortably will go.

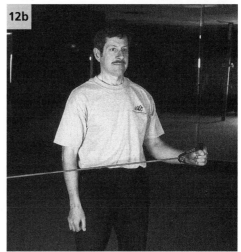

- Hold the contraction for a moment, then return to the start position. Repeat for a full set, then do the other side.

Tips. Keep your body from twisting. Occasionally perform sets with less resistance and higher reps for greater endurance.

Variations

- Lie on your side and hold a dumbbell in the hand opposite the floor, then raise and lower the weight.

- Kneel next to a weight bench so that you are face down and your back is parallel to the floor. Place your upper arm across the bench, straight out from your side, with your elbow bent at a right angle. Start with the forearm hanging straight down and rotate it up to parallel with the floor.

Precautions. Rotator cuff exercises should not be forced beyond a comfortable range of motion.

13   Curl and Press

Why? A multi-joint, multi-planar motion that works nearly all of the muscles in the arms and shoulders. Since climbers tend to underutilize the triceps, this exercise helps provide balance while also promoting shoulder stability.

Muscles. Biceps brachii; brachialis; brachioradialis; triceps long, medial, and lateral heads; anconeus; anterior and medial deltoid.

Form

- Either sit on a stability ball or stand erect with knees slightly flexed.

- Hold a moderate weight dumbbell in each hand with your upper arms at your sides, elbows slightly bent and palms facing outward.

- In one smooth motion, curl your forearms bringing the weights up to shoulder height, then continue to push upwards while rotating the hands so they face forward at the top.

- Then reverse the motion to the starting position. Repeat.

Tips. When the palms are facing up during

the curl, the large biceps brachii does most of the work. When the forearm is neutral and thumbs up (hammer curl), the weaker brachioradialis is emphasized. The brachialis is used equally for all hand positions.

Variations

■ Using kettlebells, even with the same weight, is a bit more challenging due to the change in center of gravity.

■ When lowering during the curl portion, lock off at different angles and hold for a few seconds before continuing the motion.

■ When your arms are overhead, rotate your hands so the palms face together, then lower the weight behind your head, press back up to vertical with your triceps, then go back down to the start of the curl.

■ Use a slightly heavier (about 2 pounds, 1 kg) weight in one hand. Do the exercise, then switch weights on every set. This small imbalance brings more stabilizer muscles into play.

Precautions. Emphasize control of the weight at all times; do not allow it to swing.

14 Wrist Curl

Why? Better than nothing if you can't climb or use a fingerboard. About 15 percent of the population is missing a small wrist flexor muscle (palmaris longus) on one or both arms; sometimes the muscle is there but in the "wrong" location. Flex your wrist with resistance and check for a prominent tendon in the center (another is next to it but closer to the thumb).

Muscles

Wrist flexors.

Form

■ Stand with a barbell in your hands, palms facing out.

■ Allow your fingers to relax and let the bar roll till you can just hold it.

■ Curl your fingers up, raising the bar as far as possible. Repeat.

Tips. Climbing is more fun.

14a

14b

Variations

■ Possible with dumbbells but trickier to coordinate: watch your toes.

■ When rehabbing an elbow, you may use a resistance tube by standing on the opposite end.

Precautions. Do not hyperextend your wrists backward with forearms propped on your thighs or a bench.

15   Reverse Wrist Curl

Why? These muscles are little used when climbing so they are often underdeveloped—the underlying source of many elbow pains. An ounce of prevention. . . .

Muscles. Wrist extensors.

Form

■ Grab a light dumbbell and sit with your forearm resting on your thigh.

■ Your wrist should be straight and unsupported, palm facing downward.

■ Raise your wrist as far as possible, then lower until straight. Repeat.

Tips. May also be performed with your arm extended in front of you, thus overcoming the temptation to use weights that are too heavy. A resistance tube is a good alternative to dumbbells since you can easily adjust the resistance.

Variations

■ Attach a weight to one end of a 4-foot piece of 5 mm cord. Fix the other end of the cord to the center of an 18-inch-long, 1-inch-diameter wooden dowel. Wind the weight up and then down, using your hands to alternate on the dowel.

Precautions. Do not lower your wrist below your forearm; it's an unnecessary strain.

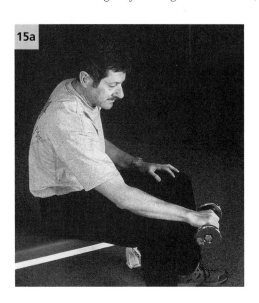

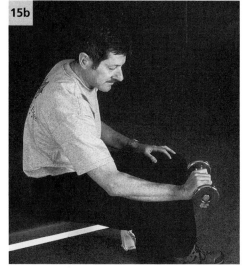

16 Finger Hangs

Why? Short of actual climbing, there is no better training for finger strength than short hangs on a hangboard. Novice climbers should only use large holds and longer hangs—you need to strengthen the ligaments and tendons before working on the forearm muscles (there are no muscles in the fingers). Hangboards are generally a poor choice for endurance training, in part due to boredom; this is best done on a climbing wall.

Muscles. Finger flexors.

Form

- Do hangs at the end of a workout or after a thorough warm-up. Prepare your muscles by hanging with both hands on large- to mid-size edges for about 30 to 60 seconds. Keep your elbows slightly bent and some tension in your shoulders (don't dead hang). Rest for a minute, then repeat.
- Move to your "problem" holds while you are still fresh. Hang for 3 to 8 seconds with an open grip, then rest for 5 seconds. If you can do one-arm hangs, then it's just a matter of moving from hand to hand. Avoid pockets unless you are an advanced climber.
- Perform six of these high-intensity reps, then rest for 2 to 5 minutes until fully recovered.
- Move to larger holds, preferably slopers, or decrease resistance. Hang for 25 to 40 seconds until you fail, then rest for about a minute. Repeat.
- Move to even larger holds or decrease resistance again. Hang for 45 to 60 seconds until you fail, then rest for about a minute. Repeat.

Tips. Place a clock with second hands directly in front of you to time the hangs. Decrease resistance with elastic cord or by using a stool to rest your legs. If you still need to increase resistance after progressing to one-arm hangs, hold a weight in the opposite hand or wear a waist pack. Do not use holds smaller than first joint; they have no training benefit but do stress the knuckles. Many fingerboards are too abrasive; either file down the holds or clog pores with chalk.

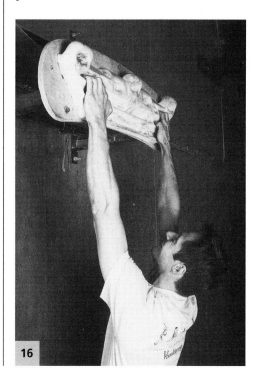

16

Variations

- Many different routines are possible on a fingerboard. You can focus an entire set on one aspect of strength or a particular type of hold.
- All of the basic resistance training principles apply—including knowing when to quit. When working on general strength, add more volume (number of reps, number of sets, or longer hangs). When working on maximum strength, increase resistance (add weight) but don't rush it.

Precautions. Avoid crimps or dead hangs when training! Crimping increases the leverage on joints and places three times more force on the A2 pulley that holds the tendons near the bone than on the fingertips. A dead hang, when the elbow and shoulder are fully relaxed, places nasty strain on the connective tissues—it's a good rest position when climbing, not when training.

BODY CORE EXERCISES

Much has been made of "core training" because all of our major movements are based upon a system of third-class levers with the torso as the fulcrum. Core stability allows maximal efficiency of our limbs—a weak core decreases overall performance.

Among the first muscles to fire at the beginning of any major limb movement are the transversus abodominis and the multifidus. These are inner core muscles (the former runs horizontally across the belly and the latter runs vertically along the spine) that stabilize the spine and are integral to the kinetic chain. These and other deep muscles—including the internal obliques, diaphragm, and pelvic floor muscles—work together to increase internal abdominal pressure to create a bag of air that protects the lower spine from heavy stress.

The superficial core muscles (rectus abdominis, external obliques, spinal erectors) help stabilize the deep muscles as well as aid with twisting and crunching motions. During typical core exercises, it is these outer muscles that get worked the most.

Many people overlook that the core is constantly trained by most of our exercises. Climbing itself is superb core conditioning, as are the major lifts (squats, deadlifts, pull-ups, etc.) and aerobic workouts (running, cycling, rowing, etc.). For many athletes in good health, additional core training is often unnecessary; it won't hurt but may not be the most productive use of time.

The people who need additional core training are primarily those who are very out of shape and starting to train, individuals with low back pain, and advanced athletes who are eking out every bit of performance. The untrained may need to develop their core simply to be able to perform exercises properly. People with chronic back pain frequently need to target their transversus abodominis and multifidus so that is often a goal of physical therapy.

The effectiveness of core training on enhancing sports performance in trained athletes is still a matter of debate and certainly not the slam-dunk that many enthusiasts claim. If a rock climber has trouble holding tension between their hands and feet, working on the posterior core muscles is likely going to help. But that time may also be more productively spent by working on better technique and economy of movement on rock.

If you are going to include core exercises in your training program, it is important to do them correctly. The last thing you want to do is knock yourself out of action with a back injury!

17 Crunch

Why? The abs are central to all outdoor sports. Climbers especially need strong abs on overhanging terrain to pull their feet up to the rock. Of course, there is also something to be said for a nice "6-pack" (actually an 8-pack) when it isn't hidden beneath a layer of fat. The rectus abdominis is a long sheet of muscle (about 54 percent Type II fibers) that contracts together, though some parts can contract harder than the others (hence the mistaken reference to upper and lower abs).

Muscles. Rectus abdominis, internal and external obliques.

Form

- Sit on a stability ball and walk your feet out until you are on your back. Knees should be bent at a right angle, shoulders higher than the hips, and neck straight.
- Place your hands behind your head. It is not necessary to interlock the fingers.
- Slowly pull your rib cage toward your pelvis, raising your torso off the ball, until you feel a strong tension in your abs. There should be no pressure against your head; hands just lightly touch.

17a

17b

- Hold the contraction for a moment (squeeze!), then reverse the motion. Repeat. Feel the burn.

Tips. For any abs exercise, if you can do 15 reps, you need to add resistance—three sets of 8 to 12 reps is best. Neither hundreds of crunches nor working abs every day will do any good.

Variations

- Doing crunches on a bench, the floor, or a larger ball is easier because of smaller range of motion and lesser demand on the obliques.

- To decrease resistance, cross your hands in front of your chest. Rolling farther out on the ball, so there is less support for your upper torso, will increase resistance, but do not allow your shoulders to drop below your hips (excessive spine flexion).
- Crunches performed using gymnastic rings or equivalent are especially effective because it involves total body tension. They can be performed with either your hands or feet in the rings and arms straight, extending your body until straight, then curling up to bring hands and feet closer together. Change resistance by moving toward or away from the plumb line of the rings.
- Crunch machines allow you to easily fine-tune the resistance for a good workout. According to an EMG study, few of the ab gadgets are worth a damn compared to ball crunches, though the wheels with handles are passable.
- Lie on your back, place your arms at your side, and grab the ball by squeezing it between your upper and lower legs. Slowly raise the ball and pull it toward your head (reverse crunch).
- Get into a push-up position with your shins on a stability ball, then roll the ball in by bending at the hips while keeping your back and legs straight. Slowly return to the starting position. Also can be performed using rings.

Precautions. Do not hyperextend your back! Too much flexion can aggravate disks between the vertebrae. Old-fashioned sit-ups performed on the floor are a good way to strain your lower back because your hip flexors pull directly on the spine.

18 Side Bridges

Why? In addition to the front and back, you can train the sides of the body's core to achieve balance.

Muscles. Internal and external obliques, rectus abdominis.

Form

- Lie sideways on the floor supported by your hip and elbow.

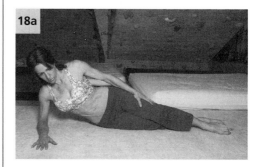

18a

18b

- Contract the obliques to raise your hips upward off the floor until you are straight.
- Hold the contraction for a moment, then reverse the motion. Repeat. After one set, do the other side.

Tips. To increase the challenge, stop the hips just short of the floor when lowering.

Variations

- Instead of raising the hip off the floor, raise both legs.

Precautions. Don't attempt this until your core strength is already developed.

19   Twist Crunch

Why? The obliques come into action on twist-lock moves and when skiing steep lines.

Muscles. External and internal obliques, rectus abdominis, psoas major.

Form

- Sit on a stability ball and walk your feet out until you are on your back. Knees should be bent at a right angle, shoulders higher than the hips, and neck straight.
- Cross your hands in front of your chest.
- Slowly pull your rib cage toward your opposite pelvis, raising your torso off the ball, until you feel a strong tension in your side abs.
- Hold the contraction for a moment, then reverse the motion. Repeat to the opposite side.

Tips. Keep your neck straight throughout the exercise. Don't use momentum to cheat; always maintain control and precision. The diameter and air pressure in the ball will affect the resistance—experiment.

19a

19b

Variations

- Use a flat bench for less resistance or a decline bench to increase resistance.
- Rotary torso machines are effective for these muscle groups but may not be appropriate for those with spinal issues.

Precautions. Be cautious if you have lower back problems.

20 Back Extension

Why? The muscles of the lower back are no less important than your abs for climbing. Without this core strength to unite the upper and lower body, all of your sports—and much of life—will be more difficult.

Muscles. Erector spinae.

Form

- Lie face down across a stability ball with your legs spread wide for balance. There should be a slight forward flex in your back and your neck is neutral.
- Cross your hands behind your back.
- Slowly raise your torso off the ball until you feel a strong tension in your lower back. Your head will only raise a couple of inches.
- Hold the contraction for a moment, then reverse the motion. Repeat.

20a

20b

Tips. To increase resistance, place your hands behind your neck, but do not apply pressure! To decrease resistance, lie on the floor or a bench to limit the range of motion. It may help to brace your feet against a wall for support.

Variations

- Start on your hands and knees. Now raise your right arm and left leg until they are straight. Hold the contraction, then return and repeat with the opposite arm and leg; this is called a quadraplex.
- Lie face down across the ball and, keeping your body and arms straight, use your hands to walk forward until only your feet are supported (cross them to make it even more challenging). Then walk back until your stomach is supported, and repeat.
- The back extension platform (called a Roman chair) is another alternative. Adjust the pad so that the top is just below your hip joint, then hook your heels under the lip on the foot platform. Cross your arms in front of you and hinge forward from the hips, keeping your back straight. Continue until your torso is vertical or you feel a stretch in the hamstrings. Then rise up until you are straight again. Hold a weight plate in your arms to increase resistance.

Precautions. Never go fast. Desist if you feel sharp pain in your back.

21 Hanging Leg Raises

Why? Leg raises train the hip flexors that are constantly used in climbing. Although these cause a burn in the abs from isometric contraction, there is little actual training effect without curling the navel toward your head.

Muscles. Iliopsoas, some rectus femoris.

Form

- Hang from a pull-up bar or gymnastic rings or use the jugs on a hangboard.
- Raise your legs by bending at the hips and knees until the thighs are past parallel to the floor.
- Lower your legs until fully extended. Repeat.

Tips. To increase resistance, hold a weight between your feet. Keeping your legs straight is also supremely challenging. Bring your knees to shoulder height if you want to also target the abs.

Variations

- Add a twist of your torso at the top of the raise to involve the obliques.

Gyms often have a device for leg raises to support your weight on your forearms so that grip strength does not become a limitation. Another option is a pair of slings hanging from a pull-up bar that cradle your upper arms.

Precautions. Do not swing your legs, maintain control at all times.

22 Stiff-leg Deadlift

Why? One of the best exercises of all for the lower back as well as the hamstrings and glutes. Climbers often tax their hamstrings when heel hooking; if they aren't trained, long-term injury can result.

Muscles. Gluteus maximus, hamstrings, erector spinae, adductor magnus.

Form

- Load a barbell (or select a pair of dumbbells) and stand with your feet hip-width apart.
- Keeping your knees slightly bent and your back straight with shoulders pulled back, bend over at the waist and grasp the bar with hands shoulder width apart. Your hips will naturally move back.
- Tighten your abdomen to protect your back and look straight ahead. Stand up by contracting your glutes and hamstrings; keep your back straight.
- Lower back down until you feel a good stretch in the hamstrings. Repeat.

Tips. This is not a straight-legged deadlift; keep the knees slightly bent. Start with light weights and increase resistance only when your form is perfect. Larger plates put the bar into a higher starting position but don't

22a

22b

go heavy until you are ready for the load. Deadlifts can also be performed with dumbbells or kettlebells.

Variations

- Raising your toes an inch or so by using a board or weight plates will increase the stretch of the hamstrings and calves at the bottom of the motion.

- In the classic power lifting deadlift, the knees bend as well as the hips. This takes some of the pressure off the back and puts more onto the thighs, allowing you to lift heavier loads and making it a total body exercise.

Precautions. A preexisting back injury rules deadlifts right out. Improper form with this exercise could cause serious injury. Never round your back when doing deadlifts!

LOWER BODY EXERCISES

Alpine climbers and ski mountaineers know how important leg strength can be. But there is a tendency for rock climbers to completely ignore all lower bodywork. They base this on the misguided fear that

lifting weights will build unnecessary bulk. Yet building power in the legs can help with dynos, better endurance is important on long routes, and the increased flexibility that comes with resistance training is useful on all types of climbs.

23   Squat

Why? The ultimate multi-joint exercise, the squat works many large muscle groups simultaneously and increases joint stability. Useful for all climbers, it is invaluable for alpinists and mountaineers. If time is short, this one exercise can replace all others for the lower body.

Muscles. Gluteus maximus, semimembranosus, semitendinosus, biceps femoris, vastus lateralis, vastus intermedius, vastus medialis, rectus femoris.

Form

- Adjust the power rack by moving the pins so the bar is just below shoulder level and the safety crossbars are just above the knees.

- Load the bar with plates and secure with spring collars.

- Place your hands on the bar several inches wider than your shoulders and tuck your head under to position the bar across the trapezius (above your shoulder blades and below the big spinal bump, C7). The elbows are pointed down, not backward.

- Bend your knees slightly to get directly under the bar and stand up.

- Take a step back and position your feet slightly wider than your shoulders, with your toes straight ahead or angled slightly outward (doesn't matter). Varying foot width can slightly alter muscle activation and knee forces.

- Slowly descend by flexing at the knees first, then the hips and ankles, in a smooth motion. Keep your spine neutral and look straight ahead, watching your form in the mirror. Knees should track directly over the toes and your heels remain flat on the floor.
- When the top of your thighs are parallel to the floor (or as low as possible while maintaining the natural arch in your spine), stand up by reversing the motion and exhaling. Do not pause at the bottom. Repeat.

Tips. Start with an empty bar, or even no bar, until you've mastered the form. Hold your breath just before you reach the bottom and while starting back up, then exhale the rest of the way. Never place a board under the heels; it is safer to increase flexibility naturally. If your gym allows it, squatting barefoot is ideal since your heels are not elevated. A plastic collar that clips to the bar, called a Manta Ray, is superb for reducing pain and keeping the bar in position when lifting heavy. Going deeper than parallel, even with perfect form, probably isn't worth the risk of knee aggravation.

Variations

- Use a kettlebell or single dumbbell held between the legs to work up to barbell squats; this is more functional than two dumbbells and removes some strain from the spine.
- A squat performed with a kettlebell held overhead in one hand requires good stabilization and balance. It's a bit safer than an overhead barbell squat should things get out of control.
- One leg body weight squats can be a good challenge that also promotes balance.

Precautions. Do not use a Smith Machine— we *want* to hit all those stabilizers. Those with a lower-back or posterior cruciate knee injury should be careful to use lighter weights and only go partway down; you may have to avoid squats altogether. The front squat (bar held before you) places more torque on the knees; best to avoid or reduce weight.

24 Leg Press

Why? An easier, though less effective, alternative to barbell squats that removes forces from your spine. With care, the leg press is the safest exercise for heavy resistance.

Muscles. Gluteus maximus, semimembranosus, semitendinosus, biceps femoris,

23a

23b

vastus lateralis, vastus intermedius, vastus medialis, rectus femoris.

Form

- Adjust the angle of the back pad.
- Sit with your back fully in contact with the pad (do not flatten the arch) and your feet hip-width apart, toes angled outward. Rest your head on the pad or tilt slightly forward.
- Push a bit with your legs, release the safety stops, and grab the handles.
- Control the descent of the sled by bending your hips and knees. The base of your spine should remain in contact with the pad and your knees track over your feet.

24a

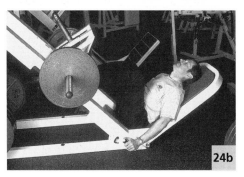

24b

- When your knees are bent at a right angle, hold for a moment, then push the sled uphill. The weight is evenly distributed between toes and heels (feet stay in full contact throughout). Your knees should not wobble or lock out at the top. Repeat.

Tips. Think about pushing with your heels to emphasize the glutes. Vary the width of feet placement and their vertical location on the platform. Some machines allow you to steepen the angle of the backrest to emphasize the quads or decrease the angle for greater hamstring involvement.

Variations

- Many gyms have several leg press machines that offer subtle differences in the movement. Try them all but experiment cautiously with lighter weights.

Precautions. Avoid the hack squat machine or reduce the load significantly; it emphasizes the quads but increases torque on the knee.

25 Static Lunge

Why? A far superior version of the forward (traveling) lunge that is less stressful on the knees, yet equally taxing on the muscles and better for improving balance. Also called a split squat, it's a great strength exercise for all backcountry sports because of the asymmetric position—ideal for telemark skiers.

Muscles. Gluteus maximus, semimembranosus, semitendinosus, biceps femoris, vastus lateralis, vastus intermedius, vastus medialis, rectus femoris.

Form

- Load a barbell and hold it across the shoulders, as in a normal squat, stand upright and take a long stride forward (about twice the distance of a normal step) with one leg. The knees of both legs are slightly bent.
- Position the forward foot with heel and toe in line with your leg and flat on the floor; the rear foot will be on bent toes; feet are about hip-width apart (not aligned) for stability. Center your hips and pelvis. This is the start position.
- Slowly descend until your forward thigh is almost parallel to the floor (adjust foot position if necessary). The rear knee will be a few inches above the floor. Keep most of the weight over the forward leg.
- Hold the contraction momentarily, then return to start position. Repeat. The up-down movement is about a foot.
- After the desired number of reps, explode back to a standing position. Then repeat with the opposite leg forward.

Tips. The front of your knee should not move forward of the toes or to either side. Pay attention that your shoulders and hips remain squared and level; look straight ahead. Raising the rear foot up on a 6- to 18-inch platform can reduce strain in that knee and increase the quad's resistance.

Variations

- Using a dumbbell in each hand is slightly easier since it requires less balance.

25a

25b

- Forward lunges are the same but you return to standing after each knee drop; another version, the farmer's walk, just keeps going forward. Both are more permissive of sloppy technique that stresses the knee. Reverse lunges, where you step back then explode forward to standing, are the best dynamic option.

Precautions. Especially when doing the forward lunge, be leery of sharp knee pains.

26 Kettlebell Swings

Why? This multi-joint ballistic exercise works most of the muscles on the backside of the lower body (posterior chain). The swing is the foundation of many advanced kettlebell exercises. For climbers, it offers the advantage of teaching the body to snap with the hips to power upward.

Muscles. Gluteus maximus, biceps femoris, semitendinosus, semimembranosus.

Form

- Straddle a heavy kettlebell with your feet about shoulder width apart.
- Bend at the hips and knees until you can grasp the handle with both hands.

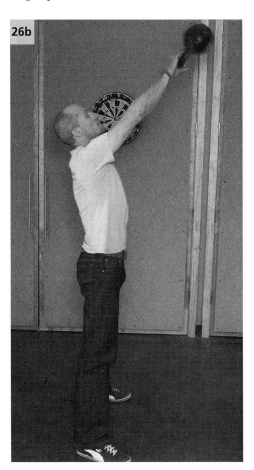

- Take a small step forward so that the kettlebell is behind your heels. Your back should be flat, not rounded, and the hips back over the kettlebell.
- With your arms straight, stand up quickly, allowing the kettlebell to swing naturally upward. When it reaches the top of the arc at around head height, allow the kettlebell to fall back between your legs. Repeat.
- As you develop momentum of the swing by snapping the hips, the kettlebell should reach head level. If it goes much higher, use a heavier weight.

Tips. Do not swing the kettlebell to vertical; this bad form weakens the exercise. Remember that this is a lower body exercise and that your arms are just holding on; all of the drive comes from squeezing the glutes and hamstrings. Breathe out as you swing up and inhale on the descent. Your back should not go past vertical at the top of the swing; if it does try adding more weight. Feet stay flat on the floor at all times.

Variations

- A one-arm swing is not really harder than using two arms if you have the grip strength.

Precautions. This exercise can hurt your lower back if performed incorrectly.

27 Hamstring Curl

Why? Many sport activities tend to build the quads more than the hamstrings. When an imbalance develops, the anterior cruciate ligament (ACL) in the knee is at greater risk of injury. Strengthening the hamstrings can also help prevent muscle strains from heel hooking on overhanging rock or mixed climbs. This movement should supplement, not replace, exercises such as squats, swings, and deadlifts.

Muscles. Biceps femoris, semitendinosus, semimembranosus.

Form

- Adjust the back pad so that the center of your knees line up with the pivot on the machine and position the lower pad to just above the ankles. Set the angle so that your knees are slightly bent.

- Sit in the machine with your spine erect and pressed against the pad. Lower the knee brace and hold the handles lightly.
- Contract your hamstrings until the knees are bent about 90 degrees.
- Hold, then slowly return to the start position. Repeat.

Tips. Don't allow your hips to rise off the pad or your back to arch. Pull your toes back to keep a right-angle bend in your ankle; point your toes straight up. If you have tight hamstrings, use the machine where you lie on your stomach until you solve the real problem. Hamstring curls can strain the knee joint and should not be done with high-loads, low-reps.

Variations

- Use both the variable- (cam) and constant- (pivot) resistance machines to work the muscles at their strong and weak points.
- An alternative is to lay on your back with your arms at your sides, hips and knees at right angles, and your heels propped on a stability ball. Raise your hips off the floor and roll the ball out until your legs are straight, then curl it back in to almost touch your butt. This can also be done with your heels suspended in gymnastic rings or webbing.

Precautions. Don't allow the machine to hyperextend your knees.

28 Hip Abduction

Why? The abductors are on the outside of the thigh and move the leg away from the body; they also help stabilize the hips.

Climbers with weak abductors will often experience cramps when stemming. Weakness in these muscles is also associated with iliotibial band (ITB) syndrome that plagues many runners and cyclists.
Muscles. Gluteus medius and minimus, tensor fasciae latae.

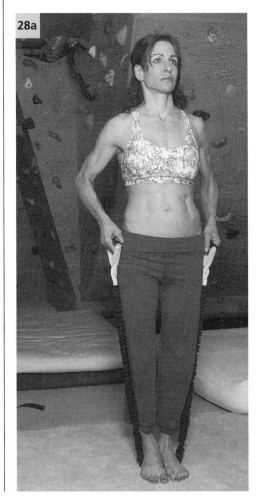

28a

Form

- With arms at your side, hold the ends of a resistance tube in your hands. Stand on the tube with both feet.
- Shift all of your weight onto the left foot. Move your right leg to the side away from the body using the tube to apply resistance to the outside of the foot.
- Bring your foot back in and repeat the motion for a full set, then do the other side.

28b

Tips. Select a resistance tube that will challenge you to do 8 to 10 reps. The low pulley on a cable machine is also great for this exercise.

Variations

- Lay on your side with your feet together, using your arms to keep you in position. Raise the upper leg away from the body, then lower it back down. To increase resistance, wear a pair of shoes, hiking boots, or ski boots.
- The hip abduction machines in a gym often place you in a sitting position and have you spread your legs against resistance. This seated position focuses more on the tensor fasciae latae.

Precautions. Find a level of resistance that is challenging but this is not a high resistance exercise.

29   Calf Raise

Why? Strong calves are essential for all climbers—we spend a lot of time on our toes. If you ever climb at Devils Tower, you're going to wish you'd done more of these. And front-pointing up a long couloir with a pack is like doing calf raises for hours! This exercise also helps protect your knees from injury because the gastrocnemius ties in with the hamstrings.

Muscles. Gastrocnemius, soleus.

Form

- Adjust the height of the shoulder pads so you need to push up slightly to enter the machine.
- Place the balls of your feet on the platform, hip-width apart, with your

toes pointed straight ahead. Your knees should be straight but not locked out throughout the exercise.

■ Start with your heels just below the toes and contract your calves to raise up your heel as high as possible.

■ Hold, then slowly lower down until level.

Tips. As flexibility increases, allow your heels to drop lower. However, do not force a stretch; allow this to come naturally. Varying foot angle has minimal effect on inner and outer sides of the calves and places unnatural stress on the knees. Don't bother.

Variations

■ When your legs are straight, the gastrocs (major calf muscle) do most of the work.

When in a sitting position with your knees bent at a right angle, the soleus muscles take more of the load. Be sure to use both machines.

■ Calf raises can also be performed free-standing with your feet elevated on a stair, block, or any other sturdy object. To increase resistance, you can do them one leg at a time or while holding a weight in one hand and bracing against a wall with the other.

Precautions. The biggest danger is not training your calves enough. Be sure to include stretching in your training program. Excessive calf and Achilles tightness is a common problem in athletes.

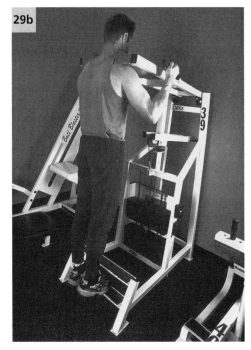

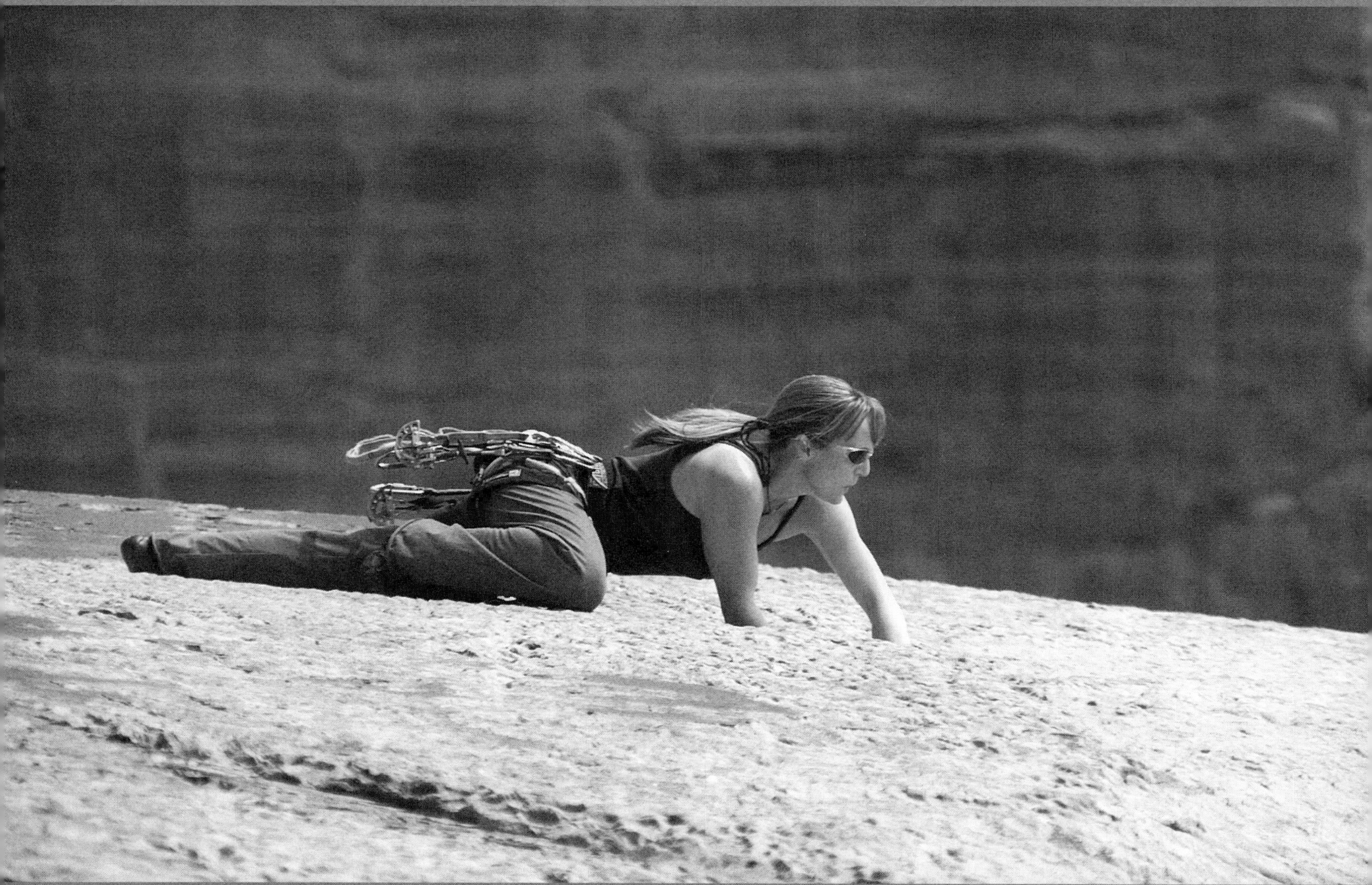

CHAPTER 7

Body Tuning: Joint Mobility, Flexibility, and Balance

Aerobic conditioning and resistance training can make you fitter and stronger. But that is only part of the equation for improving athletic performance. Fine-tuning your body with increased range of motion and superior balance is also important. While flexibility seldom determines climbing prowess outright, a more supple body moves fluidly and may be more resistant to injury. Similarly, great balance has subtle benefits that are revealed in easier movement patterns and fewer falls.

It's easy to find excuses to not stretch, hence many climbers don't bother. Perhaps you've managed just fine for years without stretching as part of your normal routine. But sooner or later, age and injuries start to catch up with you. While many people simply consider stretching as a means to increase flexibility, which does benefit your performance, there is more to it than that.

Foremost among the reasons to make the time: you can play more. Stretching properly after climbing or other strenuous exercise might decrease your chance of injury because the elasticity of muscles is increased; with proper technique, muscle strains can be significantly reduced. If a muscle becomes too tight from training, it can lead to misalignment of the joint or chronic tendon problems.

There are subtle reasons to stretch as well. Prior to launching up a difficult climb, a few minutes of gentle stretching gives you quiet time to clear your mind and prepare for the action ahead. As you concentrate on stretches, you become more kinesthetically aware of your body and learn how to relax muscles at will. And finally, stretching feels good—just ask any cat or dog.

JOINT MOBILITY

Prior to a workout, the goal should be increasing mobility in the joints. Following 5 to 10 minutes of light aerobic warm-up to elevate muscle temperature and blood flow, dynamically moving each joint with rotational movements is the best preparation to climb hard.

Once a popular pre-workout routine with athletes, traditional static stretching where a muscle is lengthened for around 30 seconds has been shown to decrease performance over an hour later. The stretched muscles don't fire as quickly (8 percent slower in one study) or as forcefully (5 to 9 percent less) compared to muscles that are unstretched. Contrary to popular belief, research has also demonstrated that stretching before athletic activities does not prevent or reduce the severity of injuries.

Climbing is a dynamic sport and it is that type of flexibility that we rely upon. Seldom do moves require us to hold in a stretched out static position for very long.

The purpose of dynamic stretching prior to climbing is to prepare both the muscles and joints for the activity ahead.

Once you have broken a light sweat from your warm-up, you can begin taking each joint through its natural range of motion. This is not ballistic stretching, which involves bouncing moves trying to exceed joint range—that only gets you hurt! Instead, these are controlled movements at a moderate to fast speed.

You can start at your neck and work down to the ankles, or vice versa; just find a routine that you will stick with. The key is to take each joint through two or three rotations in both directions (counter- and clockwise) for every angle that it is designed to move. Ideally, you would work all the joints in your body this way. But if time is short, focus on replicating the movements you will use in your workout.

If you would like a guided, systematic program, consider purchasing the Neural Warm Up Level 1 package (about $75) from Z Health. Based upon Zdorovye (an ancient Slavic health system), the DVD and manual offers clear guidance of biomechanically correct motions to both educate your body and prepare you for activity. The 10-minute program is deceptively easy but takes several months to master. The Level 2 package is indeed more challenging and athletic, however, you won't get the full benefits without starting with the basics.

The Hindu squat followed by the Hindu push-up is a combination of exercises that are particularly effective for enhancing joint mobility and warming your body.

Twenty to thirty reps of these are quite invigorating. Both the Hindu squat and the Hindu push-up are rotational callisthenic exercises that integrate breathing.

To perform a Hindu squat, start standing with your hands pulled in toward your chest. Exhaling as you go, squat down all the way while your hands move straight down, fingers almost touching the ground; unlike a barbell squat, your heels will raise off the ground and your thighs are well below parallel. Inhale as you rise and extend your arms straight out in front of you, then repeat. This is a circular motion that is performed in rapid succession.

The Hindu push-up starts with your feet and hands on the ground farther apart than a normal push-up. Your hands are also relatively close to your feet so that your butt is sticking high in the air, rather like the downward dog yoga pose. Keeping your legs straight, lower yourself toward the ground while moving your chest forward. At the bottom of the movement with hips near the ground, straighten your arms so your spine is fully arched. Then rotate back up to the starting position, keeping the arms and legs straight and exhaling as you go.

STRETCHING

The goal of stretching is to lengthen both the muscle and the fascia, which is the fibrous connective tissue that surrounds and permeates muscles. You do not want to stretch ligaments and tendons because that would destabilize the joint and increase the likelihood of injury.

In general, stretching without motion is used to maximize overall flexibility. Although called static stretching, this is more of a slow motion, deliberate movement and it doesn't necessarily mean one muscle at a time. For best athletic performance, a static-active stretch that involves the agonist muscles holding the antagonists is superior to a static-passive stretch that merely targets the antagonist.

Again, the most important rule is to never force a cold muscle; this does more harm than good. The best time to work on flexibility is shortly after a cool-down session. Particularly if you have been working your limits, it is best to spend several minutes doing light-intensity exercise to flush the by-products of metabolism.

Some people like to stretch in the morning as part of their daily routine. However, this can aggravate low back problems if performed during the first hour after waking. When you lie down at night, compressive pressure is removed from the spine, which allows the soft disks between vertebrae to absorb fluid and expand. The swollen disks are at greater risk of injury from flexion until the extra fluid is forced out again.

It is often claimed that stretching after a hard workout can reduce muscle soreness the following day. However, at least ten randomized studies have shown that the benefit is minimal to nonexistent. This post-exercise stretching is meant merely to increase your static flexibility.

Find a peaceful spot, perhaps with relaxing music, and put on some dry clothes so your muscles stay warm. A bouldering crash pad is ideal for stretching, but a closed-cell foam pad or yoga mat works well too.

Though there are several forms of stretching, the most practical involves gentle stretches: slowly sinking into position and holding for 10 to 30 seconds (a passive, static stretch). This allows the muscle to relax without stimulating muscle spindles—length sensors that form a feedback loop telling the muscle to contract. To prevent this stretch reflex, do not bounce or use fast movements. (You'll get the idea if you press firmly below your patella, the kneecap. Nothing will happen. But tap quickly in that spot, and you get the familiar knee-jerk reaction.)

You can stimulate a muscle to relax even further by contracting it tightly for a few seconds, then suddenly releasing and then stretching. The isometric contraction stimulates Golgi tendon organs, which are sensors in the junction of a muscle and tendon that tell the muscle to relax.

This can also work to stretch the opposite (agonist) muscle due to the phenomenon known as reciprocal inhibition. The body is wired so that flexing one muscle causes its antagonist to relax; for example, contracting the biceps enhances a triceps stretch by causing the triceps to relax.

If you have a partner to assist you, PNF (proprioceptive neuro-muscular facilitation) stretching has proven to offer the most rewards in the least amount of time. The techniques generally involve using an outside force, typically somebody else, to stretch the limb a bit farther than normal for 10 seconds, then you contract the muscle while they resist the motion, and then you relax as they stretch you some more for 30 seconds. PNF stretching can be done solo but not without difficulty.

STRETCHING ROUTINE

As with most aspects of conditioning, there is no single stretching routine that is ideal for everyone. The eighteen stretches offered here are a good foundation, but you may not need them all or may wish to modify or substitute some of your own. Depending on your level of flexibility and the types of training you enjoy, some stretches become more important while others take too much time and may not be as productive.

Allow about 20 to 30 minutes for a good routine so you don't feel rushed; two or three sessions per week is ideal. This is also a good time for contemplative mental training, relaxing mind and body. Alternatively, stretch for 10 minutes every day. Most stretches should be performed two or three times, though some problem areas may need more.

The order of the stretches is not particularly important, though you generally start with major muscle groups that were recently used and progress toward smaller muscles. Once you have mastered the basics, blending stretches together into a flowing movement can help integrate the whole body. Start with the side that is tighter, since many people tend to rush the second stretch.

While you are stretching, breathe easily and deeply; identify any tension in your body. As you exhale, relax and sink deeper into the stretch, but stop short of the pain threshold. Never force a stretch beyond what feels natural; trying to impress someone in yoga class is begging for trouble.

Discussions of flexibility generally refer to the hip region. Because the muscles surrounding the hip joints are among the largest in the body, many athletes tend to become tight here. This not only detracts from climbing performance due to a limited range of motion but can also lead to a variety of chronic complaints. A significant portion of your routine should concentrate on stretching the muscles and tendons connected to the hips.

Most upper-body stretches are performed to keep your body limber, not to dramatically increase range of movement. Be careful to avoid overdoing stretches involving the shoulders; you don't want the ligaments and tendons overly loose.

When climbing beyond the vertical, we sometimes contort ourselves into bizarre positions. Just as having a strong torso is essential for all sports, so too is good flexibility in this region. There are numerous possible stretches for the back that may benefit your climbing; a stretching or yoga class is recommended if you need work here. It is very important that you do not apply force to the spine when it is flexed.

STRETCHING AIDS

You can certainly achieve good stretches without any props at all. For many stretches, a stable raised object (chair, railing, etc.) and a towel will suffice. However there are a couple of products that do make it easier to achieve good, deep stretches targeted at specific muscles.

The StretchRite (around $30) is a well-designed strap with six plastic beads on each end that serve as grips, a central footrest, and loops on the ends for harder body positions. The handgrips help you judge progress; for example, you may start off at number four on a particular stretch and work your way down to two. An optional DVD gives a good description of twenty stretches.

The CoreStretch (about $70) does a remarkable job of targeting the muscles of the back, shoulders, hips, and hamstrings. Sure it's a tad pricey but using this device feels wonderful and gets at the back muscles in a way that is difficult to achieve otherwise.

While the CoreStretch elongates your back muscles, the BackMagic (about $30) flexes the spine. The relief you get from lying on this simple device is intoxicating. The arch can be set at three levels and it lies flat for transport

Many runners will already be familiar with the ProStretch (around $30) since this device is sold in most running stores. While you can use a step or a slant board to stretch the calves, the rolling action of the ProStretch allows you to sink into the stretch more effectively.

CoreStretch and StretchRite

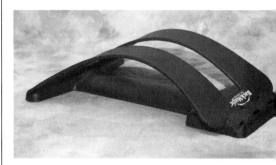

BackMagic

ProStretch

STRETCHES

30 Chest Lift

Why? This stretches the chest (pectorals), front of the shoulders (anterior deltoids), and biceps.

Form

- Interlace your fingers behind your back. Keep your elbows straight and lift your arms upward.
- May also be performed by placing your hands on either side of a doorway at shoulder height and leaning forward.

31 Behind the Back

Why? Gives a good stretch to the triceps, latsissimus dorsi, and front part of the rotator cuff.

Form

- Hold a towel in one hand and let it hang down your back, with the elbow bent at a sharp angle.
- With the other hand, reach behind your waist and grab the towel.
- Pull down gently with the lower hand to stretch the upper triceps; raised arm should be straight up in the air.
- Then pull up on the towel until you feel a stretch in the front part of the opposite shoulder. Repeat on the other side.

- Once you have sufficient flexibility, you can eliminate the towel and interlock your fingers behind your back but don't force this stretch.

32 Crossed Arm

Why? This gets at the muscles between the shoulder blades (teres major and rhomboids) and the rear part of the rotator cuff.
Form
- Either grab your upper arm just above the elbow or place one elbow in the crook of the other.
- Pull the arm across your body until you feel the stretch.

- For successive stretches, vary the angle of the arm (above parallel, parallel, below parallel) to reach different muscles. Repeat with the other arm.

33 Forearm Extension

Why? With all the gripping we do, the forearms get seriously worked. Regularly performing this stretch can prevent tennis elbow (lateral epicondylitis), which is pain on the outside when your palm is facing forward.
Form
- Straighten one arm and bend your wrist downward at a right angle.
- With the other hand, pull gently until you feel the stretch on top of your forearm. Repeat on the other arm.
- May also be performed by pressing the backs of both hands against a firm object.

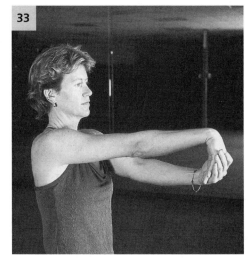

34 Forearm Flexion

Why? When your forearms are about to explode, it's the flexors that are pumped. Stretching them can prevent golfer's elbow (medial epicondylitis), which is pain on the inside when your palm is facing forward. This can also stave off joint deformities (flexion contractures) that are often seen in the middle and ring fingers.

Form

- Straighten your right arm and bend your wrist upward at a right angle.
- Place the fingers of the left hand at a right angle.
- Pull until you feel the stretch on the underside of your forearm. Press gently with your thumb to stretch the first joint of the fingers. Repeat on the other arm.
- May also be performed by pressing both hands into a pad, fingers pointed toward you. Keep the elbows straight.

35 Overhead Reach

Why? Another stretch for the triceps and shoulders that comes from a different angle.

Form

- Stand facing a wall with your feet about two feet away.
- Place your palms overhead flat on the wall (like you're getting frisked).
- Bend from the hips, keeping your arms and spine straight.
- May also be performed one arm at a time to feel the subtleties or while kneeling and using the floor.

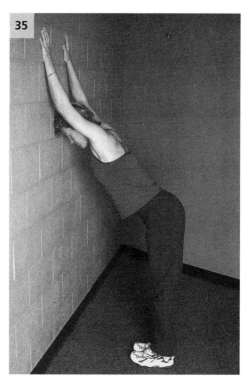

36   Neck Roll

Why? Due to the nature of the sport, climbers (and road cyclists and inline skaters in full tuck) spend a great deal of time with their necks fully craned upward. Stretching these muscles can prevent soreness.

Form

- Start with your arms at your sides, shoulders relaxed and chin pressed firmly to your chest.
- Slowly roll your head in a full, wide circle with your ear almost touching one shoulder, the back of the head trying to touch the back, the other ear reaching for the other shoulder and back to start.
- After several rotations, reverse the direction.

37   Shoulder Rolls

Why? Many of us unconsciously build up tension in our shoulders, whether from stress, work, or play. These rolls feel wonderful.

Form

- Start with your arms at your side, shoulders relaxed and head facing straight forward.
- Slowly flex your shoulders forward as far as they will go, then roll them upward trying to touch your ears, then back squeezing your shoulder blades together, and back to neutral.
- After several forward rotations, reverse the direction.

38 | Spinal Twist

Why? Making yourself into a pretzel helps stretch your side muscles (obliques), lower back (erector spinae), and hip abductors.

Form

- Sit with your legs in front of you, then bend your right leg and place the right foot outside of the left knee.
- Twist your torso to the right, placing the left elbow outside of the right knee and your right hand on the floor behind you.
- Push your elbow against the knee while trying to look far behind you. Repeat on the opposite side.
- Increase the stretch in the hips by bending the left leg so the foot is tucked underneath your right buttock.

39 | Sitting Reach

Why? Both the lower back and the hamstrings get a good stretch.

Form

- Sit with your legs out in front of you, knees slightly bent and pointing outward.
- Slowly bend from the waist and reach forward as far as possible. Exhale to increase the stretch.
- Keeping your legs straighter, but not locked, will increase the hamstring involvement and decrease that of the lower back.

40 | Lying Twist

Why? Provides a good stretch to the lower back as well as the hip abductors.

Form

- Lie flat on your back with arms outstretched.
- Raise one leg so that the hip is at a right angle.
- While keeping your shoulders on the ground, allow the leg to slowly fall across your center line to the opposite side.
- Try to touch the knee to the ground without lifting a shoulder. Repeat on the other side.

41 | Torso Side Bend

Why? A far-reaching stretch that gets at many muscles of the torso. This variation

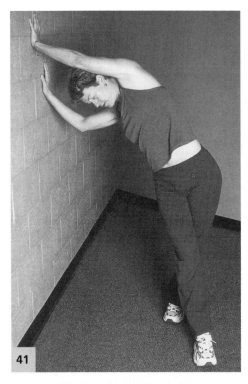

41

42

forward with your right foot, placing it a couple of inches to the left of your left foot so your legs are crossed.

- Raise your arms.
- Slowly bend your torso to the right, keeping your weight on the left leg with the foot flat on the ground and the right knee slightly bent. You should feel a stretch through your entire left side.
- Repeat on the opposite side with the left foot forward.

42   Lying Knee Flex

Why? Stretches the hip extensors (gluteus maximus and hamstrings) and the groin.
Form
- Lie flat on your back with your legs extended.
- Bend one leg until the thigh reaches your chest.
- Use your hands to pull the thigh closer but keep the other leg straight.
- Repeat with the other leg.

43   Forward Kneel

Why? Many people have tight hip flexors (iliopsoas, rectus femoris) thanks in part to a lot of chair time.
Form
- Kneel on one knee but extend it well behind you.
- Keeping your torso erect and spine neutral, press downward with your hips to achieve the stretch.
- Repeat with the other leg.

includes the iliotibial band (ITB), which extends to the knee on the outside of the thigh and often causes knee pain when tight.
Form
- Stand sideways with your right side an arm's length from a wall. Take a step

44 Butterfly

Why? An excellent stretch for the groin that will help you get your hips in closer to the rock. Men are often very tight here.

Form
- Sit on the ground and bring your feet together so the soles are touching. Pull them to within a foot of your body using your hands.
- Keeping your spine neutral, lean forward and sink into the stretch.
- Also may be performed by lying on your back with soles touching and pulling your knees to the ground with your hands.

45 Quad

Why? A long hiking or running descent really hammers the quads, as do many other aspects of fun. These large muscles can contribute to back and knee pains when overly tight.

Form

- Standing on one leg with your spine erect and neutral, grasp the other ankle (not the foot). Use a table or chair for balance.
- Pull your foot toward the butt and point your bent knee straight down (thigh is vertical).
- For maximal stretch, rotate your hips forward slightly.
- Repeat with the other leg.

46   Hamstring

Why? Probably the tightest muscles and tendons in most of us, especially men. Since these are attached to the pelvis, lower back pains can originate here.

Form

- Use a bench that is between knee and hip level to prop up one leg.
- Keeping your spine neutral and your toe pointed upward, bend from the hips to get the stretch.

- To increase the stretch, flatten the back rather than bend more from the waist.
- Repeat with the other leg.
- Also may be performed sitting on the ground by extending one leg forward with toe pointed upward and pulling the other in so the sole is against the knee and then bending forward.

47   Calf

Why? A climber's calves get a serious workout, especially on steep snow and ice. Tight calves are also the cause of many problems for runners. The ProStretch is ideal for getting at these muscles.

Form

- Brace your upper body against a wall and extend the right leg back several feet

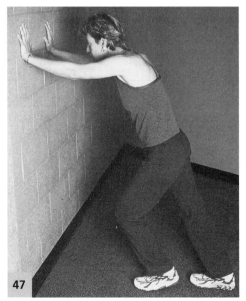

behind you while moderately bending the forward knee.

- Straighten the right leg while pressing your heel to the floor to feel a stretch in the belly of the calf. Minimal weight is on the left leg.
- Bring your right foot forward so it is only a foot or so behind the left foot.
- Bend the right knee slightly and press your heel to the floor for a stretch of the Achilles tendon.
- Repeat with the other leg.

STRETCHING ALTERNATIVES

Many climbers are drawn to, or at least curious about, different methods of stretching and conditioning. Among the beauties of these "alternative" fitness methods is their emphasis on breath control and mind-body awareness—both great things for all athletes.

Although practitioners often deny it, Pilates, yoga, and tai chi are all forms of resistance training programs. As far as your muscles are concerned, it doesn't matter if the load comes from a heavy weight, rubber tube, or body weight. Moving into and out of the positions, as well as holding them, requires contraction of muscles both large and small.

While potentially good workouts, the claims that Pilates and yoga sculpt long, lean muscles instead of the short, bulky ones created by weight lifting are pure hogwash. These sorts of statements may sell women's magazines by the gazillion, but they have

no basis in reality. Our bodies simply do not work that way; see "Resistance Training Myths" in chapter 6 for details.

Even if you are already in great shape, do not underestimate these workouts— they can kick your butt. However, despite claims about cardiovascular gains, none of these are replacements for aerobic training. See appendix C, Suggested Reading, for two excellent books on Pilates and yoga for athletes.

PILATES

This exercise system is among the most effective for targeting core muscles. It also offers many good stretches to enhance flexibility as well as light resistance training.

Developed by Joseph Pilates in the early twentieth century, his "Contrology" methods have been adapted for a broad audience. Many of the exercises rely on costly and exotic contraptions, with names like the Reformer (a spring-loaded sliding table), the Wunda Chair, and the Cadillac (looks like a kinky bondage device).

Pilates mat classes are performed without the expensive equipment but still emphasize the inner musculature. There are thirty-four original exercises that form the basis of a "true" mat class; ideally they are all performed in sequence. Some are more applicable than others to our chosen sports. And open-minded instructors have now adopted many more exercises from other disciplines. If you can find an instructor who is keyed into the needs of climbers, Pilates can be a good adjunct to your other training.

PILATES FOR CLIMBERS	PILATES FOR MOUNTAINEERS
Hundred	Hundred
Roll Up	Roll Up
Rolling Back	One Leg Circle
One Leg Stretch	Rolling Back
Double Leg Stretch	One Leg Stretch
Spine Stretch	Double Leg Stretch
Rockers with Open Legs	Spine Stretch
Saw	Rockers with Open Legs
Double Kick	Saw
Scissors	Swan-Dive
Spine Twist	One Leg Kick
Leg-Pull-Front	Double Kick
Boomerang	Shoulder Bridge
Seal	Spine Twist
Push-Up	Swimming
	Boomerang
	Seal

HATHA YOGA

Yoga certainly has much to offer climbers, though it's important to realize that there are many forms of this five thousand-year-old practice. Hatha (sun moon) yoga, a mere seven hundred years old, is the most popular form of yoga in the West. It has subdivided into many styles, but only a few are likely to help your climbing.

Compared to Pilates, yoga tends to be more spiritual while also emphasizing the mind-body balance. The poses are generally more static (depends on the style) and focus on the entire body rather than primarily the core. Yoga is more about flexibility

and relieving stress while Pilates is more about developing the body.

Some yoga positions can be injurious to joints, so use caution; a few instructors don't know what they're doing (there are no national certification standards) or push their students too hard. The purists interested in enlightenment may be contemptuous of Westernized yoga styles that lack the spiritual aspect, but it's just a matter of taste.

For climbers and other outdoor athletes, several yoga styles are the most physical, so they tend to be a better choice.

Perhaps the most commonly taught

classes involve the slow, balanced moves of Iyengar yoga, which emphasizes alignment and form using a variety of props (blocks and straps) to achieve positions. Ashtanga yoga is a fast-paced style with fluid movements in a specific sequence that require strength and flexibility; it is important to go at your own pace rather than that of those around you. Power yoga is an offshoot of Ashtanga with an emphasis on strength and stamina. Bikram yoga consists of twenty-six poses performed in humidified studios heated to 105°F, which makes it a demanding workout. Vinyasa flow yoga can be either demanding or relaxed, depending on the instructor, with movements controlled by breathing.

TAI CHI CHUAN

This Chinese form of flowing movement and breathing can take an hour to learn and a lifetime to master. Like a dance performed in slow motion, tai chi chuan (Mandarin for "supreme ultimate boxing") is remarkably peaceful and invigorating. You may come away from a good class glowing, without ever breaking a sweat. Tai chi is a contemplative martial art that can benefit climbers by slowing them down in a hectic world; subtle but worth a try.

NIA

Sometimes called Non-Impact Aerobics or Neuromuscular Integrative Action, NIA (pronounced nee-ya) is a combination of dance, martial arts, and healing arts. Specifically, it blends jazz dance, modern dance, and Duncan dance; tai chi, tae kwon do, and aikido; and Feldenkrais, Alexander technique, and yoga.

There are fifty-two basic moves performed to music, and the intensity and planes of movement can be varied to suit the individual. Primarily intended for women, the workout offers a combination of cardiovascular training and flexibility, with a strong dose of spirituality. As with martial arts, NIA instructors earn colored belts starting at white and progressing through blue, brown, black, and finally red.

BALANCE TRAINING

Although many resistance exercises can be combined with balance challenges, this is sub-optimal for both. You can't apply full force to an exercise when off balance. And using free weights can actually make some balance maneuvers easier (think of the tightrope performers who use long poles). For physical therapy, this makes combining exercise and balance ideal when rehabilitating people. But for the uninjured climber, it is better to separate the two activities.

There isn't much mystery to balance training, it just takes practice. The more you do it, the more your body learns how to stay centered and adapt to changes. As with flexibility, the direct benefits of improved balance to your climbing performance are subtle but nonetheless real.

BALANCE TOOLS

There are countless ways to work on balance. Ultimately, they all work, to some extent. But when it comes down to investing your time and money, some options are better than others.

Slacklines

The history of funambulists (tightrope walkers) goes back into ancient times; the thrill of watching someone almost die has always drawn big crowds. Between 1907 and 1974, a steel cable was strung across Eldorado Canyon, a climber's mecca in Colorado, which was walked by Ivy Baldwin eighty-seven times. His feats, and the challenge of that wire, may have inspired the current craze.

Though climbers have been using them for decades, originally walking chains in parking lots during their down times, slack-

lines have grown in popularity in recent years along with the rise of bouldering. And for many of the same reasons: both can be social activities where friends can egg each other on, they are physically and mentally challenging, and they require a minimal outlay of cash.

Slacklines are usually made from 1-inch nylon flat tubular webbing, around 50-feet long, tightly strung between two very solid anchors (stout trees for example). Even with high tension, because of the stretch of the material, the walker ends up sagging the line quite a bit in the middle.

For a 30-foot span, it requires about 400 pounds of tension to get a good walking line that won't sag too much. This can be achieved through primitive pulley systems and knots but it's a huge hassle. It's difficult to achieve sufficient tension with a 3:1 rigging system (the Z-rig many climbers know) and a 9:1 system gets complicated and loses efficiency due to friction. Anything that requires knots will be difficult to take down after it has been loaded.

The best option for stringing a slackline is one of the commercial kits that utilizes a lever-style ratchet. These can achieve a 13:1 ratio with little effort and the ratchet removed once the line is tensioned. While there are more expensive options, the Primo Kit (about $90) from Slackline Express is well suited to most slackers; it's easy to rig, has good quality components, and comes with detailed instructions.

Wobble Boards

Wobble Board

A circular board with a small semisphere attached on the bottom at the center, a wobble board provides three degrees of movement. Larger ones are designed for both feet but you will get better balance training by using a small wobble board under each foot.

The P.A.S.T. Balance System (around $100) takes the concept a bit further by using a rubber column to give a more natural feel. With wobble boards, you start out of balance and try to bring them into balance, but with P.A.S.T., you start in balance and try to maintain position. Merely balancing on the P.A.S.T. boards presents a challenge but you can also pivot on them, rotating your body in a smooth motion. Resistance tubes with handles attach to the boards to integrate some upper bodywork. The boards can also be flipped upside down to use with two comfortable pivoting handles (optional) for doing push-ups and other upper body exercises.

Balance Boards

Many of the flower-child generation will remember the Bongo Board: a wooden plank that rolled across a round log. One of the earliest successful balance products, it faded from the scene in the '80s.

Now a newer version of the rola bola offers a superior workout that is also fun. The Indo Board training package (about $125) consists of a 30-by-18-inch oval board with a traction deck and two end stops on the bottom, a 6½-inch-diameter roller, a 14-inch-diameter inflatable cushion, and an instructional DVD. When the board is used on the roller (deep pile carpet recommended at first), you can work on lateral or fore-aft stability. The feel will immediately be familiar to surfers, snowboarders, and skateboarders.

Replacing the roller with the air cushion makes the board unstable in all directions; decreasing the air makes it easier, increasing the air makes it much more difficult. The air cushion can also be used on its own for leg exercises and sit-ups. This combination gives much of the functionality as a BOSU balance trainer, so there are many training options besides balance.

The Indo Board is a great item to leave in the living room. Instead of just killing time watching television, you can work on balance and strengthening the core while having fun.

Balance Board

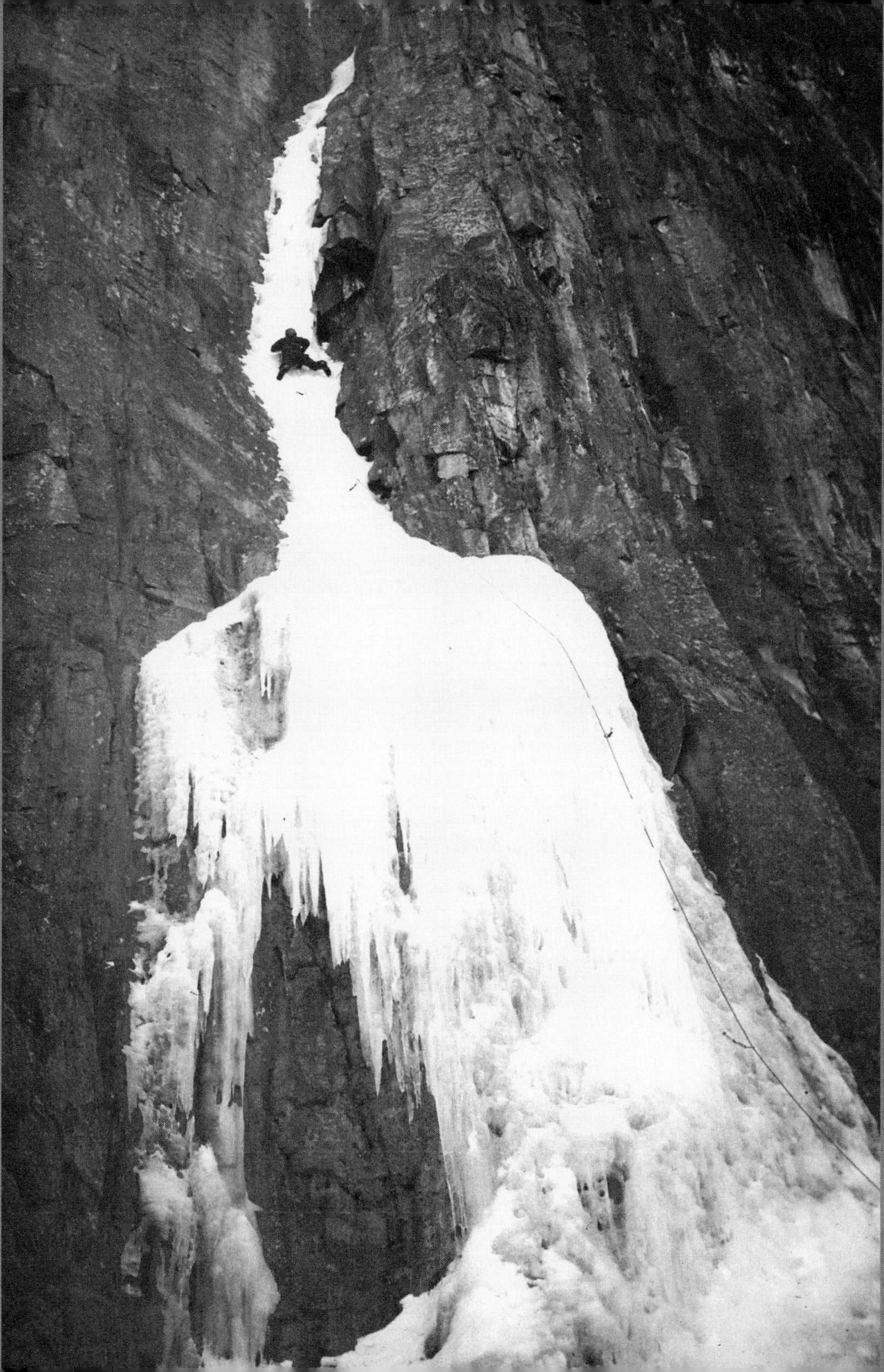

CHAPTER 8

Recovery: Rest and Rehab

Would that it were otherwise, but it is likely that you will get hurt one day. Climbing and all of the other things we do can be hard on the body. A recent survey found that 50 percent of rock climbers had been injured badly enough during the previous twelve months that they had to take at least one day off; chronic overuse injuries were mostly to blame. Much of this book has emphasized training as a means for the prevention, or at least reducing the severity, of injuries. Yet recovery is no less important: ignore it at your own peril.

REST UP

Climbers are notorious for their fanaticism, often climbing day after day with nary a break. When you're in your teens and early twenties, you can get away with this devotion—for a while. But even in the prime of your youth, the body needs time to recover for optimal performance.

Many athletes underestimate the value of rest. Taking time off is not optional! Your body gets stronger only during recovery, not when you are actually training: more, more, more is not better, just dumber. If you don't listen to your body, you will start the downward spiral of overtraining syndrome, which can take months out of your schedule.

A rest day doesn't mean lying on the couch eating popcorn (passive rest), though sometimes that's a good thing. Following a very intense workout, such as a long alpine climb or running a marathon, give yourself two full days off; you deserve it and your body needs it.

After a hard day of climbing pumpy routes, use the next two days for easy endurance climbs and aerobic play (active rest). When you look at the training schedules in chapter 9, you will see that both active and passive rest are built into even the most challenging programs. If you prefer to create your own conditioning program, be sure it deposits adequate rest into your account.

Along with gray hairs, or the lack thereof, there are some other unfortunate truths about aging. It isn't your imagination that it takes longer to recover after a hard workout. If you've stayed in shape, you can still climb as hard as the young punks, but you won't be able to do it several days in a row. Be smart and anticipate the need for additional rest.

MUSCULAR SORENESS

After a hard day's play, it's common to experience muscle soreness from by-products of exercise and edema (swelling of muscle tissue by fluid borrowed from blood plasma). Normally, if you cool down and refuel properly, this goes away within a couple of hours of stopping. Recall, however, that it takes about 20 hours to replenish muscle glycogen stores after a demanding workout.

So even when soreness abates, you may not be fully recovered.

If your pleasure included a lot of eccentric motion, such as descending a steep trail or lowering yourself down on holds, then you are likely to feel it over the next couple of days. This delayed onset muscular soreness (DOMS) results from edema and actual damage to the muscle fiber.

While DOMS is uncomfortable, it isn't necessarily bad (assuming it goes away) and may actually be required for maximum strength gains. However, the affected muscles cannot generate as much force until recovered and do not replenish glycogen reserves during the repair process.

When you experience DOMS, it is best to avoid "working through the pain," though sometimes that is unavoidable. Despite many claims, there is no proven supplement or treatment that has been shown to speed the recovery from this nuisance. Medications such as ibuprofen can alleviate some pain but may cause problems if taken in advance and even delay healing, though debate continues.

The best course of action is to limit yourself to light muscular activity until the symptoms subside—that active rest again. And try to figure out what caused your DOMS so you can start conditioning that motion to prevent future occurrences.

Although "conventional wisdom" and supplement companies maintain that cramps are caused by dehydration and electrolyte loss, there is no scientific basis for this theory. In fact, studies of marathoners and triathletes suggest that those who experienced cramps may actually be slightly over-hydrated and had higher magnesium concentrations. Likewise, lactic acid buildup in muscles does not cause cramps.

Cramps are a severe, involuntary contraction of a muscle that is caused by localized fatigue. While quite painful at times, cramps are relieved by stretching the affected muscle. It may hurt worse for a few seconds, but stretching the muscle will cause it to relax.

The best way to prevent cramps is to regularly stretch the muscles that are prone to cramping. This stretching reduces tension in the muscle that can result in over-stimulation of the nerves that stimulate the contraction (alpha motor neurons). The other preventative step is not to greatly exceed your training base; going from "zero to hero" will result in fatigue that can lock you up tight.

SLEEP TIGHT

Because it's so natural, many of us take sleep for granted, which can be a mistake. Sleep is an essential nutrient; without sufficient quantity and quality, performance suffers. While you already know this from the extreme—most everyone is familiar with the bleary-eyed feeling of too little sleep—minor disturbance has subtle effects on mental and physical performance.

While 7 to 8 hours is the standard prescription for adults, we each have different requirements and, yes, there really are early birds and night owls. Don't fight your own nature; give your body what it needs.

Another benefit of increased fitness is a higher resting metabolic rate that improves your quality of sleep, which is as important as quantity.

You should avoid eating a large meal less than 4 hours before bedtime since the digestion process revs up your engine. Also try to eliminate those late-night snacks; while they won't make you fatter (unless you exceed your calorie balance), the sugar buzz doesn't help you sleep. Since it takes stimulants (caffeine, nicotine) and alcohol (both a depressant and stimulant) about 4 to 6 hours to clear your system, be kind to yourself and hold back. And because increased body temperature lowers sleep quality, avoid engaging in a strenuous workout (other than sex) less than 4 hours prior to bed.

Although the mattress infomercials are hokey, they do have a point: you spend about a third of your life in bed, so it behooves you to make it a good one. Shop around for a quality mattress and pillows that suit you and your significant other. It's worth the time and money to make your bedroom a cool (around 65°F), dark, quiet place with good air exchange. All of these factors contribute to better, more restful sleep.

When possible, go to bed and wake up the same time every day, even on weekends. This regularity prevents "blue Monday" because it takes 24 hours to reset your body clock after sleeping late one hour. If you're dragging a little during the day, a 10- to 30-minute nap can be blissfully restorative. However, don't nap after 3:00 PM, because it may interfere with that night's sleep.

JET LAG

Traveling across multiple time zones messes with your body clock; going from west to east is particularly rough because daylight hours are reduced. Traveling north or south has little effect since the external cues about time remain the same.

In general, it takes a full day to adapt for each 2 hours of time difference. If the time difference at your destination is greater than 12 hours, then subtract that number from 24 (e.g., an 18-hour time difference means 6 hours of jet lag).

If you are about to make a long flight, you can get a head start on jet lag by slowly adjusting your sleep period at home. A specific four-day eating plan, with alternating fasting and feasting, developed by the Argonne National Laboratory showed in one study to significantly reduce jet lag. For many of us, however, the days leading up to a big trip are too hectic to start messing around with our schedule and diet.

During the flight, especially ones heading east, try to rest up. Bring an inflatable pillow, sleep mask, and earplugs or noise-cancelling headphones and request a blanket if one isn't provided. Stay hydrated (avoid too much alcohol) and keep moving your legs to prevent blood clots; take a walk.

Upon arrival, get used to the new time zone quickly; make sure your hotel room has a window and do not take a nap. Avoid heavy exercise until your resting heart rate returns to normal.

Controversy continues about whether the hormone melatonin may help reset your body clock faster, but it has a number of contraindications and potential side effects (available over the counter in the United States and Canada, it requires a prescription in many countries). If you decide to try melatonin, a standard course is 1 mg before bedtime for the first couple of nights. Avoid higher dosages or complications may arise.

No-Jet-Lag, a homeopathic product, is even more suspect than melatonin. There are no reliable studies showing that it is anything more than an expensive sugar pill.

COLDS AND FLU

It's always hard to know when it's safe to play again after suffering through a cold or the flu. First you need to decide which virus you have. If you have a slow onset of sore throat, runny nose, and congestion—but no fever—then it's likely a cold. With the flu, you tend to suddenly get a fever, chills, and body aches but your sinuses and lungs are okay. Neither illness is associated with stomach problems; if you are vomiting or have diarrhea, it's probably something else.

Although there is no cure new prescription drugs can shorten the length of the flu if taken soon after the bug bites. Over-the-counter medications can relieve flu and cold symptoms, but nothing has been shown to cure the problem; antibiotics have no effect.

The pendulum continues to swing on whether echinacea has any effect on preventing or shortening colds or flus. Some of the more recent research indicates that echinacea is no better than a placebo. But a meta-analysis of fourteen studies concluded that the herb can reduce the odds of catching a cold by 58 percent and, if you get it, shorten the duration by 1.4 days. Though echinacea is often combined with goldenseal, so far no human studies have verified the efficacy of the latter. Most everyone agrees that taking echinacea supplements does no harm . . . and who cares if it's the drug or the placebo that works, as long as you feel better faster.

Zinc lozenges have been shown in several studies to help shorten the duration of a cold, but not the flu, by two to three days. However, a popular zinc gluconate nasal spray is associated with permanent loss of smell and/or taste in a significant number of people—a harsh trade-off for fast relief.

Once you start coming down with a cold or flu, you are contagious for up to four days. Do not go to a gym during this time! You can spread the virus to others who use the same climbing holds or equipment. With the flu, don't try to work out until the fever is completely gone; that will just make the bug linger. Even though you're antsy to get back on the rock, you're better off giving yourself some extra time to recover.

MASSAGE

The harder you train, the more you will benefit from a good massage. Aside from feeling wonderful and reducing stress, bodywork can break up adhesions that occur when muscle fibers bind to each other. Sometimes called trigger points, these spots prevent full muscle function and don't usually go away on their own. Following a very hard workout, a light massage can help flush metabolism by-products from your muscles to speed recovery.

Massage therapists are usually schooled in several types of body work (certifications take 700 to 1,000 hours), but climbers will probably get the best results from either Swedish or sport massage (a blend of Swedish and Shiatsu). This is much deeper than post-workout massage; they should take you just to the edge of pain tolerance.

While massage isn't cheap (upwards of $50 per hour is common), your body should feel noticeably more fluid and relaxed. Once you find a good therapist, it's best to stick with him or her as they will learn your body and concentrate on areas that ail you; more bang for your buck.

Another expensive form of massage that may improve climbing performance is called Rolfing. This specifically targets muscle fascia, the sheath that covers each muscle like plastic wrap, and involves very deep, sometimes painful, bodywork. A complete course of Rolfing consists of ten sessions and often results in improved posture and sometimes unexpected emotional release. Not for everyone but worth considering if your body is really out of whack.

It's also possible to perform self-massage that can be quite effective. This may simply involve rubbing sore muscles, both laterally and longitudinally, and flexing joints. But to get the best results, you may want to use some massage tools to apply extra pressure and reach awkward spots.

MASSAGE TOOLS

Whether working on yourself or a partner, there are a number of tools that help do a better job. Because these can apply significant force onto soft tissue, it is important to read the instructions and view the videos to prevent causing injury.

A convenient system for self-massage is the Trigger Point Total Body Package (about $130), which is a set of rollers and tools (plus an instructional DVD) that allow you to work on tense muscles by yourself. These allow you to place the right amount of pressure where it is needed to release trigger points.

Performing self-massage on your back, neck, and shoulders is problematic at best. The Thera Cane (about $40) is a fiberglass J-shaped rod with handles and knobs for applying deep pressure at those awkward locations; it is easy to use and effective.

No matter if you believe the Chinese "three lines of energy" explanations, there is no denying that the MA Roller (about $35) delivers an incredible back massage. Moving across and sinking into this hardwood roller delivers pressure along the spine and the back muscles in a hurts-so-good manner.

Since your thumbs get tired after a while, massage on yourself or on somebody else is easier to perform for extended periods with some tools. An Omni Massage Roller (about $16) is a 2-inch, free-rolling ball in a handgrip that is great for deep tissue massage. The Knuckle-Baller Sports Massager (a little over $20) features four smaller rolling balls and a comfortable handle to allow you to apply as much pressure as desired;

it works well on skin or over clothing. The Foot Fantasy (also around $16) has a single ball on one end and a handle that is ribbed for your pleasure—it feels great after a few hours in rock shoes.

Among the biggest complaints of rock climbers are elbow problems. If you are plagued by epicondylitis or carpal tunnel syndrome, the Armaid (around $100) can be a good investment. This device is designed to administer self-massage for the entire forearm. With a high degree of precision,

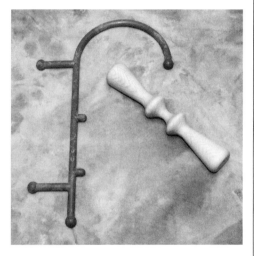

Massage cane

Armaid

you can control the amount and location of pressure to really work at problem areas.

Working on the big muscles of the lower body is easily accomplished with a simple foam roller (under $20). The typical size is 6 inches in diameter and about 3 feet long. By lying on the foam and rolling across the muscle, you can achieve a good massage to release knots.

When you really want to relieve tired muscles, short of paying for a professional massage, it's hard to beat a quality electric massager. The Thumper Mini Pro2 Massager (at around $200) is a 40-watt hand-held machine that weighs 3 pounds and sends deep percussive waves through your muscles. It has three speeds and can thump at 20, 30, or 40 pulses per second. Unlike the cheap vibrators that are more annoying than relaxing, this unit provides a serious tapotement stroke for the muscles.

So far, there is no convincing evidence that massage therapy using magnets has any real benefits.

REHABILITATION

Now ya gone'n done it—messed up and hurt yo'self. Quit your moping and be proactive about healing. With an appropriate amount of self-love, you can get back on the rock sooner and reduce the chance of reinjury. On the other hand, not paying attention to your bodily needs will result in far more downtime.

Obviously, anytime pain is severe or a broken bone is suspected, you need to see a doctor as soon as possible; the longer you wait, the worse the potential outcome. Less painful injuries involving joints should also be examined since there is a greater risk of unpleasant complications. Note that a ligament can completely rupture with minimal pain (the joint will feel unstable); these will never heal on their own; surgery is required.

If the ache is tolerable, you may be able to heal thyself. When the onset of pain is sudden, either from accident or overload, you are dealing with macrotrauma, and there is typically significant tissue damage. Acute injuries to muscles and skin, if not too severe, will heal relatively fast, while ligaments and tendons require much longer because they have less blood circulation.

The more insidious problems involve pain that may not be felt until after you stop climbing and then continues for several hours, recurring in the same place; this is an early harbinger of an overuse injury (microtrauma). As the damage intensifies, the pain will start earlier and last longer. These nasties can begin as minute tears of the tendon structure (muscle origin or insertion, musculotendinous junction, or the tendon itself) and be complicated by inflammation of the tendon (tendinitis) or the sheath surrounding it (tenosynovitis). Stress fractures

of bone are another form of microtrauma; while rare in climbers, they are fairly common in road runners and gymnasts.

Beware that it's easy to keep aggravating an overuse injury before it fully heals, thus setting yourself up for very long layoffs (more than a year in some cases). Many troublesome injuries once diagnosed as tendinitis (fairly rare) now appear to be cases of tendinosis in which the collagen structure has degenerated (common). This is bad news because of the longer recovery time and possible reinjury. Tendinitis can heal in several days to two weeks, with a low reinjury rate, but tendinosis can take six to ten weeks to heal, with a 20 percent chance of chronic problems. Another possible cause of problems is neuropathy in which the nerves are damaged; consult a physical therapist for stretches that may help.

REPAIR SCHEDULE

All soft-tissue injuries follow the same course of events, though the time period varies depending upon severity and circulation. At first, the area around the site becomes swollen as blood and fluid leak into tissues. This inflammation combined with increased pain serves to limit movement

HOMEMADE COLD PACK

As a cold pack, crushed ice inside a resealable plastic bag and wrapped in a towel will work in a pinch, as will a bag of frozen vegetables (peas or corn). But you can make a better cold pack by mixing 1½ cups (375 ml) of water with half a cup (125 ml) of rubbing alcohol in a plastic bag. Store this in a freezer; it makes a slush that molds easily.

for two or three days. The current thinking among some health professionals holds that some inflammation is a vital part of healing and reducing the swelling too quickly can actually slow the process.

Then the repair phase begins, during which new capillaries grow and collagen fibers are randomly laid down to form a matrix. By the end of this stage, pain will have mostly subsided, but the scar tissue is relatively weak. The most dangerous and frustrating period for climbers is the remodeling phase, when the collagen aligns in the direction of loading and thickens for greater strength. During this phase, you can work on increasing range of motion. However, do not attempt to stretch a damaged tendon until it is fully healed.

Once the swelling is gone and range of motion is almost back to normal, you can cautiously start working out again. Begin with a volume only one-tenth of where you were prior to injury (seriously!). Then every other workout you can increase your efforts by 10 percent. After the workout, make certain that any pain when at rest is no worse than before; if it is, stop exercising. Allow a full month to get back to where you were.

Heed these words: starting back too soon and too hard is the biggest mistake an athlete can make! You can turn an inconvenient acute injury into a debilitating chronic injury that will ultimately reduce how much you climb. Trying to strengthen a muscle while it is still healing will just keep pulling the injury apart. Use cross-play to preserve your sanity; resistance and aerobic training for limbs that are unaffected will speed recovery.

MINOR TREATMENT

The standard treatment for soft-tissue injuries, even those that require a visit to the doctor, has traditionally been RICE—rest, ice, compression, and elevation. This is still the best option for injured muscles to prevent a potentially serious condition called Compartment Syndrome. If inflammation within a muscle becomes severe, it can reduce circulation to the point that permanent damage can occur.

However, if carried out for too long, the RICE protocol can actually slow healing of injured joints and even lead to chronic problems. As soon as possible, once severe pain and swelling has subsided and the area no longer feels hot, you should shift to MICE—movement, ice, circulation, and elevation.

The post-injury movement should consist of very gentle, non-ballistic stretching of the affected joint. This is followed by about 10 minutes of icing to really numb the area. And then very light resistance isolation exercises to work blood through the affected muscles; this helps remove waste and bring nutrition into the injury. Do this MICE procedure a couple of times a day, with a few hours between sessions.

Cooling the injury will contract blood vessels, thus significantly reducing bleeding and swelling; blood is toxic outside the circulatory system and edema can hold the damaged tissues apart. The sooner you soak in a creek or apply a cold pack, the better.

Whichever method you use, the objective

is to thoroughly numb the area: 15 minutes on, 15 off, as often as possible during the first 2 hours following injury. Then for the next 24 to 36 hours, you can go with 20 minutes of ice with an hour off. Tempting though it may be, do not soak in a hot tub after trauma.

Compressing the injury with an elastic bandage will also help minimize swelling. However, this can be tricky; start wrapping well above the injury and continue well below it. The pressure should be firm but not so tight that it impedes circulation (several attempts may be necessary to get it right). By elevating the limb higher than your trunk, gravity will assist the draining of fluids; standing around on a sprained ankle is a bad idea.

If you're no stranger to injury, commercial thermal packs are more comfortable and are easier to secure than homemade cold packs. ActiveWraps are the best choice for treating joint trauma because they provide compression in addition to heat or cold therapy. There is an ActiveWrap available for the wrist, elbow, shoulder, back, knee, and ankle (from $25 to $50 each) that provides a snug, comfortable fit. These include unique gel packs that can be frozen or heated in a microwave and will not squish away from boney areas. With a couple of packs, you can alternate hot and cold treatments once swelling is gone for faster healing.

After two or three days of MICE, if the pain and swelling are mostly gone, you should apply heat either with a hot water bottle, thermal pack, or electric heat pad; despite the ad hype, warming creams do not penetrate deep enough to be effective. At this point in healing, the heat is soothing and will help disperse swelling and speed healing by increasing circulation. However, if the injury has not improved after a few days, see a doctor since you may have done more damage than you thought.

Since climbers are no strangers to muscle strains, especially in the back, it is wise to have a good heating pad around the house. The Thermophore Hot Pack (around $75 for the standard 14- by 27-inch size) is the best for producing intense, moist heat that quickly penetrates sore spots. The pad runs about 25°F hotter than most others and has a digital switch that controls the 20-minute therapeutic cycle. Because it literally draws moisture from the air (an optional stupe cover may be needed in very dry climates), the Thermophore is used directly against the skin.

Once you are back to nearly a full range of motion, you can slowly and carefully increase resistance training. This is when a gym is especially valuable because you have a wide variety of workout options that allow small increments of progress. (Many gyms also have trainers who specialize in rehab.)

When dealing with tendon injuries, either acute or from overuse, emphasize eccentric exercises; perform the motion slowly and gradually increase speed, only increasing the load after you can do the move quickly. There is some evidence that supplementing with vitamin E can speed up the regeneration of collagen by increasing the activity of fibroblasts, cells that build the structural framework of connective tissues. Also, there may be some benefit to supplementing with the amino acid arginine, which the body uses to produce nitric oxide that is used for tendon healing.

It bears repeating: don't push yourself too hard! At first, pain will be your guide. But after a while, when you are in the remodeling stage, you need to be smart. Resistance training gives you a clear indicator that it's safe to climb hard again when the injured area is back to full strength (compared to the other limb or prior performance). Unfortunately, climbing itself doesn't offer this precise feedback so the tendency is to start too soon—and get hurt all over again.

PAIN AIDS

Non-steroidal anti-inflammatory drugs (NSAIDs) are among the most commonly used over-the-counter pain medications. The other extremely popular pain and fever reducer is acetaminophen.

Everyone is different, so none of these medications is clearly superior to the others; you'll need to experiment to find what's best for you. If your goal is to reduce swelling after a soft tissue injury, you need to build up the anti-inflammatories in the bloodstream. Therefore do not skip a dose when it's due; intermittent usage is significantly less effective.

NSAIDs work by suppressing the production of prostaglandins (lipid compounds created from fatty acids) after cells have been traumatized. They do this by inhibiting an enzyme, COX-2, that is needed for prostaglandin production.

Unfortunately, NSAIDs also inhibit COX-1, which is found in the stomach lining, and can cause gastric problems with frequent use.

Newer prescription drugs only inhibit COX-2 so they are recommended for daily users. (At this writing, Vioxx has been recalled, while Celebrex is still on the market.) For sports injuries lasting a few days, COX-2 inhibitors offer no advantage and should be avoided.

Allergic or adverse reactions (such as ulcers, exacerbated bleeding, ringing in the ears, liver and kidney malfunction) are possible with any NSAID, so use these only when necessary and in the proper dosage. For most people, there's no reason not to buy generic; however, some may be sensitive to the binders found in cheaper pills. Children should avoid aspirin and naproxen sodium. Sorry, even though you may wish to drown your misery, you really should limit booze intake to no more than two drinks per day while on any of these medications.

Aspirin has been a popular pain, fever, and anti-inflammation medication for over a century; it also appears to offer heart protection. Once derived from willow bark, which has been used for at least 2,500 years, the synthetic form is more effective and less expensive. Sometimes referred to as ASA, for acetylsalicylic acid, it is still the standard against which others are judged. Unfortunately, many people cannot tolerate aspirin. Do not take aspirin if you are on other NSAIDs or Diamox.

Analgesic creams containing 10 percent trolamine salicylate have been shown to delay the onset of muscle soreness, reduce the severity of pain, and speed the demise of pain without the stomach irritation of aspirin taken orally. Unlike warming creams, these have direct action on the injury site.

OVER-THE-COUNTER PAIN RELIEVERS

Aspirin

Brands include: Bayer, Ecotrin, and St. Joseph.

Effects: Analgesic, antipyretic, anti-inflammatory, and an anticoagulant.

Common uses: Headaches, toothaches, arthritis, aches and pains from colds or flu, menstrual cramps.

Advantages: Lowest cost.

Cautions: Do not take with other anti-coagulants (bromelain, garlic, gingko biloba, etc.), Diamox, or other NSAIDs. Not recommended for children because of the risk of deadly Reye's syndrome.

Ibuprofen

Brands include: Advil and Motrin.

Effects: Analgesic, antipyretic, mild anti-inflammatory, and anticoagulant. The anticoagulant effect is less than that of aspirin.

Common uses: Headaches, muscular aches, back pain, arthritis, aches and pains from colds or flu, menstrual cramps, temporarily reducing fever.

Advantages: Can purchase to your need (e.g., Motrin for children).

Cautions: Do not take prior to endurance events.

Naproxen Sodium

Brands include: Aleve and Midol Extended Relief.

Effects: Analgesic, antipyretic, anti-inflammatory, and mild anticoagulant effect. The anti-inflammatory effect is greater than that of ibuprofen.

Common uses: Headaches, muscular aches, back pain, arthritis, aches and pains from colds or flu, menstrual cramps, temporarily reducing fever.

Advantages: Superior for minor inflammation. Longer lasting than ibuprofen and aspirin, so fewer doses are needed.

Cautions: Do not take prior to endurance events. Not recommended for children under twelve.

Acetaminophen

Brands include: Tylenol and Aspirin Free Anacin.

Effects: Antipyretic and analgesic effect. Acetaminophen is not an NSAID so it does not have an anti-inflammatory effect.

Common uses: Reducing fever, minor aches and pains, menstrual cramps.

Advantages: Great for reducing fever. Safe for children. Does not have anticoagulant effects. Frequently combined with aspirin (Excedrin and others) and cold medications.

Cautions: Do not take high dosages or combine with alcohol.

Ibuprofen is an effective alternative to aspirin, with fewer side effects. Nicknamed vitamin I, this drug has become widely overused in our society. Do not take ibuprofen with aspirin since they interfere with each other. Marathon runners and other endurance fiends who take ibuprofen before a race or activity run the risk of severe kidney problems or even death from the extra stress caused by dehydration (acetaminophen is safer).

Naproxen sodium is also effective for reducing inflammation as well as pain and fever. This lasts longer in the body than other NSAIDS, so it requires fewer dosages throughout the day.

Acetaminophen (known as paracetamol in the UK) is an analgesic (painkiller) but does nothing to reduce swelling, no matter the dosage, so it is not an NSAID. Use it for headaches, back pain, or fever if the other options bug your stomach; used properly, there are few side effects. But do not exceed the recommended dose or drink alcohol: severe liver damage is possible.

ALTERNATIVE MEDICINE

If your injury hasn't responded well to standard treatment, and surgery has been ruled out, alternative medicine or faith healing—much the same in some cases—may be acceptable choices. Promoters of alternative medicine seldom support their claims with hard evidence. Just because it's "natural" or a thousand years old doesn't mean it's safe or even works.

There are certainly good aspects to alternative practices, and traditional medicine doesn't have all the answers. Some procedures used in acupuncture and chiropractics have been scientifically proven effective for treatment of specific ailments.

In a study of 1,100 patients with back pain, 47 percent of those who received acupuncture got relief compared to 27 percent who received conventional treatment (physical therapy, massage, etc.). However, in the same study, 44 percent of the patients in the placebo group (sham acupuncture with only partial insertion of the needles) said their pain was relieved.

Another new healing technique uses low-level lasers to focus energy on specific points to stimulate the cells. Because there is no heating of the tissue, this is sometimes called cold laser therapy. Due to the precise nature of the beam, this treatment is somewhat like acupuncture, but the goal is to help the body heal itself. However, there are many unsubstantiated claims (weight loss, smoking cessation, etc.) and a wide range of technologies. Some of the machines are little more than glorified flashlights, while the high-end models generate up to 500 milliwatts (surgical lasers generate 3,000 to 10,000 milliwatts).

Unfortunately, alternative practitioners are often big on show and light on credibility; the tests some chiropractors use to diagnose maladies belong in a grade school science fair. Don't rely solely on the diagnosis of a chiropractor for a serious problem; go to a medical doctor too. Avoid chiropractors who try to sell routine manipulations or treat anything beyond neuromusculoskeletal problems of mechanical origin. Ideally, they should do all manipulations by hand and be a member of the National Association for Chiropractic Medicine, the only chiropractic organization grounded in science.

While the advocates may seem sincere and will be quick to deny it, many of the "cures" are likely related to the placebo effect and the patients giving their bodies much-needed rest. The best prescription for many maladies is TOT (tincture of time). Little to no credible evidence supports homeopathy, crystal healing, magnet therapy, healing hands, aromatherapy, applied kinesiology, energy balancing, hair analysis, iridology, phrenology, or reflexology.

If you have the disposable income, alternative medicine in most cases will do no harm and might help if standard medicine has been ineffective. However, serious problems can arise if a patient delays seeking an M.D.'s opinion at the onset of an injury or illness. Even more foolish is the patient who combines standard and alternative medicine without informing caregivers; drug interactions with herbal medicines can be fatal.

LEARN TO FALL

'Tis a far, far better thing to avoid getting hurt in the first place. The mental training discussed in chapter 3 is an important first step: stay focused. But climbers also need to learn how to fall—something rarely taught.

Whenever you are leading, top-roping, or bouldering, watch your drop zone. This means constantly being aware of your impact area, whether it's the ground below or a wall that you might vector into because of the rope. While you don't want negative thoughts to interfere with your ascent, somewhere in the back of your mind should be a contingency plan.

Though you shouldn't give up prematurely, once you're off, completely free yourself from the rock or ice in that instant. Allowing a body part to linger can result in tweaked fingers, torn shoulder or knee joints, or a nasty head injury from being flipped upside down.

As with a cat in midflight, you must contort your body to anticipate the landing—then go soft in that last split second. Tensing your muscles leads to greater injury, which is why drunks often walk away from car crashes that kill others. Land on both feet with hip and knees flexed to absorb the impact and reduce the chance of joint or bone injury.

Those on the ground must stay sharp as well. When belaying a leader on an overhanging route, it's often best to pay out some slack should they come off. If you lock off the rope or try to take in, they will swing violently into the rock instead of dropping straight down.

Bouldering has become a much safer sport now that the macho era is over and most people are using crash pads. But spotters still play a vital role of directing the falling climber and protecting the head and neck. Spotting is a truly essential skill to develop.

Wear a helmet; the advantages far outweigh the disadvantages.

COMMON CLIMBING INJURIES

With proper education and caution, climbing is far safer than the general public thinks. But as with any sport, if you do it often enough, there are certain problems that tend to arise. Knowing what they are ahead of time allows you to take preventive action.

SKIN

Scratches and abrasions are certainly the most frequent damage we inflict upon ourselves. These are little concern when small; perhaps apply a dab of chalk to the wound while midpitch to stop the bleeding. Larger gashes should be cleaned and protected by a flexible bandage. If it's a big abrasion (palm-size or larger, aka road rash), then you need to be aggressive about cleaning out debris and applying a topical disinfectant.

Keeping skin wounds airtight will speed healing and make the scar tissue more pliable. The new high tech bandages, such as Liquid Band-Aid, stay on better and promote faster healing than old-fashioned strips.

Calluses often form on the fingers. If these become too thick, they may tear off, creating a painful "flapper." Since calluses are merely dead skin, you can trim them with flat nail clippers. Washing dishes the old-fashioned way (in a sink) is also effective for getting rid of calluses. The drying effect of chalk is hard on the skin, so it's a good idea to regularly use hand lotion.

Many climbers worship the sun and are convinced that they, themselves, are immune to melanoma. Yet skin cancer is still on the rise throughout the world, despite better awareness and skin care products. There is no such thing as a "safe" tan, and that bronze skin you flaunt in your invincible teens and twenties may very well come back to haunt you decades later. Even if you luck out on the cancer front, there is still the undeniable aging effect from sun overdose that wrinkles and dries skin. Anymore, a deep tan is an indication of foolishness not sexiness.

When selecting sunscreens, be sure that they are "broad spectrum," which means they filter both UV-A and UV-B rays. Unfortunately, the sun protection factor (SPF) number only apples to UV-B and provides no information about filtration of UV-A. An SPF 15 sunscreen blocks 93 percent of the UV-B rays (280–320 nanometers), while SPF 30 blocks 97 percent, and higher SPFs do nothing more.

To complicate matters further, there are both short and long UV-A rays (320–340 nm and 340–400 nm, respectively) and some compounds (such as oxybenzone) only absorb the latter. And others, such as avobenzone, tend to break down in the sun after a couple hours. To get full UV-A protection requires both avobenzone (Parsol 1789) and oxybenzone, plus reapplying every few hours. Newer chemicals, such as Mexoryl SX, are even more effective at absorbing UV-A but are expensive.

The other alternatives are the total blockers: zinc oxide and titanium dioxide. These work well, if you don't mind the pasty look. Some that go on invisible use nanoparticles, which raises a whole other range of health concerns because they are so small they get in the bloodstream.

HANDS

Since climbing is a hands-on sport, it should be little surprise that's where most of the injuries occur. Surveys have shown that about 40 percent of all injuries in rock climbers occur to the fingers. Since there are no muscles in the fingers, the damage is usually in structures with limited blood circulation so they tend to be slow healing, possibly as long as two years.

The most common injuries in experienced climbers involve either tears of the finger's flexor tendons ("climber's finger") or the second annular (A2) pulley, a fibrous ring that holds the tendons near the bone. These are primarily caused by overstressing the joints on small holds (or one-finger pull-ups) and usually affect the middle and ring fingers—often with an audible pop.

With a torn tendon, pain will occur near the site on the palm side of the finger and is increased by movement. Damage to the A2 pulley is accompanied by pain and swelling at the base of the finger. If the A2 is fully blown, the tendon will pull away from the bone on the palm side, called "bow-stringing," as the finger is flexed against resistance. With either injury, depending on the severity, you are likely facing two to six months without climbing. In the case of complete rupture, surgery may be required.

Contrary to popular belief, wrapping tape around a finger offers minimal protection against pulley rupture, absorbing only 12 percent of the force when done properly (many don't achieve this). Taping may be useful as a reminder against over-crimping, but it's unlikely to prevent an injury. Don't let tape make you overconfident or pretend it will allow you back on the rock faster after injury.

Another common injury among climbers is a tweaked knuckle, which is damage to the collateral ligaments that run on either side of the joint. This usually occurs from sharp sideways pressure on the knuckle, as in over-cranking or falling on a finger jam. For minor cases, follow standard therapy and prevent reinjury by taping adjacent fingers. If the joint feels very loose, but there isn't much pain, you may have really messed up and need surgery.

Overuse injuries of the fingers are relatively rare but can be especially difficult to treat. Pay attention to pain that begins after you stop climbing; it may be time to switch sports for a while. More frequent is inflammation of the sheath around the wrist tendons, which is indicated by swelling and a creaking feeling that you may even hear. This tenosynovitis may be brought on by a lot of ascending vertical fixed lines since most mechanical ascenders place the wrist in a non-ergonomic position.

Finger injuries can be particularly frustrating for climbers because you often feel great otherwise. Instead of rushing back to the rock too soon, you can maintain fitness with resistance training. To use heavy resistance without stressing your hands, consider trying a product like the Harbinger Lifting Hook (at around $20), a pair of padded wrist straps with a steel hook that fits over barbells and pull-up bars.

Purposely or accidentally cracking your joints, while obnoxious, increases range of motion but does not appear to cause arthritis. When the joint is manipulated, dissolved gases (about 15 percent of the joint's volume and made of 80 percent carbon dioxide) are suddenly released from the synovial fluid, causing the noise. While not as bad for you as it sounds, there is a correlation between popping your knuckles and a temporary reduction in grip strength followed by swelling.

Of course, prevention is the best solution to finger injuries. If you are working hard on grip strength, it is wise to balance it out with extensor training. Some simple exercises three times a week can save you from months of no climbing.

The IronMind Strong and Healthy Hands Kit (about $35) can be a good investment. This contains a soft, anatomically shaped egg that is designed for squeezing comfortably. It also contains a collection of color-coded rubber bands with gradated resistance; slip one over all five fingers at fingernail height and expand your hand.

ELBOWS

Nearly all elbow aches among climbers can be traced to overuse and muscle imbalances; often pronator teres is underdeveloped. With your arm at your side, face your palm forward: if the pain is on the outside (thumb side), then you may have lateral epicondylitis (tennis elbow); pain on the inside may indicate medial epicondylitis (golfer's elbow but also common in climb-ers); and pain in the middle could be anterior epicondylitis (climber's elbow).

In mild cases, the treatment will involve reducing inflammation and taking time off to heal. Reverse wrist curls with a therapy band may help balance muscles once the swelling is down. Weighted forearm rotations (hold a claw hammer horizontally with your palm down and rotate until it is vertical, then lower) can solve some elbow problems. The Armaid device (see "Massage Tools" earlier in this chapter) can also be a great help.

If you didn't heed the warnings and allowed the condition to progress, more aggressive therapy will be required. This may consist of ultrasound and painful cross-friction massage, which will really make you wish you'd listened to your body (and hate your physical therapist). If this still doesn't help, you may need prolotherapy (injections of an irritant or platlet-rich plasma [PRP] into a joint to force inflammation and start a natural healing process), steroid injections, or even surgery.

SHOULDERS

The shoulders of climbers are at high risk of trauma due to the odd positions and torques we sometimes apply. The shoulder socket (glenoid) of the scapula is very shallow, which gives this complex of joints (it's actually made up of four joints) greater range of motion than any other, with more than 1,600 positions. While large, superficial muscles do most of the work, relatively small, deep muscles—collectively known as the rotator cuff—keep the head of the upper arm bone (humerus) in position.

The rotators are most vulnerable when your arm is raised out to the side and rotated forward (thumb down, elbow moving upward); do this now so you know what it feels like. Be especially careful to avoid loading your shoulder in any manner while reaching up and back! Likewise, never do an arm bar with your thumb pointed down: a slip could be disastrous. No move or climb is worth a partial dislocation (subluxation) or full dislocation; the latter can be near the top of the pain scale.

Two of the most common shoulder injuries involve the glenoid labrum, which is the tissue surrounding the glenoid (commonly known as the shoulder socket). A Bankhart tear (front, lower) of the labrum typically results from shoulder dislocation. A superior labrum anterior-to-posterior (SLAP) lesion is on the top of the socket where the biceps tendon attaches and is often the result of a fall with arms outstretched or overuse.

Another common injury is acromioclavicular (AC) joint separation in which the clavicle (collar bone) is dislocated from the scapula (shoulder blade), typically by landing on the "point" of the shoulder after a fall. Depending upon the severity of damage, it may merely hurt to raise your arm or there may be a big lump on top. Surgery is rarely necessary but it can take a long time to fully heal.

Once you've damaged the tendons or ligaments of the shoulder, you are facing a long rehab and several months of no climbing, if you're smart. Assuming the damage

wasn't too severe (partial tear), you'll need to work on strengthening all the remaining muscles of the shoulder region. Should your shoulder go out a second or third time, surgery is probably your best option; doctors have a lot of practice, so the success rate is good.

A common overuse injury among climbers shows up as impingement of tendons (or nerves) that run across the top of the shoulder joint. These tendons run through a tunnel between the clavicle and scapula, and irritation from repeated overhead stress can cause swelling that further aggravates the problem. This may start as minor soreness at the front of the shoulder, especially when the arm is raised, and continue to worsen without adequate rest.

Somewhat less common, but still prevalent (particularly in the over-forty crowd), is damage of the tendon used to raise the arm to the side (supraspinatus tendinosis). Again, these microtraumas are often the result of muscle imbalances, overuse, and improper training, so pay attention to yourself. Avoid sleeping with your hand behind your head; the additional shoulder strain can slow recovery.

BACK

Many climbers suffer from lower back pain, though this is often more life-related than the result of climbing. By some estimates, more than 80 percent of the adult population will experience back pain that interferes with activity; half of those sufferers will experience a flare-up within three years of the initial injury. There are numerous causes, including: weak back and abdominal muscles; tight muscles of the upper legs and buttocks; poor posture when sitting or standing; and obesity. All those little stresses add up over time until the proverbial straw breaks the camel's back.

Proper training and stretching can solve the majority of back pains and prevent future episodes. This is a far better option than spinal manipulations that don't solve the underlying problem—a weak core. However, bad lifting technique can result in a stress fracture of the spine (spondylolysis) or ruptured disk.

If you work at a desk, be sure your desk and computer screen are set up at an optimal height and that you have a high-quality chair; sitting on a stability ball is an affordable alternative. For those who spend a lot of time on their feet, pay careful attention to your footwear (good cushioning, no high heels). Preventive action is far superior to follow-up care for back injuries.

Climbers should pay attention to their sit harness; the more you weigh, the greater the lumbar support (wide, firm back) it should offer. Many sport harnesses are woefully inadequate, sacrificing support to reduce weight. Considering that ropes in rock gyms are notoriously worn out and have lost much of their elasticity (though they won't break) and belays are often fairly static—a double whammy for more impact on your spine—a more supportive harness is best for indoor practice. Mountaineers should be sure that their internal frame pack is properly fitted; minor tweaks can make a big improvement.

LEGS

Rock climbers seldom suffer from overuse injuries in the legs. However, mountaineers may experience "trekker's knee" from long descents with a heavy pack; use trekking poles to prevent this. If you also cycle or run a lot, beware of a tight ITB (iliotibial band), which can cause knee pains if you don't stretch. Another common complaint is patellofemoral syndrome (chondromalacia), which results from muscle imbalances that prevent the kneecap from tracking properly in its groove. Runners should also watch out for Achilles tendonitis, and the more insidious tendinosis, resulting from too many miles and inadequate calf stretching.

Due to extreme contortions, climbers are subject to various traumas. Groin pulls are possible from very wide stemming; this is another injury that can become quite nasty if not allowed to heal. Heel hooking can result in a strain of the hamstrings, often near the back of the knee. The most significant problems come from applying a twisting force while attempting a drop-knee or high rock-over; these positions place a great deal of pressure on the ligaments in their weakest position, when the knee is severely bent.

Women in general have more problems with torn ACLs (anterior cruciate ligaments) in the knees than men; possible reasons include less training, greater angle of the thigh bone (due to wider pelvis), and hormone influences. One large study showed that female alpinists run the same risk of knee injury as downhill skiers and basketball players. No matter your gender, learn to fall safely when skiing. Among the most knee-damaging are slow, backward, twisting falls when the ski tail cannot move; this can even pop an ACL when you're stopped.

ANKLES

The main risk to a climber's ankles is landing wrong while bouldering or swinging into the rock after a fall on lead or top-rope. Crash pads have certainly made bouldering safer, though some of them have cheap foam, which does little to absorb impacts, or gaps to allow folding that can turn an ankle. Always try to land on the balls of your feet so your ankle acts as a crumple zone. Heel landings can result in a broken heel bone (calcaneous), which will put you on crutches for months; take this injury seriously since improper healing can require ankle fusion.

Sprained ankles are fairly common among runners, especially those making the transition from road to trail, but climbers turn their share on talus approaches and descents. Rehab is the same as with other connective tissue injuries. To increase range of movement, write the alphabet with your toes. Once recovered, trail running in proper shoes is among the best strengthening options.

FEET

Climbing ranks with ballet for unkindness to feet. Years of cramming feet into shoes, especially if you start early in life, can lead to significant problems such as bunions (a painful swelling of the first toe joint leading to displacement of the toe) and neuroma (tumorous mass of nerve tissue). Fortunately rock shoes have improved anatomically so an ultra-tight fit is no longer necessary; indeed it can decrease performance since you lose sensitivity.

Spend the time to shop around for the shoes that best fit your feet and ignore the recommendations of anyone else. What some hotshot climber wears is immaterial unless he or she happens to have a foot shaped identically to yours. Most dedicated climbers have several pairs of rock shoes: snug, sensitive shoes or slippers for sport and gym climbing; stiffer shoes for edging and crack climbing; perhaps a looser all-around shoe for long traditional climbs.

Rock shoes are perfect breeding grounds for all manner of microorganisms that emit vile, toxic odors. Be certain to remove shoes from your pack after a day of climbing so they can dry out. Occasionally sprinkle the insides with foot powder; washing with soap and warm water will help in more extreme cases.

Toenail fungus (onchomycosis) is ugly, highly contagious (about 7 percent of the population has it), and persistent, so it's a good idea to avoid walking barefoot in damp, public areas, such as showers and rock gyms. Prescription drugs are expensive, might not work, and can be harsh. If you have a mild case, you might try painting on tea tree oil or grapefruit seed extract for several months.

Mountaineering boots can be a source of blisters or black toenails if you do not shop carefully. Be sure your heel lifts no more than an eighth-inch inside the boot when you walk and that your toes do not hit the front when you kick a solid object. Generally, boots for high-altitude mountaineering are purchased a full size larger than those for technical alpine or ice climbing; it's a matter of circulation versus precision.

Select high-quality wool-blend socks and wear them during the testing and break-in period; your feet will be happier. Vapor-barrier socks (and inner boots) can result in clammy feet and even trenchfoot unless you are religious about changing liner socks; avoid neoprene socks for mountaineering because they can expand at higher altitudes, thus reducing blood flow. Dry your socks and boots at every opportunity on an expedition; some climbers apply antiperspirant to their feet (your tent mate will appreciate it).

Most boots come with chintzy foot beds that offer poor support and break down quickly. Excess foot movement in stiff boots is tiring and can lead to heel spurs (bony lumps). While often unnecessary in softer shoes and boots, custom foot beds can improve comfort and performance because mountaineering boots are often worn for long walks and hours of front-pointing. Custom foot beds also may be helpful in rigid cycling shoes on long rides.

If you are also a serious runner, beware of plantar fasciitis, a very painful and difficult-to-treat condition resulting from excessive tightness (or looseness) in the feet. This typically starts as a small pain under the heel when you wake in the morning and becomes progressively worse if you don't heed the warning for rest. A new shock-wave therapy machine offers sufferers potential relief without surgery.

AFTER MAJOR INJURY

Broken bones and completely torn ligaments or tendons are a bad deal, no doubt. But in most cases, they don't spell the end of your climbing career—just a long vacation. Consider your experience a lesson in mental fortitude.

When dealing with the medical establishment, understand that most doctors already think that climbers are nuts (or worse), though professionalism prevents them from saying so. Thus you often run into a wall of resistance if you even mention that you still want to hang by your fingernails over oblivion (your doctor's concept of all forms of climbing). While it's important to disclose all vital information relevant to your case, they don't need to know the rest of what you do (same goes for your parents).

After the initial go-round in the emergency room, you will need to consult with a specialist; check with your insurance provider to see who is on their list. If at all possible, seek out a sports medicine doctor, because this specialist will better understand your needs. Since all doctors are not created equal, you might get recommendations from several physical therapists in your area; they see the results of various doctors' handiwork. Healthygrades.com, a website offering detailed reports on more than 600,000 physicians in the United States, is another option.

The more you know about your condition, the greater the odds of a superior outcome since you can ask the right questions and know your options. Once a diagnosis has been made, and before you commit to the knife (assuming time permits), try to learn all you can, including the precise medical terminology. You can find a wealth of information on the internet and in libraries; however, be skeptical and check medical-studies references on MEDLINEplus (medlineplus.gov).

Even if they seem innocuous, be sure to inform your anesthesiologist before surgery of any medications, herbs, or megadoses of vitamins you are taking. For example, excess vitamin C can cause anesthesia to wear off faster than normal (so a heavier dose is needed and recovery delayed), while vitamin E or ginkgo biloba can interfere with blood clotting.

For broken bones, in many cases full immobilization has thankfully given way to minimal casting, which reduces muscle atrophy. Do yourself a favor and request a waterproof cast or removable splint with a Gore Procel liner, even if it costs extra, so you can take showers and even swim. Although it may seem logical, drinking extra milk or taking calcium supplements does not speed bone healing.

Following a bad break, the bones of the lower leg (especially the tibia, talus, and fifth metatarsal) are at risk of nonunion, which means they don't heal properly.

This is such a bad prospect that you should take your doctor's advice seriously when he tells you non-weight bearing for X weeks!

If you will require crutches for more than a few days, be sure to get forearm crutches (aka, Canadian crutches). Though cheaper, underarm crutches are much less comfortable due to chaffing in the armpits. Select a forearm crutch with a full cuff that hinges, such as the Model 490 from Walk-easy.com (about $100).

Following surgery or non-surgical severe trauma, your best friend—and worst enemy—is the PT (aka physical therapist, physiotherapist, or painful terrorist). He or she is absolutely critical for faster recovery and minimizing aftereffects. While you typically only follow up with your doctor a couple of times, you may visit the PT a few times a week for a month or more. Unlike doctors, many PTs do understand the desires of climbers and outdoor athletes and will encourage your goals.

In addition to the therapy, you should start some form of aerobic conditioning as soon as possible. The increased circulation will aid the repairs, and the stress relief will preserve your sanity. With a bit of ingenuity and pluck, you may be able to resistance-train your unaffected limbs as well; consult with your PT first. Use your downtime for intellectual and philosophical pursuits you wouldn't have time for when healthy; don't get "TV remote thumb."

CHAPTER 9

Synergy: Coalescing and Planning

If you have read everything up to this point, you should have a good understanding of *what* to do for improving your climbing performance, as well as *where* and *when*. Equally important, you'll know *why* you're doing some things and not others. Now it's time to synthesize this knowledge into a time-efficient plan of action. In other words, here's *how* to do it. Don't forget to have fun!

PUTTING IT ALL TOGETHER

Once you decide to get serious about improving your climbing, you must make some hard decisions, not the least of which is what do you mean by *climbing*. While many tend to think only of difficult rock routes, this is a narrow-minded view of the sport. A skier can choose from many very different aspects of snow sliding, each with its own set of gear: giant slalom, all-mountain, randonée, telemark, backcountry touring, general touring, light touring, classic track, and skate. Our sport is no less diversified—from bouldering at Hueco to summiting Everest—and you need to adjust your training to your goals.

Just as no one in modern times will win an Olympic gold medal in both alpine and Nordic skiing, no climber can truly excel at all aspects of the sport. So you must decide if you are going to be a specialist or a generalist. And if the latter, whether you want to focus more at one end of the climbing spectrum—from rock to alpine—or can accept being a jack-of-all-trades-master-of-none. Of course, those who make climbing their lifestyle (guiding, bumming, etc.) can attain a fairly high level of proficiency at many different things. However, these folks are the minority and everyone else must fit climbing into everyday life.

No matter how dedicated you are to climbing, choose at least two other sports for aerobic cross-play. In fact, the more specialized your interest, the more important these outlets become for recovery and recuperation. The cross-play options in chapter 4 are well suited to climbers, but if swimming, kayaking, or whatever turns you on, then go for it. The key is to embrace the activity: learn proper technique, acquire good equipment, and play often.

If you really want to improve, keep track of your progress with a training journal. Without this reference, everything becomes guesswork, and it's difficult to pinpoint weaknesses. This can be a full diary entry every day, if you wish, or simply a few benchmarks jotted down in a notebook every couple of weeks.

Whether you are climbing, lifting weights, stretching, or cross-playing, every workout is an opportunity to improve. A half-assed attitude gives half-assed results.

MAKING THE TIME

Yeah, yeah . . . you're busy. So who isn't? After the excuse scrolls are recited, you must say the magic words: "I want to climb better." Problem solved. Passion takes over. Once you commit to the major goal—create a more specific mantra if it helps—the time will appear. Perhaps it means getting up an hour earlier, making your lunch break a workout, or getting to the gym after dinner.

There will be days when you have to drag yourself out the door for a run or a trip to the gym. And if you manage that, you spend the first 10 minutes of the workout asking, "Why am I doing this?" But if you repeat the magic words and stick with it, everything gets better. Really.

Ever so rarely, too many other life pressures intrude and you just can't get psyched—in this case, call it a day. Missing a workout here and there will not ruin your conditioning, and a rest may very well help.

Don't expect overnight miracles! In fact, they should be avoided; because sudden changes indicate a problem with what you're doing. Sudden dramatic weight loss, such as 10 pounds in a week, is absolutely not sustainable and will come back to haunt you. Similarly, massive strength gains in a short time mean you likely have muscle imbalances and your tendons are relatively weak; overuse injuries are just around the corner.

When you are training smart, significant results take time. Since you have realistic expectations, this doesn't disappoint. Knowing that it may take three or four months for your body to fully adapt to a substantial program change, you take the long view.

This is what gets you to the top of major climbs, too. But the ultimate goal is to put young climbers to shame when you're sixty-five, and still be climbing when you're ninety-five.

TRAINING FOR ROCK

If you've decided that your interests lay more toward the rock end of the climbing spectrum, you can adjust your training accordingly. Of course, within the general term *rock climbing* there are subspecialties: sport climbing and bouldering, which are mostly about power; trad, which is about power and endurance; and big wall, which is mostly about endurance—plus the distant relatives, canyoneering and caving. Each of these has its own training requirements, though there may be considerable overlap and they are by no means exclusionary.

The overriding rule for all forms of the sport: Climb first, train second. Strength and aerobic conditioning are for naught without technique, which can only be learned by doing.

The first corollary: Climb at as many areas as possible. For the best technique, it is essential to encounter different types of rock and styles of climbing. It's a dirty job, but ya gotta travel and have fun to be a better climber.

The second corollary: Don't train on the sharp end. Training should be a separate activity from leading; the goals are different. When you are leading, put all of your mental and physical energy into reaching the top.

So given this Prime Directive—climbing before training—the rest of your conditioning adjusts to forays that are often determined by time of year, climbing partners, and job/school/family realities. Since fall and spring are often the best times to do hard projects due to weather, summer and winter may be when you want to train more. Plan your training to accomplish major goals and tweak it to hone weaknesses.

This emphasis on climbing must also be tempered by a dose of reality. If you have a good fitness gym that is 10 minutes from home while the nearest rock gym or crag is 2 hours away, then resistance training may need to form the bulk of your weekday workouts. It will be incumbent upon you to train smarter, build a home wall if possible, and get out on real rock at every opportunity. Perhaps you and a few others in the same boat can pool your resources to create a deluxe garage rock gym.

While resistance training is an important part of any program, it is only one component that will vary in significance over the course of a year. Used thoughtfully, not just as a playground, rock gyms can be fantastic training tools. Integrating the two forms of gym training can yield greater results than either alone. Neither, however, prepares you fully for the real world; for example, learning crack or slab technique generally requires getting outside.

For the best results, isolate areas of weakness and concentrate on improving them. If your arms routinely give out on climbs, determine which aspect of strength suffers most. Then do lat pulls, pull-ups, and other arm exercises at the appropriate intensity. But do not attempt to train your arms on a hangboard or while bouldering since quality will suffer. On the other hand, if grip strength is a weakness (which is common), then focus on those exercises without combining arm work.

ENDURANCE

Though climbers often feel they need to get stronger, muscular endurance is frequently their major limiting factor. This aspect of strength is emphasized on trad climbs where you hang on while placing protection and when there are multiple sustained pitches. Big-wall climbing also requires muscular endurance for a day of nailing overhead, hauling the "pig," and jugging fixed lines.

As discussed in chapter 6, training for muscular endurance requires low resistance and high numbers of repetitions. Because endurance training is fairly time consuming, this is best performed by actual climbing, rather than with weights, so that technique also becomes ingrained. The exception is for specific small muscles—shoulder rotators and wrist extensors—that do not get worked by climbing.

Rock gyms are ideal for training endurance because there are often several routes of desired difficulty. Warm up on some fun, easy climbs in preparation for your workout. If possible, select a moderate yet long climb that you can top-rope. With a cooperative belayer, do as many laps as possible—climbing up and down—without stopping for at least 10 minutes. The auto-belay devices in rock gyms are ideal for endurance training because you can keep climbing without wearing out your belayer from boredom.

When down-climbing, use slow, controlled movements and do not drop down onto holds (bad for the joints). Some climbers will climb up, then lower off, and climb again, but this neglects an important skill—retreat—and emphasizes concentric movements to the exclusion of the eccentric. Use big holds on the way down to rest your fingers. If you can stay on your course for more than 20 minutes, then either increase the level of difficulty or start wearing a fanny pack with weights.

When endurance training, focus on steady breathing; if necessary, have your belayer remind you not to hold your breath. Long bouldering traverses (30 to 50 moves in each direction) are an acceptable substitute for enduro-roping if a patient belayer is unavailable. However, other people often get in the way, so you may need to hop off, then find a free section of wall with minimal rest.

POWER ENDURANCE

When you go to the rock gym without a plan, chances are most of your time will be spent unsystematically working power endurance, the transition stage that uses both aerobic and anaerobic energy systems. In general, if you can walk up to a route you've never seen and flash up it (an onsight ascent), you will mostly be using low-intensity power endurance. Working a harder route for an eventual no-falls climb (redpoint ascent) calls upon high-intensity power endurance.

Likewise, the power endurance zone is where many people routinely train at a fitness gym since this is where maximum muscle gain is attained. While this is certainly an important aspect of strength, and a good starting point for a conditioning program, you don't want to spend too much time here either.

If you find that you have trouble with onsighting routes that should be within your capabilities, then you may need to work on your ability to sustain an extended pump. Since few rock gyms have routes long enough, this means climbing a route near your onsight level, then lowering off and climbing it again without a rest. Overall, you want to spend about 5 to 10 minutes in action before you flame out, so it may take two or three laps. Take a good long rest while belaying your partner, then repeat the pumpfest on a slightly harder route. If there is time, go through the cycle again, but be sure to warm down afterward.

Improving your redpoint ability, if you are falling because of the pump, may require increasing your fatigue tolerance. This calls for high-intensity interval workouts lasting 1 to 3 minutes followed by brief rests of about half that duration. Relating this to a climb, it means selecting a pumpy route right at your limit and climbing until you fall. Then lower a few moves, and after a short hang, start climbing again and try to get higher. Should you reach the top, lower and repeat until you've managed 5 to 10 intervals. Needless to say, this is a painful workout and thorough recovery is essential.

POWER

Many climbers can do quite well with general fitness and finesse; these attributes may be sufficient for everything you wish to do. But as you progress to more difficult climbs, greater power is required. At the highest levels, technique will only get you so far. Raw strength alone is also insufficient since the ability to generate maximal force has limited practical value. Climbers often need to create the most force early in a move to counteract gravity; this high-speed strength reaches a maximum in the explosive thrust of dynoing for a hold.

Although strength is not the primary goal, you must be strong before you can start to train for power. The number of reps and rest intervals for strength and power are very similar (see the sidebar "Muscle Magic" in chapter 6). The major difference is that strength sets are performed at maximum resistance so that you can just barely complete the last rep with good form. When training for power, the resistance is significantly decreased, but you are completing each rep as fast as possible. Although you are not drained by the end of power sets, these are very taxing workouts that require thorough rest afterward.

Bouldering is a great way to train power, though you can also use a campus board. The goal is to link a few very hard moves into a problem that takes 10 to 40 seconds to complete, then do nothing (complete rest) for 3 to 5 minutes before doing another problem. A full power session will involve from 6 to 10 of these intervals, but you should never get a pump; this is targeting the phosphocreatine system.

When fully committing to high-end sport climbing (roughly 5.12c and above, UK 7a) and bouldering (V5 and higher), a major change in training may be required. The shorter and harder the climb, the more power is required. However, muscular endurance training has a negative effect on power (fortunately for everyone else, the converse is not true: power training does not harm endurance). Thus sport climbers have less need for aerobic conditioning but should find some outlet that suits their tastes. Since excess muscle mass below the waist seldom enhances climbing performance on overhanging routes, legs may not need as much resistance training.

TRAINING FOR ALPINE

As with rock, alpine climbing is a generic term that encompasses several sub-disciplines, including ice and mixed climbing, technical alpine climbing, general mountaineering, high-altitude mountaineering, and possibly even ski mountaineering. While these are all interrelated, they are distinct enough that you can train for each.

One major difference between preparing for alpine climbing versus rock is you often don't have the luxury of practicing even simulated conditions on a regular basis. Few climbing gyms offer artificial ice (special sheets of foam formulated to withstand abuse) and most will not allow dry tooling, due to the danger of somebody getting hit by a tool.

Most forms of alpine climbing demand endurance and power endurance, so these should form the bulk of your training. However, as with rock climbing, power plays a greater role at the highest levels of the sport.

PLANNING YOUR PROGRAM

Some climbers require rigid structure in their life and map out every aspect of their training—the so-called Type A personality. If you desire, there are numerous computer programs available that allow you to create charts and plot data. Some heart rate monitors can even guide you through different workouts and allow you to download the info to your home computer. Be especially cognizant of the need to periodize your training with planned variations on a weekly, monthly, and quarterly basis.

Other climbers are Type B and are much more relaxed about training. You may find charts and schedules abhorrent but still recognize the benefits of a conditioning program. While you may not stick to a set routine, following the basic form of one is better than going about things haphazardly; consider it a planless plan. It is helpful to establish benchmarks in performance so you can evaluate the effectiveness of your efforts.

For either personality type, you want to start preparing for the upcoming season well ahead of time. Thus, begin getting ready for rock season in the winter and thinking about skiing and ice climbing when there are still leaves on the trees.

BASIC PROGRAMS

The following are a selection of training routines that can serve as stepping-stones to greater levels of climbing performance. Don't try to skip ahead too fast or you could be setting yourself up for trouble. You will need to at least complete an intermediate program (one here or an equivalent) before beginning any of the peaking programs described later in this chapter.

No single routine is appropriate for everybody. These programs are merely guidelines to help you develop your own customized routines. Based upon your self-evaluation, there will be certain weaknesses that need greater emphasis and strengths that may need less effort.

Even after you start in on a routine, it should not be cast in stone: your body isn't. If you stick with the exact same workout for too long, two things are inevitable: a plateau and boredom. In order to make gains, your muscles and nervous system constantly need to be challenged anew. Without variations in motion, intensity, and volume, you will stagnate. Given the countless exercise options—the ones presented here are just the tip of the iceberg—there is little reason to become bored unless you have limited imagination.

Don't just do an exercise because a trainer, friend, article, or book told you it would help. Always ask the question "what does this actually do for me?" If there is no sound physiological reason for the exercise, including specific muscles and energy systems involved, you may be wasting your time or risking injury.

For details on the zones that are mentioned with each of these programs, see the sidebar "Zone Play" in chapter 4.

Approach: Beginning Fitness

If you've become the proverbial couch potato, this is the program to begin your comeback (or new life). Before you can start working toward your major goals, you need to establish a base of fitness. This means strengthening major muscles, stabilizing joints, and reducing body fat. At this stage, climbing is purely for fun and is not part of your training.

Depending on how out of shape you are, this program could last from one to six months, maybe more. Don't rush it, particularly if you have a lot of weight to lose. During this time, you are also phasing in better

---

APPROACH: BEGINNING FITNESS

Climbing: For fun, as you can fit it in.

Stretching: 10 minutes a day, or three 20-minute sessions per week.

Aerobic conditioning: 30 to 45 minutes of cross-play, three times a week, mostly in Zone 2 with some Zone 3.

Resistance training: Two or three 45-minute sessions per week of the following exercises:

Exercise	Volume, Intensity	Rest Period
Cycling, Running, or Rowing	5–10 minutes (Zone 2)	
Squat or Leg Press	2 sets, 12–15 reps	1.5 minutes
Calf Raise	1 set, 12–15 reps	
Lat Pull or Pull-up	2 sets, 12–15 reps	1 minute
Bench Press	1 set, 12–15 reps	
Bent-over or Seated Row	2 sets, 12–15 reps	1 minute
Shoulder Press or Rear Delt Row	1 set, 12–15 reps	
Internal Shoulder Rotations	1 set, 12–15 reps	
External Shoulder Rotations	1 set, 12–15 reps	
Crunch	2 sets, 12–15 reps	1 minute
Back Extension	1 set, 12–15 reps	

nutrition and adding cross-play to your lifestyle. If you are seriously overweight, have your doctor check your heart health, then emphasize resistance training and low-impact, higher-intensity aerobic fun.

When starting out, you might only resistance train two times per week, cross-play for a half hour three times, and sneak in some stretching. That isn't much—less than 6 out of 120 waking hours—but it's enough to get your mind and body ready for more. As your fitness improves, and it will, you should try to add one more day of resistance and either add an extra day of cross-play or extend the duration to 45 minutes.

This program includes a full-body resistance routine with plenty of options. If you have a choice of gym exercises, perform one the first day and the other exercise the next. If only one exercise is listed (bench press, calf raise, crunch), try its variations on different days (for instance: incline, normal, and decline bench press). Use free weights most of the time as well as machines for variety.

Don't expect to see major changes: you should lose some fat, but increased muscle mass can balance it out on the scale. However, you should feel better and find that simple things, like walking up the stairs, are easier. Perhaps that sore back will be less bothersome or you won't be as tired after a weekend of play.

Crankin' Up: Intermediate Fitness

If you already are in reasonable shape, or are feeling comfortable with the beginning fitness (Approach) plan, then this program can take you to the next level of climbing performance. The goal here is to significantly strengthen the climbing muscles while continuing to improve the weak links. Because this includes an all-around gym routine tailored for climbers, it also serves as the foundation for those who intend to progress to even higher levels.

This program should take about six to eight weeks, possibly less if you are reasonably fit. Again, don't rush things, since your tendons and ligaments need time to catch up with the muscles. Hopefully by now you are eating healthier and look forward to cross-play. Climbing is still recreational, but you are doing more of it and the grades are getting harder.

Since you are looking to really improve, a greater time commitment is required. This calls for about 60 minutes of resistance training two or three days per week. You are still cross-playing, too, but the sessions are 45 to 60 minutes each and at higher intensity. It's also important to maintain flexibility with at least an hour of stretching per week. Thus you are looking at around 8 hours each week, in addition to climbing.

The resistance training described here is a full-body routine featuring both ascending and multiple sets. Three days a week is preferred for strength gains but missing a day every now and then shouldn't mess up your training, particularly if the reason was climbing or cross-play.

By the time you complete this program, you should be cranking harder climbs and notice significant changes in your body. Not only will you have visibly lost body fat, but also your muscles will be more defined. Maybe you aren't quite "ripped" yet, but you're getting there. Most people think you're "normal," but would say you're in good shape.

If you can plot out your life for several months, even greater progress can be made with a periodization program in the gym (see "Periodization" and the sidebar "Muscle Magic," both in chapter 6). Using the same set of exercises, or variations thereof, you would spend four to six weeks training low-intensity power endurance (15 to 20 reps), the same amount of time doing high-intensity power

---

CRANKIN' UP: INTERMEDIATE FITNESS

Climbing: For fun, as you can fit it in.
Stretching: 10 minutes a day, or three 20-minute sessions per week.
Aerobic conditioning: 45 to 60 minutes of cross-play, two or three times a week, in Zones 3 and 4.
Resistance training: Two or three 60-minute sessions per week of the following exercises:

Exercise	Volume, Intensity	Rest Period
Cycling, Running, or Rowing	5–10 minutes, Zone 2	
Lat Pull or Pull-up	1 set, 15–20 reps 1 set, 8–10 reps 2 sets, 4–6 reps	1 minute 2 minutes 3 minutes
Bench Press or Fly	3 sets, 8–12 reps	1 minute
Bent-over or Seated Row	3 sets, 6–10 reps	1 minute
Shoulder Press or Rear Delt Row	2 sets, 10–12 reps	1 minute
Side Bridges	2 sets, 10–12 reps	1 minute
Squat or Leg Press	1 set, 12–15 reps 2 sets, 8–10 reps	1.5 minutes
Static Lunge	3 sets, 10–12 reps	1 minute
Calf Raise	1 set, 8–10 reps	
Crunch	3 sets, 8–12 reps	1 minute
Back Extension or Deadlift	2 sets, 8–12 reps	1 minute
Internal Shoulder Rotations	1 set, 8–12 reps	
External Shoulder Rotations	1 set, 8–12 reps	
Wrist Curl	3 sets, 8–12 reps	30 seconds

endurance (8 to 12 reps), and end the cycle with strength and power exercises (4 to 6 reps). The cycle can be repeated following a week of rest. The time spent in each stage will depend upon you and your goals. Consider hiring a coach or personal trainer to get the most out of periodization.

Weekend Warrior: Intermediate Maintenance

Once you have raised the bar on your fitness, you have the option of holding it there or taking it even higher. After completing an intermediate fitness program you should be fairly pleased with your climbing ability—and

---

WEEKEND WARRIOR: INTERMEDIATE MAINTENANCE

Climbing: Three to four days per week (weekend excursions and a gym session or two).
Stretching: 10 minutes a day, or three 20-minute sessions per week.
Aerobic conditioning: 45 to 60 minutes of cross-play, two or three times a week, in Zone 3.
Resistance training: One or two 45-minute sessions per week of the following exercises:

Exercise	Volume, Intensity	Rest Period
Cycling, Running, or Rowing	5 minutes, Zone 2	
Pull-up or Lat Pull *alternating with sets of* Dips or Shoulder Press	3 sets, 6–10 reps 3 sets, 8–12 reps	15 seconds
Seated or Bent-over Row *alternating with sets of* Bench Press or Fly	3 sets, 6–10 reps 3 sets, 8–12 reps	15 seconds
Curl and Press *alternating with sets of* Finger Hangs	2 sets, 8–12 reps 2 sets, 8–12 reps	15 seconds
Squat or Static Lunge *alternating with sets of* Calf Raise	3 sets, 6–10 reps 3 sets, 8–12 reps	15 seconds
Stiff-leg Deadlift *alternating with sets of* Hip Abduction	2 sets, 8–12 reps 2 sets, 8–12 reps	15 seconds
Crunch *alternating with sets of* Twist Crunch	3 sets, 8–12 reps 3 sets, 8–12 reps	15 seconds
Wrist Curl or Internal Shoulder Rotation *alternating with sets of* Reverse Wrist Curl or External Shoulder Rotation	2 sets, 8–12 reps 2 sets, 8–12 reps	15 seconds

your appearance. But all that gym time hasn't improved your technique, and you know there's room to improve.

This program will allow you to maintain those gains and prevent imbalances. Equally as important, greater emphasis on climbing-specific training at a rock gym (or home wall) develops the muscles and neural pathways necessary for serious fun on the weekends.

Because this is a maintenance program, it can last more or less indefinitely, though you need to mix it up enough to prevent stagnation. When necessary, you should be able to launch into any of the peaking programs (detailed later in this chapter) to prepare for an upcoming climbing trip. While climbing is your main release, cross-play is also a significant part of life.

The emphasis here is on time efficiency, but you can still make progress on strength. Warning: this is a demanding full body routine—don't try it until you are ready! If the alternating agonist/antagonist sets are too hard, give yourself more time by alternating upper and lower body exercises. Switch between alternative exercises on different training days.

Ideally, this superset routine should be performed twice a week, but you can hold even with just one day if you are playing often. Cross-play can be reduced to 2 hours a week, but you'll like it so much you may do it more often. Stretching is still important at the end of workouts. So at a minimum, we're talking about 5 hours of focused training each week—plus as much climbing as you can squeeze in.

Although you aren't working for major changes, an active athletic lifestyle results in continued adaptations. After a while, your body reaches a weight equilibrium, but your endurance continues to increase. By now, co-workers who don't know you well think you're nuts but are secretly jealous when you return from weekend climbing epics and still have energy.

Slammed: The Too-Busy-To-Work-Out Workout

Hey buddy, can you spare 45 minutes? Although you will get the best training effect from resistance-training sessions lasting about an hour, life has a way of getting in the way. Rather than blow off exercise altogether—the easy, but wrong, answer—you can maximize efficiency. These bare-essentials routines will get you in and out the gym door in under an hour, including changing clothes and a quick shower. If you have a few more minutes, add a set or two of rows after the presses.

Hard Rock: Injury Prevention

During the height of the season, especially when the weather is good, few climbers are interested in working out in a gym of any type. While you may not be a fan of lifting weights, you're probably even less excited about getting sidelined by an injury.

This short routine can be done at home, or on a road trip, with a few dumbbells. All of these exercises may also be performed with a set of resistance tubes when you are traveling.

Even during a climbing vacation, you need to take rest days occasionally. Use a

SLAMMED: THE TOO-BUSY-TO-WORK-OUT WORKOUT

Climbing: For fun, as you can fit it in.
Stretching: 5 minutes a day, or three 10-minute sessions per week.
Aerobic conditioning: 30 to 45 minutes of cross-play, two or three times a week, in Zones 3 and 4.
Resistance training: Two 30-minute sessions per week of the following exercises:

Exercise	Volume, Intensity	Rest Period
Cycling, Running, or Rowing	5 minutes, Zone 2	
Pull-up or Lat Pull	2 sets, 6–10 reps	30 seconds
Bench Press	1 set, 8–10 reps	
Squat	2 sets, 6–10 reps	30 seconds
Crunch	2 sets, 8–12 reps	15 seconds
Cycling, Running, or Rowing	5 minutes, Zones 2 to 3	

HARD ROCK: INJURY PREVENTION

Climbing: 4 or 5 days per week.
Stretching: 10 minutes a day, or three 20-minute sessions per week.
Aerobic conditioning: 45 to 60 minutes of cross-play, two times a week in Zone 3.
Resistance training: Two 45-minute sessions per week of the following exercises:

Exercise	Volume, Intensity	Rest Period
Cycling or Running	3 minutes, Zone 3	
Static Lunge or Squat	2 sets, 8–10 reps	2 minutes
Bench Press	2 sets, 8–10 reps	1 minute
Shoulder Press	2 sets, 12–15 reps	1 minute
Internal Shoulder Rotations	2 sets, 12–15 reps	15 seconds
External Shoulder Rotations	2 sets, 12–15 reps	15 seconds
Reverse Wrist Curl	2 sets, 8–12 reps	15 seconds
Stiff-leg Deadlift	2 sets, 8–12 reps	1 minute

fraction of this time to do a little preventive maintenance. Incorporate some cross-play and stretching into your rest days as well. Your body will thank you.

Climber's Circuit: Advanced Intermediate Fitness

Circuit training is as old as the hills. This well-proven concept of working fast and furious has been getting more attention lately as research demonstrates the benefits of high-intensity interval training.

When performing a circuit routine, the goal is to get the heart rate up and keep it there. Each exercise is performed for 30 seconds with heavy resistance so that you are challenged by the end. Then you only get 30 seconds rest before moving to the next set or exercise. The circuit is repeated six times in a row. By the end of 45 minutes, you should be breathing hard, sweating profusely, and ready to collapse.

Because this is a demanding workout, you need a fair level of fitness to begin with. Equally important, you need experience to judge the amount of resistance required and to perfect your technique. It is recommended that you frequently vary the routine

---

CLIMBER'S CIRCUIT: ADVANCED INTERMEDIATE FITNESS

Climbing: For fun, as you can fit it in.
Stretching: 10 minutes a day, or three 20-minute sessions per week.
Aerobic conditioning: 45 to 60 minutes of cross-play, one or two times a week, in Zones 3 and 4.
Resistance training: Two or three circuits per week of the following exercises:

Exercise	Volume, Intensity	Rest Period
Cycling, Running, or Rowing	5 minutes, Zone 3	
Overhead Squats	1 set, 30 seconds	30 seconds
Pull-up or Lat Pull	1 set, 30 seconds	30 seconds
Stiff-leg Deadlift	1 set, 30 seconds	30 seconds
Crunches	1 set, 30 seconds	30 seconds
Static Lunge with Curl and Press	1 set, 30 seconds	30 seconds
Push-ups or Dips	1 set, 30 seconds	30 seconds
Hip Abduction	1 set, 30 seconds	30 seconds
Back Extension	1 set, 30 seconds	30 seconds
Repeat circuit six times.		

by selecting different exercises for the circuit: just keep in mind what body parts and energy systems you are training. No matter what, do not sacrifice quality or range of movement just to complete the workout!

Fun Hog: Advanced Fitness

Admit it, you have a problem: being in pretty good shape isn't good enough. You know that the harder you train, the harder you can play. This means you aren't content with the routes for the masses but are looking to put up your own climbs or establish new records (faster times, longer linkups, higher fun quotient).

Since you are committed (or committable), then you are willing to put in the time and effort it takes for four to six weeks to get maximum results. At this level of fitness, individual goals will determine the specifics of your training program. But you should also know enough about your body that you can decide what areas need improvement.

This routine assumes that much of your endurance training comes from climbing and cross-play. By splitting resistance workouts into two days, your body has more time to recover. The amount of cross-play will range from a great deal for an alpinist to very little for a sport climber. With this much activity, rest days are critical and stretching should be an integral part of your workouts. Including climbing, you may well be putting in 20 or more hours each week.

With this routine, you may see little change in your body. But you should find that you have more energy in reserve on harder climbs and can pull through more difficult moves. Non-climbing friends wonder aloud what drives you, and when you'll grow up.

PEAKING FOR GOALS

Climbers are twisted. Instead of spending our vacation time relaxing on a warm beach drinking cold beer, we go and punish ourselves on crags and mountains. Of course, those cold drinks do taste better after a good round of suffering. But we all enjoy our climbing vacations more when our minds and bodies perform at optimal levels.

If you have adopted a healthy athletic lifestyle, peaking for an upcoming goal is usually just a matter of tweaking and intensifying your current regimen. Here are a half dozen programs—out of an infinite realm of possibilities—that can help maximize your performance.

Important: The following plans all assume a solid base of fitness and therefore start at a moderately high level of intensity. Do not jump into these training schedules until week 1 is something you can do comfortably. Thus, if you aren't in great shape but decide to make an attempt on Denali, it's going to take at least six months of serious training instead of the four outlined here. Be careful not to hurt yourself before the big trip; back off the training if necessary.

The tables that follow give suggested training activities for each day of a program that lasts anywhere from two months (for rock climbing) to four months (for a high-mountain expedition). Here's what is meant by the abbreviations used in the tables:

ST = Strength training: 1–1.5 hours of resistance exercises in the gym.

FUN HOG: ADVANCED FITNESS

Climbing: Possibly four or five days per week.

Stretching: 10 minutes a day, or a few longer sessions of stretching or yoga.

Aerobic conditioning: 45 to 60 minutes of cross-play, three or four times a week, in Zones 3 and 4 (with some Zone 5 intervals); longer sessions (over 90 minutes) once a week.

Resistance training: Two 60-minute sessions per week of the following exercises:

Day 1 (Torso)		
Exercise	**Volume, Intensity**	**Rest Period**
Cycling, Running, or Rowing	5–10 minutes, Zone 3	
Lat Pull or Pull-up	1 set, 15–20 reps 3 sets, 4–8 reps	1 minute 3 minutes
Bench Press or Fly	2 sets, 8–12 reps	1 minute
Bent-over or Seated Row	3 sets, 6–10 reps	1 minute
Shoulder Press or Rear Delt Row	3 sets, 10–12 reps	1 minute
Stiff-leg Deadlift	2 sets, 8–12 reps	1 minute
Hanging Leg Raises	2 sets, 10–12 reps	1 minute
Internal Shoulder Rotations	2 sets, 8–12 reps	30 seconds
External Shoulder Rotations	2 sets, 8–12 reps	30 seconds
Back Extension	3 sets, 8–12 reps	1 minute
Crunch	3 sets, 8–12 reps	1 minute
Day 2 (Arms and Legs)		
Exercise	**Volume, Intensity**	**Rest Period**
Cycling, Running, or Rowing	5–10 minutes, Zone 3	
Squat or Leg Press	1 set, 12–15 reps 3 sets, 4–8 reps	1 minute 3 minutes
Static Lunge	3 sets, 8–12 reps	1 minute
Hamstring Curl	3 sets, 8–12 reps	1 minute

Day 2 (Arms and Legs), continued		
Exercise	Volume, Intensity	Rest Period
Calf Raise	3 sets, 8–10 reps	1 minute
Curl and Press	3 sets, 6–10 reps	1 minute
Dips	3 sets, 6–10 reps	1 minute
Wrist Curl	3 sets, 6–10 reps	1 minute
Reverse Wrist Curl	3 sets, 8–12 reps	15 seconds
Reverse Crunch	3 sets, 8–12 reps	1 minute
Twist Crunch or Side Bridge	3 sets, 8–12 reps	1 minute

FH = Finger hangs: 10–15 minutes of focused training.

CE = Climb endurance: 1–4 hours on long, easy routes, preferably outdoors; this could be termed "active rest."

CS = Climb strength: 1–1.5 hours of power endurance or power.

AB = Aerobic base: Cross-play in Zone 2 (about 70–80 percent MHR) with some occasional forays into Zone 3 and even 4.

EI = Endurance intervals/fartleks: Either 4–5 intervals of 8- to 15-minute bouts at moderate intensity followed by 5 minutes of cool down, or 5–6 intervals of 2- to 8-minute bouts at high intensity followed by 4–6 minutes of cool down.

S = Sprint intervals/fartleks: Either 5–20 intervals of 10- to 30-second full-intensity bursts followed by 3–5 minutes of complete rest, or 5–10 intervals of 1- to 3-minute bouts at near-maximum intensity followed by 1 minute of cool down.

Rock Climbing: Two Months

When heading off for a week or more of trad or sport climbing, you want to arrive at your destination prepared for the type of climbing that you'll encounter. Obviously the pocketed limestone crags of southern France and Thailand have different demands than Indian Creek cracks or Joshua Tree face climbs. Tuning your body and climbing technique ahead of time can maximize your fun.

At home, it's likely that you seldom get more than two full days of climbing in a row. If this is the case, it's unrealistic to expect your body to suddenly be able to climb day after day without falling apart. This program aims to get you in a rock gym

ROCK CLIMBING: TWO MONTHS							
	M	**Tu**	**W**	**Th**	**F**	**Sa**	**Su**
Week 1 Base	CE	0.5 hr AB and ST	CS	0.5 hr AB and ST	off	CE	0.75 hr AB and CS
Week 2 Intensity	off	0.5 hr AB and ST, FH	CS	0.75 hr AB and ST, FH	CE	CS	0.75 hr EI and CE
Week 3 Intensity	off	0.5 hr AB and ST, FH	CE	0.75 hr AB and ST, FH	CE	CS	1 hr AB and CE
Week 4 Intensity	off	0.75 hr AB and ST, FH	CS	0.75 hr EI and ST, FH	CE	CS	1 hr AB and CE
Week 5 Intensity	CE	0.75 hr AB and ST, FH	CE	0.75 hr AB and ST	CS	off	1.25 hr EI and CS
Week 6 Peak	CE	0.75 hr AB and ST	CS	0.75 hr AB	CS	CE	1.25 hr AB and CS
Week 7 Peak	off	0.75 hr AB and ST	CS	0.5 hr EI and CE	CS	CE	CS
Week 8 Taper	off	0.75 hr AB and ST	CS	0.5 hr AB and CE	off	CE	off

as often as possible prior to your trip. There are more days of intense training in a row than you may be used to: when it's time to rest, make it good.

This schedule should help trad climbers prepare for a serious climbing vacation. If you will mostly sport climb, your training will necessitate more power endurance and power training while backing off on endurance and aerobic training.

Big-Wall Climbing: Two Months

Whether adventuring to Yosemite, Greenland, or the Baltoro, the big stone requires significant preparation and a mountain of gear. While demanding overall, climbing a big wall requires good endurance, particularly when leading in blocks (multiple pitches in a row instead of alternating each time).

Upper-body and core strength are certainly important. If you anticipate a lot of nailing or hand drilling, be sure to include shoulder presses, triceps extensions, and wrist curls. Prepare for a lot of jumaring with reverse wrist curls. Your legs had better be ready too; humping haul bags to and from a climb can be serious work.

BIG-WALL CLIMBING: TWO MONTHS							
	M	**Tu**	**W**	**Th**	**F**	**Sa**	**Su**
Week 1 Base	ST	0.5 hr AB and CS	ST	0.5 hr AB and CS	ST	CE	0.75 hr AB
Week 2 Intensity	ST	0.5 hr EI and CE	ST	0.75 hr AB and CS	ST	off	0.75 hr EI and CE
Week 3 Intensity	ST	0.5 hr AB and CS	ST	0.75 hr AB and CS	ST	CE	1 hr AB
Week 4 Intensity	ST	0.75 hr AB and CE	ST	0.75 hr EI and CE	ST	CS	1 hr AB
Week 5 Intensity	off	0.75 hr EI and ST	CS	0.75 hr AB and ST	CE	CS	1.25 hr AB and CE
Week 6 Peak	off	0.75 hr EI and ST	CS	0.75 hr AB and ST	CE	CS	1.25 hr AB and CE
Week 7 Peak	off	0.75 hr AB and ST	CS	0.75 hr EI and ST	CS	off	1.5 hr AB and CE
Week 8 Taper	CE	0.75 hr AB and ST	CS	0.75 hr EI	off	CE	off

Ice Climbing: Two Months

Modern ice tools and crampons have certainly made this sport easier, and high-tech clothing has made it less miserable. But the newfangled gear just means we can all push our personal limits a bit further. During a trip to playgrounds like Ouray, Valdez, and Banff, multiple days of ice climbing can fry your forearms and calves, work the rest of your body, and leave your face bloodied.

Preparation for ice season involves total body conditioning with an emphasis on endurance. Those interested in high-end, mixed climbing will train for greater power.

When possible, perform the climbing endurance and climbing strength sessions while dry-tooling and wearing your climbing boots. Resistance training should include a significant amount of shoulder presses, triceps extensions, wrist curls, and calf raises. To really get specific, attach a 1-inch-thick rope to the lat pull machine and do one-handed pulls with a few extra seconds (2 to 20) of contraction at the bottom to simulate a lock-off.

ICE CLIMBING: TWO MONTHS

	M	Tu	W	Th	F	Sa	Su
Week 1 Base	CE	0.5 hr AB and ST	CS	0.5 hr AB and ST	off	CE	0.75 hr AB and CE
Week 2 Intensity	CS	0.5 hr AB and ST	off	0.75 hr AB and ST	CE	CS	0.75 hr EI and CE
Week 3 Intensity	off	0.5 hr AB and ST	CE	0.75 hr AB and ST	CE	CS	1 hr AB and CE
Week 4 Intensity	off	0.75 hr AB and ST	CS	0.75 hr EI and ST	CE	CS	1 hr AB and CE
Week 5 Intensity	CE	0.75 hr AB and ST	CE	0.75 hr AB and ST	CS	off	1.25 hr EI and CS
Week 6 Peak	CE	0.75 hr AB and ST	CS	0.75 hr AB	CS	CE	1.5 hr AB and CS
Week 7 Peak	off	0.75 hr AB and ST	CS	0.75 hr EI and CE	CS	CE	1 hr AB and CS
Week 8 Taper	off	0.75 hr AB	CS	0.75 hr AB and CE	off	CE	off

Ski Mountaineering: Two Months

Leaving the piste behind for a week or more gets you into some fantastic ski country. Whether hut touring the Haute Route (Argentière to Saas Fee) or crossing the Columbia Icefield, you will encounter significant vertical gain and descent while wearing a moderate to heavy pack. Light, fluffy powder is the exception rather than the norm. Expect heavy crud, breakable crust, bottomless depth hoar, and frozen sastrugi.

Good aerobic conditioning is vital to your happiness—inline skating is great preparation. This is certainly quad-burning skiing, so place a heavy emphasis on squats and static lunges to strengthen the muscles and knee joints. Strengthening hamstrings is important to protect the ACLs in your knees. But you also need significant upper-body and core strength for poling uphill and extricating yourself after a fall; lat pulls, dips, and crunches now will reward you later.

If you have snow, try to go skiing on your "off" days. If you have great snow, ski all weekend!

Alpine Climbing: Three Months

For the ultimate form of climbing—nothing else is as demanding of technique, endurance, mental power, and physical strength—your body should be tuned to its highest potential. Whether going to the Tetons, the Alaska Range, Chamonix, or Peru, you will

SKI MOUNTAINEERING: TWO MONTHS

	M	Tu	W	Th	F	Sa	Su
Week 1 Base	ST	0.75 hr AB	ST	0.75 hr AB	ST	off	1 hr AB
Week 2 Intensity	ST	0.75 hr EI	ST	0.75 hr AB	ST	off	1.5 hr AB
Week 3 Intensity	ST	1 hr EI	ST	1 hr AB	ST	off	1.5 hr AB
Week 4 Intensity	off	ST	1.25 hr AB	ST	1 hr EI	off	2 hr AB
Week 5 Intensity	off	ST	1 hr EI	ST	1 hr S	off	2 hr AB
Week 6 Peak	1 hr AB	ST	1.25 hr EI	ST	1.25 hr S	off	2.5 hr AB
Week 7 Peak	1 hr AB	ST	1.25 hr AB	ST	1.25 hr EI	off	2 hr AB
Week 8 Taper	off	ST	1 hr AB	off	0.75 hr EI	off	off

be using everything you've got—and sometimes more.

The problem (and part of the attraction) with remote wilderness climbing areas such as the Wind Rivers or Bugaboos is you have to get there with all of your stuff—and the gear required for 15-pitch climbs isn't light. Porters aren't an option, and horse and llama packers don't come cheap. Which leaves you and your partners with big, heavy packs.

In addition to a fair amount of climbing and resistance training, this plan calls for a lot of aerobic conditioning. The long days should be a low-impact activity—power hiking, road biking, rowing, ski touring, snowshoeing—and include hills if you have them.

It takes a demanding training program to prepare for a demanding sport. In the alpine world, you need to be ready for anything and must perform at a high standard, sometimes for days on end. As Mark Twight puts it, your goal is "to make yourself as indestructible as possible."

High Mountain Expedition: Four Months

The lack of oxygen turns the big peaks—Denali, Aconcagua, the Eight-Thousanders—into a struggle against time. Most climbers have a very limited window of opportunity when logistics, weather, and health all come together for a summit bid. Although the climbing usually isn't very technical, it

ALPINE CLIMBING: THREE MONTHS							
	M	**Tu**	**W**	**Th**	**F**	**Sa**	**Su**
Week 1 Base	1 hr AB and CS	ST	off	ST	1 hr AB and CS	CE	2 hr AB
Week 2 Intensity	ST	1 hr EI	ST	1.25 hr AB and CS	ST	off	3.5 hr AB
Week 3 Intensity	ST	1.25 hr EI and CS	ST	1.25 hr AB and CS	ST	CE	4.5 hr AB
Week 4 Intensity	off	ST	1.25 hr AB and CS	ST	1.25 hr EI	CE	3.5 hr AB
Week 5 Intensity	0.75 hr AB and CS	ST	1 hr EI and CS	ST	1 hr AB	CE	3 hr AB
Week 6 Intensity	0.75 hr AB and CS	ST	1.25 hr EI and CS	ST	1.25 hr EI	off	3.5 hr AB
Week 7 Intensity	0.75 hr S	ST	1.25 hr AB and CS	ST	1.25 hr EI	CE	4 hr AB
Week 8 Peak	off	1 hr S CS	ST	1.25 hr EI and CS	ST	CE	4 hr AB
Week 9 Peak	1 hr S	ST	1.25 hr AB and CS	ST	1.25 hr EI and CS	off	4.5 hr AB
Week 10 Peak	1 hr AB and CS	1 hr S	1 hr AB and ST	1 hr EI and CS	1 hr AB	off	4 hr AB
Week 11 Peak	ST	1 hr S	ST	1.25 hr EI and CS	1 hr AB	CE	3.5 hr AB
Week 12 Taper	1 hr AB	ST	1.25 hr AB and CS	ST	1.25 hr EI	off	1.5 hr AB

is always physically demanding and often very exposed.

Obviously, aerobic and muscular endurance are essential for high-altitude climbing. But you also want big, strong muscles when you head in, partly because physical strength is useful up there and partly because your muscles may wither.

For this type of climbing, you must be prepared to work hard day after day when the weather is good. Since summit snow slopes seem to last forever, it takes mental stamina to tough them out. Those long, sweaty hours of training will reward you at the top—even more so when you make it down in one piece.

HIGH MOUNTAIN EXPEDITION: FOUR MONTHS

	M	Tu	W	Th	F	Sa	Su
Week 1 Base	1 hr AB	ST	1 hr AB	ST	off	CE	2 hr AB
Week 2 Base	ST	1 hr EI	ST	1.25 hr AB	ST	CE	2 hr AB
Week 3 Base	ST	1.25 hr EI	ST	1 hr AB and CE	ST	CE	2.5 hr AB
Week 4 Base	off	ST	1.25 hr AB	ST	1.25 hr EI	CE	2.5 hr AB
Week 5 Intensity	off	ST	1 hr EI and CE	ST	1 hr AB	off	3 hr AB
Week 6 Intensity	CE	ST	1 hr EI and CE	ST	1.25 hr EI	off	3 hr AB
Week 7 Intensity	1hr AB	ST	0.75 hr S and CE	ST	1.25 hr EI	CE	3.5 hr AB
Week 8 Intensity	off	1.25 hr AB and CS	ST	1.25 hr EI CE	ST	off	3.5 hr AB
Week 9 Intensity	1 hr AB	ST	1 hr S and CE	ST	1.25 hr EI	off	4 hr AB
Week 10 Intensity	CE	1 hr S	1 hr AB and ST	1 hr EI	1 hr AB and ST	off	4.5 hr AB
Week 11 Intensity	1 hr AB and ST	1 hr S	ST	1.25 hr EI	1 hr AB and ST	off	4 hr AB
Week 12 Intensity	ST	1 hr S	ST	1.25 hr EI	ST	off	4 hr AB
Week 13 Peak	ST	1 hr S	ST	1.25 hr AB	1.25 hr EI and ST	off	3.5 hr AB
Week 14 Peak	1 hr S	ST	1.25 hr AB	ST	1.25 hr EI	CE	3 hr AB
Week 15 Taper	1 hr S	ST	1.25 hr AB and CE	ST	1.25 hr EI	off	2 hr AB
Week 16 Taper	1 hr AB	ST	off	ST	1.25 hr EI	off	1.5 hr AB

Appendix A: Glossary

abduction. The movement of a limb away from your body, such as raising your arm or leg straight off to the side.

adduction. The movement of a limb toward your body, such as lowering your arm or leg back to the side.

aerobic capacity. See *VO₂max*.

aerobic exercise. Anything that elevates the heart rate to over 50 percent of the maximum heart rate without making you gasp for air.

aerobic metabolism. Chemical pathways in muscle cells that consume oxygen to produce energy.

agonist. The muscle (or group) that moves a limb, such as the biceps that contract to flex the elbow. See *antagonist*.

anabolic. The building of larger molecules and body tissues. Medium-intensity resistance training tends to be anabolic, so muscles get bigger.

anaerobic metabolism. Chemical pathways in muscle cells that do not consume oxygen to produce energy.

antagonist. The muscle (or group) that opposes the prime mover, such as the triceps that slows the flex of the elbow. See *agonist*.

antioxidant. Enzymes that remove free radicals from within cells. Supplementing your diet with antioxidants may be beneficial to health, but the evidence is not as strong as many people believe. See *free radical*.

ATP (adenosine triphosphate). A molecule that is the ultimate source of energy to make muscles move. When a phosphate is released, energy is produced that contracts the filaments in a muscle fiber. The resulting molecule, ADP, must be restored by aerobic or anaerobic processes before it may be reused for energy.

bioavailability. The ability of a food to be utilized by the body. When you consume a food or supplement, the body digests a portion and the rest is excreted. Higher bioavailability means greater absorption and utilization. However, different tests can change the ranking of products, so marketers often abuse the term.

calorie. For biological systems, energy is measured by the amount of heat a reaction produces. A nutritional calorie is the amount of heat energy it takes to raise 1 kilogram of water by 1 °C at 15 °C.

capillarity. The ratio of the smallest blood vessels (capillaries) to muscle fiber. The capillaries are vital for providing oxygen and removing wastes to and from muscle fibers. With endurance training, the capillarity increases.

carbohydrate. A major source of energy for animals, these are organic compounds made of carbon, hydrogen, and oxygen in a 1:2:1 ratio. Sugars and starches are carbohydrates that are the body's most readily accessible form of energy. Each gram of carbohydrate provides 4 calories.

catabolic. The breakdown of big things into little things, such as proteins into amino acids, often with a release of energy. High amounts of endurance training tend to be catabolic to muscles—making them wither.

closed chain. A movement where the last segment in a kinetic chain is fixed; for example, the squat is a closed-chain exercise because the feet are immobile. Generally considered more functional exercises that promote joint stability. See *open chain* and *kinetic chain*.

compound movement. A movement that involves bending two or more joints, such as a pull-up (elbows and shoulder). Compound exercises are considered more functional because muscles work in coordination. See *simple movement*.

concentric. A movement that shortens the muscle(s), such as flexing the biceps. Also called the positive phase. See *eccentric*.

distal. The part of a limb that is farthest from the heart. See *proximal*.

DOMS (delayed onset muscle soreness). Pain that sets in two or three days after a workout. It is generally harmless (unless pain persists) and is not a requirement for strength gains nor is it a gauge of effectiveness.

eccentric. A movement that lengthens the muscle(s). Also called the negative phase. See *concentric*.

ergogenic. Used in reference to a supplement that is said to increase performance. Some work, most don't.

extension. Usually the movement of bones farther apart, such as straightening a bent elbow or knee. However, raising your arm straight behind you is also considered shoulder extension. See *flexion*.

fartlek. A Swedish word for speed-play. It basically means to throw occasional bursts of hard effort into your aerobic workouts and have fun.

fat. The densest form of energy and the slowest to digest. Eating too much fat does not make you fat; eating too many calories does. Each gram of fat contains 9 calories.

flexion. Generally means bringing bones together, such as upper and lower arms or legs. However, raising your arm straight in front of you is also considered shoulder flexion. See *extension*.

free radical. A molecule containing oxygen and an unpaired electron that makes it highly reactive. Free radicals can cause oxidative damage to cells but proper training and nutrition mollify the effects. Reactive oxygen species (ROS, the technical term) are not inherently evil; they are only bad for you in excess quantities.

glycogen. This is the form of carbohydrate that your body stores in your muscles and liver for fast energy. This power source can quickly be converted to glucose, but the supply is limited to around 90 minutes.

hypertrophy. To grow larger; commonly describes an increase in muscle size.

hypoxia. Reduced oxygen content of the air, generally from increased altitude.

isokinetic. A contraction that occurs at a constant velocity while the resistance varies. Hyper-expensive hydraulic isokinetic machines are often found in physical therapy clinics but are rare in gyms.

isometric. A static contraction of the muscle (neither shortens nor lengthens), such as a lock-off when climbing. Strength gains tend to be very localized and specific to the angle of force.

isotonic. The term means "same tension," but it's often misapplied as a reference to free weights. Although the weight of a dumbbell is constant, the resistance a muscle feels varies considerably within the range of movement.

kinetic chain. A linkage that consists of all the joints involved in a movement, such as the shoulder, elbow, and wrist when pulling up on a hold. In the real world, our joints seldom work in isolation but often work together. A weak point in the chain makes the entire movement less effective. See *closed chain* and *open chain*.

lactate threshold. The point during exercise where lactate accumulates faster than it is metabolized. This is an indirect measure of fitness that is sometimes used to prescribe training regimens. A better term in performance threshold.

lactic acid. One of the by-products of anaerobic energy production that is immediately converted into a salt called lactate, an important energy source. See *anaerobic metabolism*.

lateral. Close to the body's middle.

medial. Farther from the body's middle.

open chain. A movement where the last segment in a kinetic chain is free to move; for example, the quad extension is an open-chain exercise because the feet are mobile. Generally considered less functional exercises that isolate muscles. See *closed chain* and *kinetic chain*.

pronation. Inward rotation of a limb about its horizontal axis. The elbow pronates when your thumb rotates inward, and the ankle pronates when it rolls toward the arch. See *supination*.

protein. The source of amino acids, which are the building blocks of the body. Each gram of protein provides 4 calories, but this is an inefficient source of energy.

proximal. The part of a limb that is closest to the heart. See *distal*.

simple movement. A movement that only flexes a single joint, such as a biceps curl. Simple exercises isolate muscles that need to be targeted. See *compound movement*.

supination. Outward rotation of a limb about its horizontal axis. The elbow supinates when your thumb rotates outward, and the ankle supinates when it rolls away from the arch. See *pronation*.

vitamins. Molecules that make things happen in the body, serving as catalysts. You don't burn vitamins, nor are they a source of energy, but you do need an adequate intake.

VO_2max. The maximum amount of oxygen that the body can consume during heavy exercise. Usually measured in milliliters per kilogram of body weight per minute (ml/kg/min), it can be a good estimation of fitness but a poor predictor of athletic performance. Also called aerobic capacity.

Appendix B: Product Sources

Chapter 2: Nutrition Foundation
InnerScan Body Fat Scales
Tanita Corporation of America, Inc.
2625 South Clearbrook Drive
Arlington Heights, IL 60005
847-640-9241
www.tanita.com

Chapter 4: Aerobic Conditioning
Bike Trainer
Kurt Kinetic
395 Ervin Industrial Drive
Jordan, MN 55352
877-226-7824
www.kurtkinetic.com

Cardio Coach
VO2 Maxed Inc.
1-877-348-4968
www.cardiocoach.com

Indoor Cycle
CycleOps/Saris Cycling Group
5253 Verona Road
Madison, WI 53711
800-783-7257
www.cycleops.com

Indoor Rower
LifeCORE Fitness
242 Bingham Road #101
San Marcos, CA 92069
888-815-555
www.lifecorefitness.com

PowerLung
PowerLung, Inc.
800-903-3087
www.powerlung.com

Spinerval DVDs
Lifesports
913 Ridgebrook Road
Suite 106
Sparks, MD 2115
888-288-0503
www.spinervals.com

Suunto Heart Rate Monitors
Suunto USA, Inc.
2030 Lincoln Avenue
Ogden, UT 84401
800-543-9124
www.suunto.com

Chapter 6: Resistance Training
Bosu Ballast Ball
BOSU Fitness, LLC
3745 Third Avenue
San Diego, CA 92107
619-702-2678
www.bosufitness.com

Captains of Crush and IMTUG Grippers
IronMind Enterprises, Inc.
PO Box 1228
Nevada City, CA 95959
530-272-3579
www.ironmind.com

Dry Ice Cubes
Woody's Holds, LLC
1393 Old Dairy Road
Summerville, SC 29483
843-376-3693
www.woodysholds.com

Dry-tooling holds
MR & CO. d.o.o.
Cesta v Zgornji Log 67
SI - 1000 Ljubljana
Slovenia
+386-(0)1-4236755
www.mrclimbing.com

Elite Rings
Power Athletes, LLC
1301 1st Avenue, #1907
Seattle, WA 98101
www.ringtraining.com

Kettlestack handles
Kettlestack
PO Box 750081
Arlington, MA 02475
866-423-0922
www.kettlestack.com

Lebert Equalizer
Lebert Fitness Inc.
33 Elm Street, Suite #356
Champlain, NY12919
905-785-0626
www.lebertequalizer.com

PlateMate add-on weights
Benoit Built, Inc.
12 Factory Cove Road
Boothbay Harbor, ME 04538
800-877-3322
www.theplatemate.com

PowerBlock dumbbells
SportBlock
1071 32nd Avenue Northwest
Owatonna, MN 55060
507-451-5152
www.sportblock.com

Pro Fitter Leg Trainer
FitterFirst
2600 Portland Street SE
Calgary, Alberta
Canada T2G 4M6
800-348-8371
www.fitter1.com

Rock Rings and hangboards
Metolius Climbing
63189 Nels Anderson Road
Bend, OR 97701
541-382-7585
www.metoliusclimbing.com

Slastix resistance tubes
Stroops
Building A-15 Freeport Center
PO Box 160327
Clearfield, UT 84016
800-344-2756
www.slastix.com

Super Gripper
Ivanko Equipment
PO Box 6224
Reno, NV 89513
800-759-6399
www.ivanko.com

TRX Trainer
Fitness Anywhere, Inc.
1660 Pacific Avenue
San Francisco, CA 94109
888-878-5348
www.fitnessanywhere.com

Chapter 7: Body Tuning: Joint Mobility, Flexibility, and Balance
BackMagic
SMC-Innovations
330 SMC Drive
Somerset, WI 54025
866-450-0200
www.backmagicworks.com

Indo Board Balance Trainer
Indo Board
131 Tomahawk Drive, Unit 15-A
Indian Harbour Beach, FL 32937
321-777-6021
www.indoboard.com

Neural Muscular Warm-up
Z-Health Performance Solutions
251108 8th Place South
Des Moines, WA 98198
888-394-4198
www.zhealth.net

P.A.S.T. Balance Board
Functional Innovations, LLC
14478 I-25 Frontage Road
Longmont, CO 80504
303-666-0505
www.balance2posture.com

Primo 50 Slackline
Slackline Express LLC
835 Kimbark Street
Lafayette, CO 80026
720-890-5088
www.slacklineexpress.com

StretchRite, CoreStretch, ProStretch
Medi-Dyne
1812 Industrial Boulevard
Colleyville, TX 76034
800-810-1740
www.medi-dyne.com

Chapter 8: Recovery: Rest and Rehab
ActiveWrap cold packs
ActiveWrap Inc.
5550 Cerritos Avenue, Suite F
Cypress, CA 90630
714-527-7129
www.activewrap.com

Armaid forearm massager
The Armaid Company
658 Pleasant Street
Blue Hill, ME 04614
800-488-550
www.armaid.com

MA Roller
The Ma Roller
3635 Old Court Road, Suite 311
Pikesville, MD 21208-3907
800-830-5949
www.themaroller.com

Mini Pro 2 Massager
Thumper Massager Inc.
1241 Denison Street, Unit #40
Markham, Ontario
Canada L3R 4B4
800-848-6737
www.thumpermassager.com

Omni Massagers
Omni Massage Systems
PO Box 4554
Odessa, TX 79760
432-334-4900
www.omnimassage.com

Strong and Healthy Hands Kit
IronMind Enterprises, Inc.
PO Box 1228
Nevada City, CA 95959
530-272-3579
www.ironmind.com

Thera Cane
Thera Cane Company
PO Box 9220
Denver, CO 80209-0220
www.theracane.com

Thermophore heating pad
Battle Creek Equipment Co.
307 W. Jackson Street
Battle Creek, MI 49037
800-253-0854
www.thermophore.com

Trigger Point massage tools
Trigger Point Technologies
7801 North Lamar Blvd, Suite C65
Austin, TX 78752
888-312-2557
www.tptherapy.com

Appendix C: Suggested Reading

General

MEDLINEplus (medlineplus.gov). A free resource operated by the National Library of Medicine and the National Institutes of Health. Contains a wealth of information on health, diseases, and drugs.

The Physician and Sportsmedicine Online (www.physsportsmed.com). Medical review articles (technical, but not overly so) in addition to many excellent articles for the layperson in the Personal Health section.

PubMed (www.ncbi.nlm.nih.gov/pubmed). The largest online database of scientific research articles. Operated by the National Library of Medicine. Before trusting ad claims, verify references here, because they are often taken out of context or misinterpreted.

SportScience (www.sportsci.org). A superb, peer-reviewed collection of information on all aspects of the science of sport.

Wilmore, Jack, and David Costill. *Physiology of Sport and Exercise*, 4th edition. Champaign, Illinois: Human Kinetics, 2007. A superb college text that provides an overview of human performance.

Chapter 2: Nutrition Foundation

Antonio, Jose, and Jeffrey Stout. *Sports Supplements*. Philadelphia: Lippincott Williams & Wilkins, 2001. A well-referenced text that gets into the nitty-gritty of what supplements do and don't do.

Burke, Louise. *Practical Sports Nutrition*. Champaign, Illinois: Human Kinetics, 2007. This textbook goes over the most recent nutrition science in the first couple of chapters, and then focuses on specific sports in the next eleven. Not climbing specific but a great resource if you are really interested in maximizing performance.

Clark, Nancy. *Sports Nutrition Guidebook*, 4th edition. Champaign, Illinois: Human Kinetics, 2008. Clear explanations for the layperson, with a lot of good recipes.

Dorfman, Lisa. *The Vegetarian Sports Nutrition Guide*. New York, New York: John Wiley & Sons, 1999. Though a bit evangelical, this is a good source of information and recipes for non-meat-eating athletes.

Food and Nutrition Board, Institute of Medicine. *Dietary Reference Intakes*. Washington, DC: The National Academies Press. If you really need to know all the details behind the new recommendations for vitamins and minerals, here they are. The online version is free (www.nap.edu), or you can buy the six printed volumes.

Girard Eberle, Suzanne. *Endurance Sports Nutrition,* 2nd edition. Champaign, Illinois: Human Kinetics, 2007. Written for serious athletes, this is a very good source of nutrition information with excellent advice for vegetarians.

Manore, Melinda, and Janice Thompson. *Sport Nutrition for Health and Performance.* Champaign, Illinois: Human Kinetics, 2000. A college textbook for those who want a strong science background to decipher the mumbo jumbo.

Quackwatch.com. Perhaps a bit zealous in the battle against evil, but full references are provided, so you can decide for yourself (www.quackwatch.com).

Ryan, Monique. *Sports Nutrition for Endurance Athletes*, 2nd edition. Boulder, Colorado: Velopress, 2007. Another good book that is written for the serious athlete. Includes specific nutrition advice for a variety of sports including adventure racing.

Supplementwatch.com. An independent website that isn't selling anything and doesn't accept advertising. Well-researched and referenced articles. (www.supplementwatch.com).

Chapter 3: Mental Power

Ilgner, Arno. *The Rock Warrior's Way: Mental Training for Climbers*, 2nd edition. La Vergne, Tennessee: Desiderata Institute, 2006. One of the few books that delves into the subject.

Murphy, Shane, editor. *The Sport Psych Handbook.* Champaign, Illinois: Human Kinetics, 2005. This text contains many chapters on sport psychology that apply to climbers as well as other athletes.

Williamson, Jed, editor. *Accidents in North American Mountaineering.* Golden, Colorado: American Alpine Club Press, annual. Learn from other people's mistakes.

Chapter 4: Aerobic Conditioning

Armstrong, Lawrence E. *Performing in Extreme Environments.* Champaign, Illinois: Human Kinetics, 1999. A compilation of research on how the body reacts in less-than-ideal conditions.

Friel, Joe. *The Cyclist's Training Bible*, 3rd edition. Boulder, Colorado: Velopress, 2003. Since cycling is one of the best ways to get in shape for mountaineering, this book is a good resource for anyone who wants to get serious. The workouts may seem complicated, but there is a lot of information to help customize your program.

Galloway, Jeff. *Marathon: You Can Do It!* Bolinas, California: Shelter Publications, 2001. A good beginner's guide to running the distance.

Noakes, Timothy. *Lore of Running*, 4th edition. Champaign, Illinois: Human Kinetics, 2002. Basically the bible for runners. It's a huge book with a vast amount of information.

Sleamaker, Rob, and Ray Browning. *SERIOUS Training for Endurance Athletes*, 2nd edition. Champaign, Illinois: Human Kinetics, 1996. A book for the dedicated athlete willing to plan life months in advance.

Chapter 5: Climbing at Altitude

Bezruchka, Stephen. *Altitude Illness: Prevention and Treatment*, 2nd edition. Seattle, Washington: The Mountaineers Books, 2005. A small book with a lot of valuable information.

Houston, Charles. *Going Higher: Oxygen, Man, and Mountains*, 5th edition. Seattle: The Mountaineers Books, 2005. A superb book that explains the challenges of high altitude in layman's terms.

Ward, Michael, J. S. Milledge, and J. B. West. *High Altitude Medicine and Physiology,* 4th edition. London: Oxford University Press, 2007. This definitive medical text is not for the lay reader, but it has exceptional content for those seriously interested in performance at altitude and the history of altitude research.

Chapter 6: Resistance Training

Aaberg, Everett. *Muscle Mechanics,* 2nd edition. Champaign, Illinois: Human Kinetics, 2005. One of the better introductions to resistance training, this provides good explanation of the pros and cons of exercises that are safe and effective.

Baechle, Thomas, and Roger Earle. *Essentials of Strength Training and Conditioning,* 2nd edition. Champaign, Illinois: Human Kinetics, 2000. The National Strength and Conditioning Association's textbook for personal trainers. It is an excellent reference for those interested in the science of training.

Brooks, Douglas. *Effective Strength Training*. Champaign, Illinois: Human Kinetics, 2001. Intended for personal trainers but useful for athletes, this provides a good analysis of resistance exercises.

Fleck, Steven, and William Kraemer. *Designing Resistance Training Programs,* 3rd edition. Champaign, Illinois: Human Kinetics, 2003. A good textbook for those interested in the research behind the theories.

Newton, Harvey. *Explosive Lifting for Sports*, enhanced edition. Champaign, Illinois: Human Kinetics, 2006. The next best alternative to hiring a coach for learning the Olympic lifts. This book and DVD carefully take you through the steps for safely learning proper technique.

Chapter 7: Body Tuning: Joint Mobility, Flexibility, and Balance

Alter, Michael. *Sport Stretch*, 2nd edition. Champaign, Illinois: Human Kinetics, 1998. A more technical approach with many advanced stretches for dancers and martial artists.

Anderson, Bob. *Stretching*, 20th anniversary edition. Bolinas, California: Shelter Publications, 2000. The latest edition of this classic book has more than fifty routines, including one for rock climbing, that only take 2 to 8 minutes each.

Cook, Gray. *Athletic Body in Balance*. Champaign, Illinois: Human Kinetics, 2003. Written by a physical therapist, this is a good resource for working on weak links such as muscle imbalances, mobility restrictions, and stability problems. The optional DVD takes you through five assessment tests, helps you correct problems, and illustrates core training techniques to enhance athletic performance.

Frederick, Ann, and Chris Frederick. *Flexibility for Sports Performance*. Champaign, Illinois: Human Kinetics, 2007. This excellent 51-minute DVD demonstrates a wave-like style of stretching that is somewhat like yoga but from the scientific viewpoint.

Rountree, Sage. *The Athlete's Guide to Yoga.* Boulder, Colorado: Velopress, 2007. This is a superb book for climbers who wish to integrate yoga into their training. The poses shown are those most useful for performance while the Sanskrit and philosophy are kept to a bare minimum. It comes with a 15-minute sampler DVD that contains two routines (warm-up and cool-down).

Stricker, Lauri Ann. *Pilates for the Outdoor Athlete.* Golden, Colorado: Fulcrum Publishing, 2007. An outstanding resource for anyone who wants to develop their core musculature.

Chapter 8: Recovery: Rest and Rehab

Gotlin, Robert, editor. *Sports Injuries Guidebook.* Champaign, Illinois: Human Kinetics, 2008. Each chapter deals with a different area of the body, giving the common causes of injury, identification of the problem with detailed illustrations, treatment suggestions, and guidelines on when to return to action.

Horrigan, Joseph, and Jerry Robinson. *7-minute Rotator Cuff Solution.* Los Angeles: Health for Life, 1991. Provides a good explanation of shoulder problems and exercises to help them. If you have recurrent shoulder issues, this is a must-have.

Musnick, David, and Mark Pierce. *Conditioning for Outdoor Fitness,* 2nd edition. Seattle: The Mountaineers Books, 2004. Good source for functional exercises used in rehabilitation.

Chapter 9: Synergy: Coalescing and Planning

Goddard, Dale, and Udo Neumann. *Performance Rock Climbing.* Mechanicsburg, Pennsylvania: Stackpole Books, 1993. Though some of the information is dated, this remains a good starting point for sport and high-level trad climbers.

Hague, Dan, and Douglas Hunter. *The Self-Coached Climber.* Mechanicsburg, Pennsylvania: Stackpole Books, 2006. An excellent manual for the advanced rock climber. The included DVD is particularly helpful for its content on movement skills.

Horst, Eric. *Training for Climbing.* Helena, Montana: Falcon Books, 2003. An update of his popular book for sport climbers.

Sagar, Heather Reynolds. *Climbing Your Best: Training to Maximize Your Performance.* Mechanicsburg, Pennsylvania: Stackpole Books, 2001. Another viewpoint for sport climbers.

Twight, Mark. *Extreme Alpinism.* Seattle: The Mountaineers Books, 1999. An excellent how-to-push-the-envelope manual. Those with no desire to imitate Dr. Doom can still pick up some good tidbits. However, the training information is outdated. See www.gymjones.com and www.mtnathlete.com for the latest in hardman workouts.

Index

acetaminophen 219-20
acetate 32
acetazolamide 117-18
acromioclavicular joint separation 225
acute mountain sickness (AMS) 113, 116
adaptogens 66
adenosine triphosphate (ATP) 80
adipose triglyceride lipase 26
aerobic capacity 80-81, 89, 111
aerobic energy 128
aerobic training
    adaptations from 80-82
    after injury 230
    amount of 82
    cardio planning 86-88
    definition of 80
    goals of 81
    health benefits of 80
    in intervals 90-92
    performance threshold 89-90
    physiological changes 81-82
    principles of 82-83
    programs 237-53
    progress monitoring 85
    timing of 83
    training zones 86-88
    warm-up for 83
aging climber 16
alcohol 32, 212
alfalfa 67
alpha-linolenic acid 36
alpine climbing 236-37, 251-53
alternative medicine 221
altitude climbing 110-18, 251-53
amenorrhea 26-27
amino acids 34, 62-63, 117

amygdala 77
anatomy 123-27
ankle injuries 227-28
anterior cruciate ligament tears 227-28
antibiotics 115
antidiuretic hormone 47
antioxidants 55, 57, 59, 117
aspartame 38
aspirin 117, 219-20
astragalus 67
Atkins Diet 21-22
atmospheric pressure 110

back
    exercises for 178
    injuries to 226-27
backcountry skiing 105-06
balance training 205-08
barbells 134
bars 46-47
BCAAs (branched chain amino acids) 62-63, 117
bee pollen 67
beer 54-55
bench press 162-63
bent-over row 159-60
beta-carotene 56
bicarbonate 63-64
biking 99-101
bioelectrical impedance analysis (BIA) 22-23
biotin 58
blisters 228
blue-green algae 67
body core exercises 174-80
body fat
    percentages of 13-14, 16
    reductions in 22-23
body fat scales 22
body mass index 23

body weight 27
bouldering 236
breads 41
breakfast 28-29
broken bones 229-30
brown rice syrup 38-39

caffeine 59-60
calcium 59-60
calf raise 187-88
callus 223
calories
    for altitude climbing 116
    daily intake of 24-25
    food sources of 27
campus board 145-46
canned foods 42
carbohydrates 27, 38-39, 52, 113, 116
carbo-loading 45
cardiac output 81
cardiovascular conditioning 14
carnitine 64
casein 62
catecholamines 72
cereals 28, 41
Cheyne-Stokes pattern 112
children 132
chiropractics 221-22
chitosan 67
chlorophyll 67
cholesterol 35
choline 58
chondroitin 62
chromium 59, 64
circuit routines 244-45
climber's elbow 225
climber's finger 224
climbing wall 145-46
coaching 13
coenzyme Q10 64

coffee 60
cold laser therapy 221
cold pack 216
colds 213
colloidal silver 67-68
colostrum 68
conditioning 13
conjugated linolenic acid 36, 64
copper 59
cordyceps 68
core exercises 174-80
COX-2 inhibitors 219
cramps 51, 211
creatine 60-61
cross-country skiing 104-05
cross-play 15, 92-108, 232
crunch 175-76
curl and press 170-71
cycling 102-03

dairy products 42
dehydration 47, 85, 110, 112
delayed-onset muscular soreness (DOMS) 131, 211
dexamethasone 118
DHA (docosahexaenoic acid) 36
DHEA (dehydroepiandrosterone) 16, 65
Diamox. See acetazolamide
diarrhea 115
diet
    basics of 20-27
    fad 21-22
    fats in 24-25
    hype about 20-21
    styles of 18-20
dietary fiber 40-41
dietary reference intakes (DRI) 58
Dietary Supplement Health and Education Act 63
dining out 30-31
dinner 32
dips 165-66

disordered eating 26-27
distractions 73
drinking water 29, 47, 51-53
dumbbells 134, 138-39

eating disorders 26-27
echinacea 68, 213
elbow injuries 225
elliptical trainers 96
endorphins 80
endurance 128
endurance training 81, 152-53, 235
energy bars 46-47, 49-50, 53
energy drinks 48
EPA (eicosapentaenoic acid) 36
ephedrine 60, 68
erythropoietin 111, 114
excess post-exercise oxygen consumption 90
exercise(s)
    body core 174-80
    breathing during 148, 235
    caloric intake for 25
    dangerous types of 155
    form during 148
    lower body 180-88
    resistance 156-88
    timing of 24
    tips for 147-48
    upper body 156-74
    weight loss through 24
    workout structure 149-50, 152-53
exercise programs 237-53

fad diets 21-22
failure 78
falls 222
Fartlek 91
fast food 30
fasting 26
fast-twitch muscle fibers 16, 129
fatigue 46, 128

fats 24-25, 35-36
fat-soluble vitamins 55
fear 75-77
feet injuries 228-29
fermented malt beverages 54-55
fiber 40-41
finger hangs 173-74
finger injuries 223-25
fish oil 36
fitness clubs 135-37
flexibility 192-93
"flow" 74-75
flu 213
fluoride 59
fly (exercise) 164-65
focus 72-74
folate 57-58
folk remedies 118
food
    after climbing 54
    during altitude climbing 114-18
    dining out 30-31
    energy density of 33
    organic 33-34
    shopping for 32-44
    for wall climbing 53
forearms 143-44
free weights 133-35
frozen foods 42
fructose 37-38, 54
fruits 41
functional training 147-48

garlic 118
gastric emptying 52
gels 47-48, 53
general conditioning 13
genetically modified organisms 34
germanium 68
ginkgo biloba 68-69, 118
ginseng 69
glucosamine 62
glutamine 64-65

glycemic index 37
glycerol 65
glycogen 45, 81-82
glycolysis 128
goal setting 12-13, 75
golden root 69
granola 28
grippers 144
guarana 69
gym 134-46

hamstrings 185-86, 202
hand injuries 223-25
hangboard 143
hanging leg raises 178-79
Hatha yoga 204-05
heart rate
    altitude-related adjustments 111
    maximum 84-86
    at rest 81, 83-84
    target 86
heart rate monitors 85
heart rate reserve 86
hemochromatosis 61
herbal antioxidants 57, 59
high altitude climbing 52
high altitude pulmonary edema 118
high fructose corn syrup 37-38
high-intensity interval training 26, 90
hiking 96-98
hill repeats 91
Hindu squat and push-up 191
hip abduction 186-87
HMB 64
holism 14-15
home climbing wall 145-46
home gym 138-45
honey 38
hornet juice 69
human growth hormone 26
hydration 47, 52, 113
hyperventilation 110
hyponatremia 51

ibuprofen 219-20
ice climbing 249-50
iliotibial band 227
indoor cycling 102-03
indoor rowing 107-08
indoor running 95-96
inflammation 216
injuries 217-18, 223-30
inline skating 103-04
interval training 90-92
intuition 77-78
iodine 59
ion-exchange whey protein 62
iron 59, 61
isoflavones 62
isometric training 131

jet lag 212-13
joint mobility 190-91

Karvonen method 86
kettlebells 134, 140, 184-85

lactate 65, 82, 128
lacto-ovo vegetarians 19
lat pull 156-58
lateral leg trainer 144-45
leg injuries 227
leg press 181-82
low-calorie diets 23
lower body exercises 180-88
lunch 29
lunge 182-84

Ma Huang 68
machines, resistance-training 133
macronutrients 27
magnesium 59, 65
maltodextrin 38
manganese 59
maral 69
massage 213-15
maté 69
maximum heart rate 84-86
MCT oil 65

meats 44
medium-chain triglycerides 65
melatonin 212-13
men
    body fat levels for 14
    fear and 76-77
    ideal body weight for 27
    water percentages 47
mental focus 72-74
metabolic syndrome 16
MICE 217
milk 28
milk thistle 70
minerals 56, 59
molybdenum 59
mountain biking 100-101
multivitamins 56-57, 117
muscle
    adaptations by 129-30
    glycogen used by 45, 81-82
    list of 126-27
    physiology of 123
muscle cramps 51, 211
muscle fibers 16, 129
muscle strain 218
muscular soreness 131, 211
myoglobin 81

naproxen sodium 219-20
natural supplements 66-70
NIA (non-impact aerobics) 205
niacin 56, 58
nifedipine 118
non-steroidal anti-inflammatory drugs (NSAIDs) 63, 219-20
nutrition
    during altitude climbing 114-18
    basics of 18-20
    breakfast 28-29
    before climbing 44-45
    during climbing 45-47
Nutrition Facts label 25, 34

octacosanol 70

oils 36
omega-3 fatty acids 35-36
omega-6 fatty acids 35-36
organic foods 33-34
osmolality 47
osteoporosis 16, 120
overuse injuries 216, 224, 226

pain relievers 219-21
Paleo Diet 21
pantothenic acid 58
parallettes 142
performance threshold 89-90
periodization 155-56, 240
personal trainer 137-38
phosphorus 59, 62
phytochemicals 43
pilates 203-04
plantar fasciitis 229
plasma osmolality 47
plyometric box 144
polyunsaturated fatty acids 35
potassium 39, 51
power cage 139
power endurance 235-36
power hiking 96-98
prebiotics 40
pressure breathing 14
probiotics 61-62
progressive overload 131
prohormones 65
proprioceptive neuromuscular
    facilitation (PNF) stretch-
    ing 192
protein 19-20, 34-35
protein powder 62
pull-up 158-59
push-ups 163-64, 191
pyruvate 66

raw food diets 22
rear delt row 161-62
recovery fuels 53-55
rehabilitation 215-22
reishi mushroom 70
relaxation 74-75

resistance training
    after injury 218
    benefits of 120-21
    exercises 156-88
    form during 148
    frequency of 150-51
    getting started 131-32
    intensity of 151
    by kids 132
    machines for 133
    muscle adaptations 129-30
    myths about 121-22
    periodization 155-56, 240
    principles of 130-46
    programs 237-53
    purpose of 14
    rest periods 154
    for rock climbing 234-35
    volume of 154
    warm-up before 147
    workout structure 149-50,
        152-53
respiration training 92
rest 210-14
resting heart rate 81, 83-84
resting metabolic rate 16
riboflavin 58
ribose 66
RICE 217
road biking 99-100
road running 94-95
rock gyms 135-36, 138, 234-35
rock training 233-37, 247-49
Rolfing 214
rowing 107-08
royal jelly 70
running 93-96

safety 10
salmeterol 118
salt 39-40
sarcopenia 16
saturated fats 35-36
seafood 18, 32, 36, 44
seated row 160-61
selenium 59

self-massage 214-15
shoes 228
shoulders
    exercises for 167-70
    injuries to 225-26
side bridges 176-77
sildenafil 118
skating, inline 103-04
ski mountaineering 250-51
skiing 104-06
skin cancer 223
skin injuries 223-24
skinfold caliper 23
slacklines 73, 206
sleeping 112-13, 211-12
slow-twitch muscle fibers 16, 129
snacks 29, 31, 40, 44
snowshoeing 106-07
sodium 39-40, 51
soy 19, 62
soy milk 28, 42
specialization 14-15
specific adaptation to increased
    demand 14
specific aerobic capacity and
    capillarity (SACC) 128
specific conditioning 13
squat 180-81
stability ball 142
stairs/stair-steppers 98-99
static stretching 190
stiff-leg deadlift 179-80
strength 123, 128-29. *See also*
    resistance training
stress fractures 120
stress test 85
stretches/stretching
    alternatives to 203-05
    benefits of 190-93
    post-exercise 192
    routine for 193-94
    types of 195-203
sugar 37-39
sunscreen 223
superior labrum anterior-to-
    posterior lesion 225-26

supplemental oxygen 118
supplements 55-70, 116-18, 211
suspended resistance 141-42
sweat loss 51
sweeteners 38

tai chi 205
target heart rate 86
testosterone 16, 32
thiamin 58
time management 233
trail running 93-94
trainer 137-38
training. *See specific training*
training cults 15-16
training zones 86-88
trans fatty acids 35
"trekker's knee" 227
trekking poles 113
tubing, resistance 140-41
twist crunch 177

ubiquinone 64
upper body exercises 156-74
urination 52-53
urine 47, 51
urochrome 47

vanadyl sulfate 66
vegans 19, 35
vegetables 41-43
vegetarians 19, 35
ventilatory threshold 81
Viagra. *See* sildenafil
visualization 75
vitamin A 55, 58
vitamin B-6 58
vitamin B-12 19, 58
vitamin C 57-58, 117
vitamin E 57-58, 117
vitamin K 58
VO$_2$ max 80-81, 89, 111

wall climbing 53
warm-up 83
water
    during altitude climbing
    52, 113
    drinking of 29, 47, 51-53
    during wall climbing 53
water-soluble vitamins 55
weight lifting. *See* resistance
    training

weight loss
    during altitude climbing
    112
    description of 23-24
    exercise for 24
    fasting for 26
wheat germ oil 70
whey protein 62
whole-body vibration machines
    145
wobble board 207-08
women
    body fat levels for 14
    fear and 76-77
    ideal body weight for 27
    water percentages 47
wrist curl 171-72

yerba maté 69
yoga 204-05
yogurt 28-29, 42
yohimbe 70

zinc 59
zinc lozenges 213
Zone Diet 21

About the Author

Clyde Soles is a writer, photographer, and consultant with a passion for adventure (www.clydesoles.com). Prior to going freelance, he was an editor at *Rock & Ice* magazine for seven years. He also founded *Trail Runner* magazine and has contributed many articles to that publication.

Soles is the author of *Rock & Ice Gear: Equipment for the Vertical World* (The Mountaineers Books, 2000), *Climbing: Expedition Planning* (The Mountaineers Books, 2003), and *The Outdoor Knots Book* (The Mountaineers Books, 2004). He co-authored *The Land Navigation Handbook*, 2nd edition (Sierra Club Books, 2005).

After three decades of climbing, Soles enjoys all aspects of the sport—from bouldering to Himalayan summits. He is equally devoted to trail running, road biking, mountain biking, telemark skiing, track skiing, scuba diving, and whitewater rafting.

THE MOUNTAINEERS, founded in 1906, is a nonprofit outdoor activity and conservation club, whose mission is "to explore, study, preserve, and enjoy the natural beauty of the outdoors. . . ." Based in Seattle, Washington, the club is now the third-largest such organization in the United States, with 15,000 members and five branches throughout Washington State.

The Mountaineers sponsors both classes and year-round outdoor activities in the Pacific Northwest, which include hiking, mountain climbing, ski-touring, snowshoeing, bicycling, camping, kayaking and canoeing, nature study, sailing, and adventure travel. The club's conservation division supports environmental causes through educational activities, sponsoring legislation, and presenting informational programs. All club activities are led by skilled, experienced volunteers, who are dedicated to promoting safe and responsible enjoyment and preservation of the outdoors.

If you would like to participate in these organized outdoor activities or the club's programs, consider a membership in The Mountaineers. For information and an application, write or call The Mountaineers, Club Headquarters, 300 Third Avenue West, Seattle, WA 98119; 206-284-6310.

The Mountaineers Books, an active, nonprofit publishing program of the club, produces guidebooks, instructional texts, historical works, natural history guides, and works on environmental conservation. All books produced by The Mountaineers Books fulfill the club's mission.

Send or call for our catalog of more than 500 outdoor titles:

The Mountaineers Books
1001 SW Klickitat Way, Suite 201
Seattle, WA 98134
800-553-4453
mbooks@mountaineersbooks.org
www.mountaineersbooks.org

The Mountaineers Books is proud to be a corporate sponsor of Leave No Trace, whose mission is to promote and inspire responsible outdoor recreation through education, research, and partnerships. The Leave No Trace program is focused specifically on human-powered (nonmotorized) recreation.

Leave No Trace strives to educate visitors about the nature of their recreational impacts, as well as offer techniques to prevent and minimize such impacts. Leave No Trace is best understood as an educational and ethical program, not as a set of rules and regulations.

For more information, visit www.LNT.org, or call 800-332-4100.

MORE CLIMBING TITLES FROM THE TOP ATHLETES AND ORGANIZATIONS IN THE SPORT

Climbing: Expedition Planning
Clyde Soles and Phil Powers
Guide to planning, organizing, and leading
climbing expeditions

The Outdoor Knots Book
Clyde Soles
Techniques for hikers, campers, paddlers,
and climbers

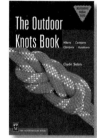

Forget Me Not: A Memoir
Jennifer Lowe-Anker; foreword by Jon Krakauer
A narrative of love, travel, adventure, and
loss, against a backdrop of mountains from
Montana to Nepal; this is the true story of
Jennifer Lowe-Anker, Alex Lowe and Conrad Anker.

Rock Climbing Anchors: A Comprehensive Guide
Craig Luebben
Modern anchoring ideas and techniques for
top-roping, rappelling, sport climbing, traditional
rock climbing, and mountaineering

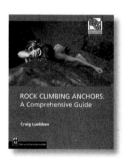

Accidents in North American Mountaineering
American Alpine Club
The classic source of climbing-related
accidents for 50 years

Conquistadors of the Useless
Lionel Terray; foreword by David Roberts
Classic autobiography of one of the greatest
climbers of the 20th century. One of *National Geographic
Adventure Magazine's* "100 Greatest Adventure
Books of All Time."